The Brain and Learning

One of the five books in the *Mental Health and Wellbeing Teacher Toolkit*, this practical resource is designed to help young children understand how the brain affects ways we see and interpret the world. The book offers research-driven, practical strategies, resources and lesson plans to support educators and health professionals. Key sections include Development of the Brain, How the Brain Works, The Brain and Learning, The Brain and Emotions and How the Brain Can Influence Behaviour

A complete toolkit for teachers and counsellors, this book offers:

- Easy-to-follow, and flexible lesson plans that can be adapted and personalised for use in lessons or smaller groups or 1:1 work.
- Resources that are linked to the PSHE and Wellbeing curriculum for KS1, KS2 and KS3.
- New research, 'Circles for Learning', where the introduction of baby observation into the classroom by a teacher is used to understand and develop self-awareness, skills for learning, relationships, neuroscience and awareness of others.
- Learning links, learning objectives and reflection questions.

This book is an essential resource for practitioners looking to have a positive impact on the mental health and wellbeing of the children and young people in their care; both now and in the future.

Alison Waterhouse has worked in mainstream, special education and the independent sector for the past 30 years, specialising in working with children with AEN including Mental Health and Wellbeing. She has set up and developed an Independent Therapeutic Special School; developed a role as Teacher in Charge of the Social and Emotional Wellbeing of the Whole School Community, and has been an Inclusion Manager and Deputy Head in mainstream schools. She now works as an Independent Educational Consultant for SEN and Wellbeing; is involved in staff training, and has her own Educational Psychotherapy practice. Alison works with children who are referred due to difficulties with self-esteem, anger, anxiety, depression and other Mental Health needs as well as children with learning differences. Alison is developing the 'Circles for Learning' Project in schools and has already undertaken a Primary Research Project and is now working on a Secondary Research Project. The resources were put together to support staff with these projects.

Emotional literacy
Self-discovery
Skills for effective learning in school
Positive relationships in school
The brain and learning
The invisible roots of learning

The Brain and Learning

Supporting Emotional Health and Wellbeing in School

Alison Waterhouse

Routledge
Taylor & Francis Group
LONDON AND NEW YORK

First published 2020
by Routledge
2 Park Square, Milton Park, Abingdon, Oxon OX14 4RN

and by Routledge
52 Vanderbilt Avenue, New York, NY 10017

Routledge is an imprint of the Taylor & Francis Group, an informa business

British Library Cataloguing-in-Publication Data
A catalogue record for this book is available from the British Library

Library of Congress Cataloging-in-Publication Data
Names: Waterhouse, Alison, 1963– author.
Title: The brain and learning : supporting emotional health and wellbeing in school / Alison Waterhouse.
Description: Abingdon, Oxon ; New York : Routledge, [2020] | Series: The mental health and wellbeing teacher toolkit | Includes bibliographical references.
Identifiers: LCCN 2019025308 (print) | LCCN 2019025309 (ebook) | ISBN 9781138370326 (paperback) | ISBN 9780429428050 (ebook)
Subjects: LCSH: Learning, Psychology of. | Cognition in children. | Cognitive neuroscience. | Students—Mental health.
Classification: LCC LB1060 W384 2020 (print) | LCC LB1060 (ebook) | DDC 371.7/13—dc23
LC record available at https://lccn.loc.gov/2019025308
LC ebook record available at https://lccn.loc.gov/2019025309

ISBN: 978-1-138-37032-6 (pbk)
ISBN: 978-0-429-42805-0 (ebk)

Typeset in Avant Garde
by Apex CoVantage, LLC

To David, who taught me to listen and think and have the courage to stand up and say when things are not right.

Contents

Introduction

NEUROSCIENCE

Neuroscience is the scientific study of the nervous system. It combines physiology, anatomy, molecular biology, developmental biology and psychology to understand neurons and neural circuits within the body. It explores the biological aspects of learning, memory, behaviour, perception and consciousness. Most of the research is focused on understanding the fundamental processes within the brain, both in health and disease.

Research in the latter part of the 20th century has shown that the brain has the ability to change throughout life (Rakic 2002). This finding is in contrast with previous scientific thinking that the brain only develops during a critical period in childhood and then remains relatively unchanged (Pascual-Leone 2005).

The brain is an interconnected system made up of different subsystems. Each of our experiences shapes our brain structure and therefore brain development is an experience-dependent process. Experiences activate pathways, strengthening existing connections or creating new ones. A wide range of research has shown that brain development is a product of the effects of experience on the developing genetic potential. Genes are affected by experience and the nature of our genes and how they regulate us impacts on our experience: genes and experience are interwoven (Siegel 2015a).

Brain research can help us to understand learning in a variety of ways. If we look at the cognitive, emotional and relational circuits in the brain we are able to understand learning in more detail. In 1949 Donald Hebb found that things that we experience cause a network of neurons to fire together. These complex networks span the brain and the body like a fine net. The more often the net of neurons fires the more likely they will fire in the same pattern, hence the saying 'What fires together wires together'. This is the same for positive experiences and negative ones (Olson 2014). If a child continually experiences asking questions with a negative response from an adult they will soon link questions with a negative outcome – the net has been formed.

Siegel (2015a) argues that because the brain is a complex system of interconnecting systems, using the term 'brain' for the skull based structure alone makes no sense. He argues that the body is connected and regulated by the skull-based structure and so the two cannot be separated (Siegel 2015a).

Understanding the brain and how it affects relationships, emotions and learning is important for CYP. Research is showing that mental health problems are starting at a much earlier age. Hawkins (2017) suggests that if we want to support our CYP in understanding how their minds work and give them more strategies to cope with stress, regulation, learning and relationships, helping them understand neuroscience can support this. Judy Willis became a teacher after 20 years as a neurologist. She argues that when we teach children to understand what is happening in their brain it can give them the power to make choices for themselves in the future (2009). She has found that explaining how the brain works can be particularly important to those CYP who believe they are not clever and that nothing they do can change this. The knowledge that they can change the brain by improving how they engage with and undertake their learning becomes an idea that engages them with learning again.

Lori Desautels is an assistant professor at Butler University in Indianapolis. Her passion is engaging her students through neuroscience in education. She argues that when we teach CYP about the brain and how the different parts work, it gives the brain a scientific context which then extends into learning. Lori taught an Education Neuroscience course to CYP at the Butler Laboratory School in 2016 and found that the CYP engaged and became fascinated by the topic and that for many, understanding how they felt and why had a calming response as well as supported learning (Desautels 2016).

Olson (2014) shares his belief that by sharing and teaching CYP about the brain and how it works, it can support CYP in managing difficult situations and events later on in life. He argues that teaching about negative bias, explanatory styles and how the brain remembers events are all supportive to CYP by giving them the ability to understand their way of viewing things and gives them the ability to challenge themselves to change this. He believes that this work also leads to discussions on self-talk and the impact this can have on our thoughts, behaviours and emotions.

Cozolino (2013) describes the body's response to stress. By helping CYP understand that the hypothalamic-pituitary-adrenal (HPA) system that regulates the body's response to stress has developed to support survival and that stress for a short time is not dangerous can help CYP learn strategies to manage.

Siegel (2015a) suggests that knowing about how the brain works can empower people to choose to transform their lives and move towards greater health and wellbeing.

There is very little literature on the impact of understanding the brain on either learning or wellbeing. Research is now showing that toxic stress has a biological impact on the growing brain which then has a developmental impact for CYP.

> Insecure attachment and a dangerous environment and chronic stress can create a perfect storm of biological and epigenetic consequences that can turn the brain off to learning. On the other hand caring and supportive others can

> create a state of body and mind that primes the brain for curiosity exploration and learning.
>
> (Cozolino 2014, p. 50)

In a report by the Wellcome Trust in 2014, 82 per cent of teachers asked said that they were interested in neuroscience and 75 per cent said they used their knowledge about neuroscience to inform their classroom practice, with 65 per cent saying that they used this knowledge for planning.

Teaching changes the structure of the brain and the understanding of basic brain processes can help teachers understand both the learning and the behaviour of CYP better. Cozolino (2013) describes teachers as neuro-scientific sculptors who, through their personal and pedagogical skills, create learning environments and internal connections in the students that sculpt the synaptic framework of our brains.

> The brain influences both our minds and our relationships, knowing about the brain can help us with our inner experience and our social connections . . . . Learning the steps to strengthen the brain in practice ways can help us build a more resilient mind and more rewarding relationships with others.
>
> (Siegel 2015b, p. 6)

Each child enters the classroom with a vastly different experience of the world and people in it. Neuroscience invites us to think about their attitudes, beliefs and behaviours as neural networks that have been created by past experiences but which can be altered by new experiences and positive relationships. Olson (2014) suggests that new positive experiences with a trusting adult can create disconfirming experiences for CYP who have had negative experiences which have created negative neural networks. Disconfirming experiences can weaken previously developed neural networks or traumatic memories (Ecker et al. 2012).

Cozolino (2013) states that the position of the teacher is similar to that of a parent or carer in building the brain of CYP and creating a supportive environment with a safe and trusted relationship is important for learning. Just as we think about parent-child attunement as being important in development he also argues that this is important for the teacher-child relationship.

Areas that research has shown are important for teachers to understand are:

1 Neurodiversity: This is the idea that students all have natural differences in brain function and behaviour just as they have differences in academic skills and personality (Whitehead 2017).

2 Memory: This is more than what we can consciously recall about events from the past – it is also the way that past events affect future function (Siegel 2015a).

3 Mental Models: These generalisations from past experiences are the essence of learning. These models shape our understanding of the present and help us to work out the best ways to act in the future.

4 Co-constructing narratives: By teaching CYP about the narratives that they create about situations or learning we can help them to understand that these self-narratives become the blueprint for their thoughts, feelings and behaviours.

5 Stress: By understanding what happens in the brain when we are stressed and teaching strategies to reduce stress, we can support CYP with difficulties they may encounter in the future (Joëls et al. 2006).

6 Feeling safe: This depends on our interpersonal environment more than our physical environment. The connection and attunement created between teacher-student is vital for students to feel safe.

7 Attention: The capacity to pay attention is described by Olson (2014) as a torch in the dark. You choose what you light up and what you leave in the dark. Helping CYP understand that they are in control of where they point the torch and providing them with strategies and understanding to stay on task enables learning to progress.

8 Trust is the 'firm belief in the reliability, truth, or ability of someone or something.' Brown puts forward the belief that '[t]rust is a product of vulnerability that grows over time and requires work, attention, and full engagement.' She uses the analogy of the marbles in the jar. Each small act adds or takes away from the marbles in the jar. The level ebbs and flows. She argues that trust in schools is '[t]he need to feel trust to be vulnerable and we need to be vulnerable in order to trust' (Brown 2010).

9 Motivation: This is the internal process that causes a person to move either towards a goal or away from something they do not want to experience (Churches et al. 2017).

THE CIRCLES FOR LEARNING PROJECT

Circles for Learning is a unique research-based, whole class or small group project that builds the positive foundations for Mental Health and Wellbeing. It supports and strengthens learning skills alongside the development of social skills, emotional literacy and wellbeing. It facilitates and encourages children to experience how learning happens and explore brain development, relationships and emotions. This includes how other people might feel or experience situations, how to manage emotions, discover our sense of self and understand how our beliefs influence our behaviour.

Circles for Learning has been developed by Alison Waterhouse over the past five years. Alison initiated the Circles for Learning Project in primary schools in East Sussex, where she led and developed this innovative way of working with children. As colleagues became aware of her work, they asked to get involved, so Alison set up the Primary Research Project for five schools in East Sussex where she worked closely with the class teachers to both design and develop the project in their schools. This enabled her to work in both small rural schools and very deprived large urban schools as well as with a variety of teachers. As a result of the interest of professionals in the Secondary field, Alison has just completed a research project with 4 different secondary schools to explore and measure the impact of the work within their environment. This work has been the core of a research MA in Education with the University of York.

The project trains and then supports teachers to bring a parent and baby into the classroom once a month for a year. The children and young people are supported in observing the interactions, learning, relationships and the baby's early developing sense of self. Then, with the support of the teacher, they explore and think about what they have seen and how this may link to their own development, thinking, behaviour and ways of interacting with others.

These observations are the provocation or stimulus to follow-up work led by the teacher exploring one of the Circles for Learning's five areas of work:

1 Emotional competencies: including recognising emotions, managing our own emotions, recognising emotions in others and developing strategies to cope and deal with these emotions.

2 Relationships: including social skills, the learning relationship, social inclusion and empathy.

3 Self-discovery: including self-concept, self-esteem, self-efficacy, self-regulation, self-talk, self-compassion, mindsets and resilience.

4 Skills for effective learning.

5 Neuroscience and learning.

These five key areas form the foundations for Mental Health and Wellbeing. The follow-up work is not a scheme of work to be followed regardless of the needs of the children or young people but a wide range of activities that the teacher can refer to and use that supports the needs of the group at that time.

The resources within each of the five books in the *Mental Health and Wellbeing Toolkit* can be used as standalone resources to support the five key areas that create the foundations for Mental Health and Wellbeing or as part of the Circles for Learning Project.

TRACKING SHEET

NAME/GROUP:		
DATE:		**TERM:**
ASSESSMENTS UNDERTAKEN:		**OTHER INFORMATION:**
Date	Lesson:	Comments
Date	Lesson:	Comments
Date	Lesson:	Comments
Date	Lesson:	Comments
Date	Lesson:	Comments
Date	Lesson:	Comments
Date	Lesson:	Comments
Date	Lesson:	Comments
Date	Lesson:	Comments
Date	Lesson:	Comments

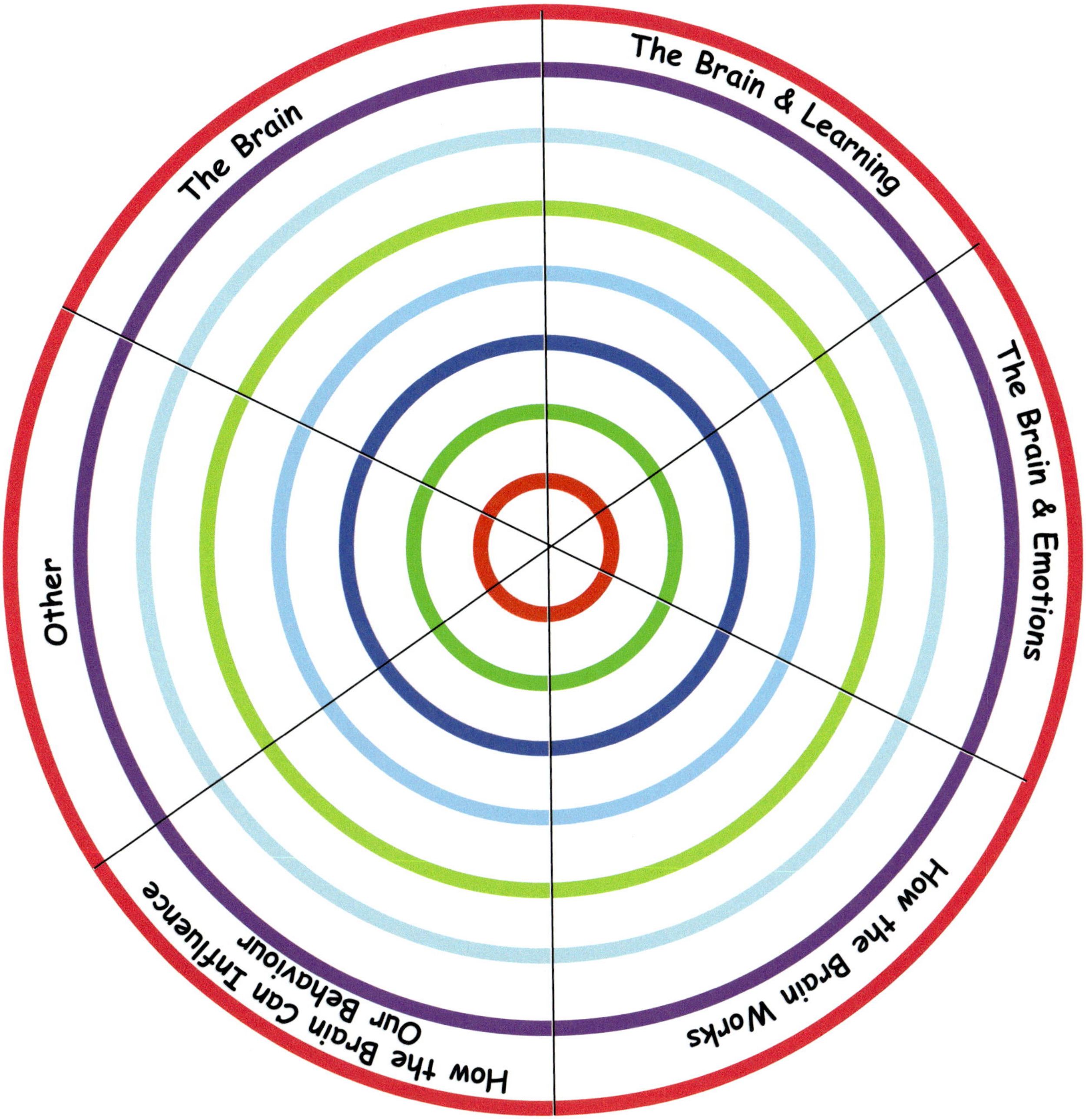

The circular tracking document has been designed to allow practitioners to monitor and track the areas that they have covered with the children. As each lesson is covered they are entered onto the document within the focus section. This enables practitioners to see the particular focus they are taking with their group. For some classes they may present a high need within a particular area or a strength in another area and so this can be shown and monitored. The document also allows for other lessons/activities to be added to the document that may have extended knowledge and understanding in this area from PSHE or Circle Time focus.

The document allows the flexibility to meet the needs of the children as they arise rather than having to follow a pre-set curriculum and in so doing allows practitioners to clearly see the areas of need and what they are doing to meet them.

Chapter 1

Development of the brain

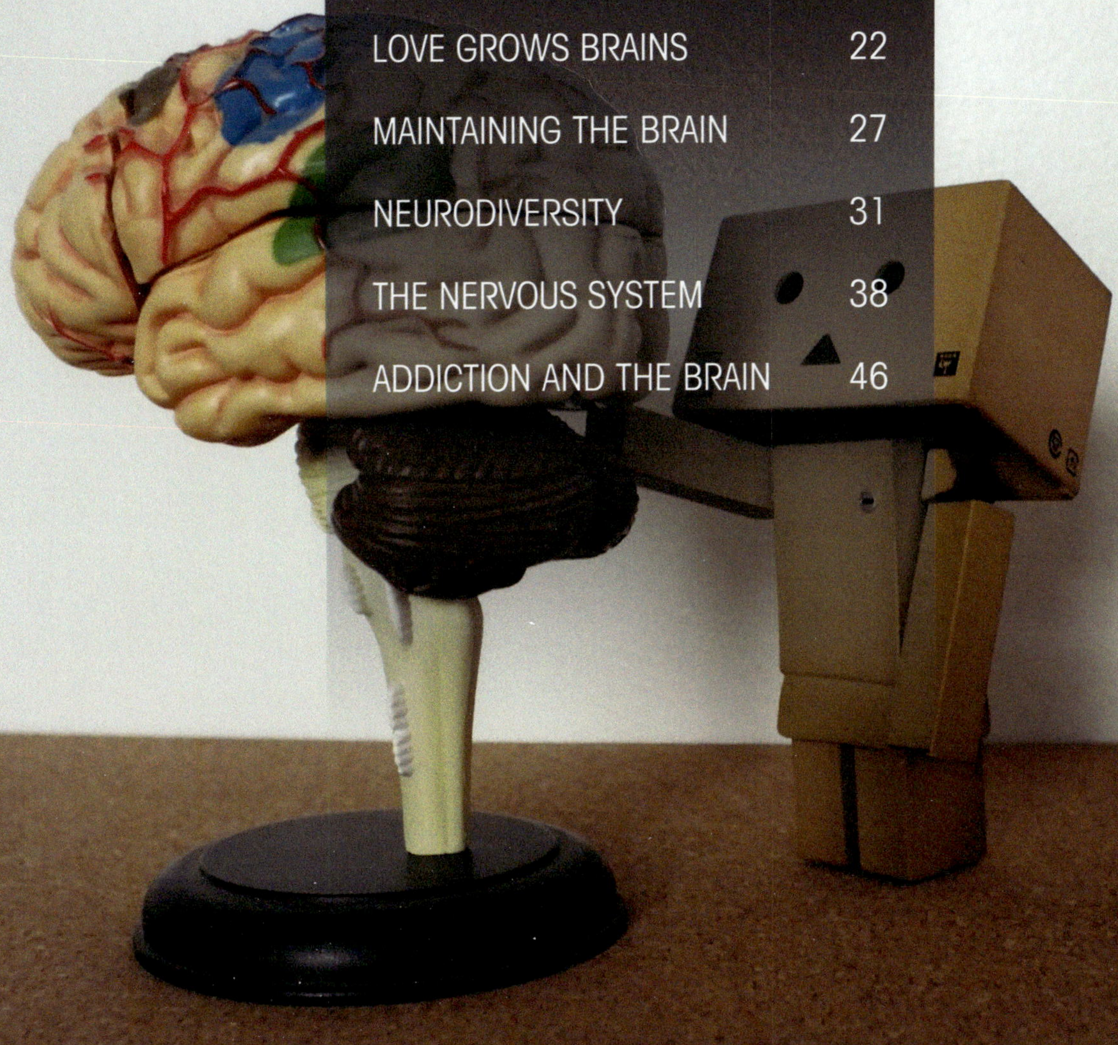

The brain

1 2 3

SESSION OBJECTIVES

To understand that the brain has many areas and that each area is responsible for different things.

SESSION OUTCOMES

- ✓ To be able to identify and talk about the different areas of the brain.
- ✓ To be able to discuss what each area of the brain does.

LESSON PLAN

- ➢ Ask the children to share some of the things that their class baby has learnt to do since they have been observing them.
- ➢ Ask why they think this is and how the brain has learnt these new things.
- ➢ Help them understand that a human baby is born with a brain which is not fully developed and that the first few years of life are really important as the brain is learning.

For those classrooms not able to undertake the Circles for Learning Project, video clips or photographs can be used to support the discussion around the topic and stimulate thoughts and ideas from the children and young people.

Task

KS1: To make a brain hat showing the different areas of the brain.

KS2: To make a model brain.

KS3: To create a large class brain poster with lift-up flaps showing what each part of the brain does.

KS1

1. Work with the children to collect all the things they know about the brain and then one thing they would like to know.
2. Discuss how scientists know about the brain – brain scans, people who have had a brain injury, operations, etc.

3 Show a picture of the brain. Discuss how very delicate it is and explore what protects it – the skull.

4 Show the children some of the parts of the brain and share the names and what they do.

5 Give the children the templates for the brain hat and ask them to make them in pairs.

KS2

1 Share a picture of a human brain with the children and then fill in the 'What I know about the brain' sheet in pairs.

2 Share what the children already know about the brain and what they would like to know.

3 Collect the questions they have asked and put them on a large piece of paper – these can be used as research questions when children have completed work or for homework.

4 Share brain scans and brain images and link to diagrams of what neuroscientists have found out about areas of the brain and their functions.

5 Ask the children to work in pairs and create a model of the brain from clay (like a jigsaw) that can be moved around and put together to make a complete brain.

6 Ask the children to number each piece and then, when dry, paint them.

7 Once dry, draw round each piece on a large sheet of card. Write information about each part of the brain on the card. The pieces can then be placed on their shape to form the complete brain.

KS3

1 Share a photograph and a brain scan with the children. Ask them to work in pairs and fill in the 'What I know about the brain' sheet.

2 Share what they know and write the questions they would like to know on a large sheet of paper – these can be used as research questions when they have completed work or for homework.

3 Ask the children to research areas of the brain:

- Find the different areas
- The name of the different areas
- What each area does

4 Ask the class to create a giant brain poster with lift-up flaps that shows the different areas of the brain and what they each do.

5 Create a display and put around the brain the questions and answers they collected at the beginning.

RESOURCES

1 Two sections of the brain hat – left and right. Instructions on how to make the brain hat.

2 'What I know about the brain' record sheet

3 Simple brain areas and names

4 Access to the internet

5 Brain scan

6 Photograph of a human brain

IMPORTANT POINTS

Different areas of the brain have different roles. Neuroscientists have been able to work out which areas do what from brain scans, people who have suffered head injuries and through dissection. There is still a lot that we do not know.

LEARNING LINKS

Learning, research, knowledge and understanding, working together, collaboration

REFLECTION

Questions:

Positive comment from child:

Positive comment from adult:

LEARNING DIMENSIONS		SOCIAL & EMOTIONAL SKILLS	
Strategic awareness		Emotional literacy	
Learning relationships		Neuroscience	
Curiosity		Self-regulation	
Creativity		Self-development	
Meaning making			
Changing & learning			
Resilience			

Brain Hemisphere Hat

TARGET AGE RANGE:

Ages 8–13

WHAT YOU WILL NEED:

Copies of the left and right brain

Clear tape

Glue

NOTES:

When using glue it is useful to use clothes pegs to hold the paper until the glue has dried.

It is useful when working with a class to have 2 or 3 hats assembled at different stages so that the children know what they should look like.

HOW TO ASSEMBLE:

Cut out both hemispheres, then snip in on the 'V' lines. Don't snip the dashed lines, just the solid ones. Then pull the 'flaps' you have created over the dashed lines and glue or tape. After you have pulled the flaps over to the dashed lines, the hat will start to take on a rounded shape. To put the two halves together, simply choose one side to overlap onto the other by about 0.5 cm and secure with tape.

You might want to write 'Left' and 'Right' on the inside of the hat after you have cut them out so you don't forget which is which.

Have fun and enjoy.

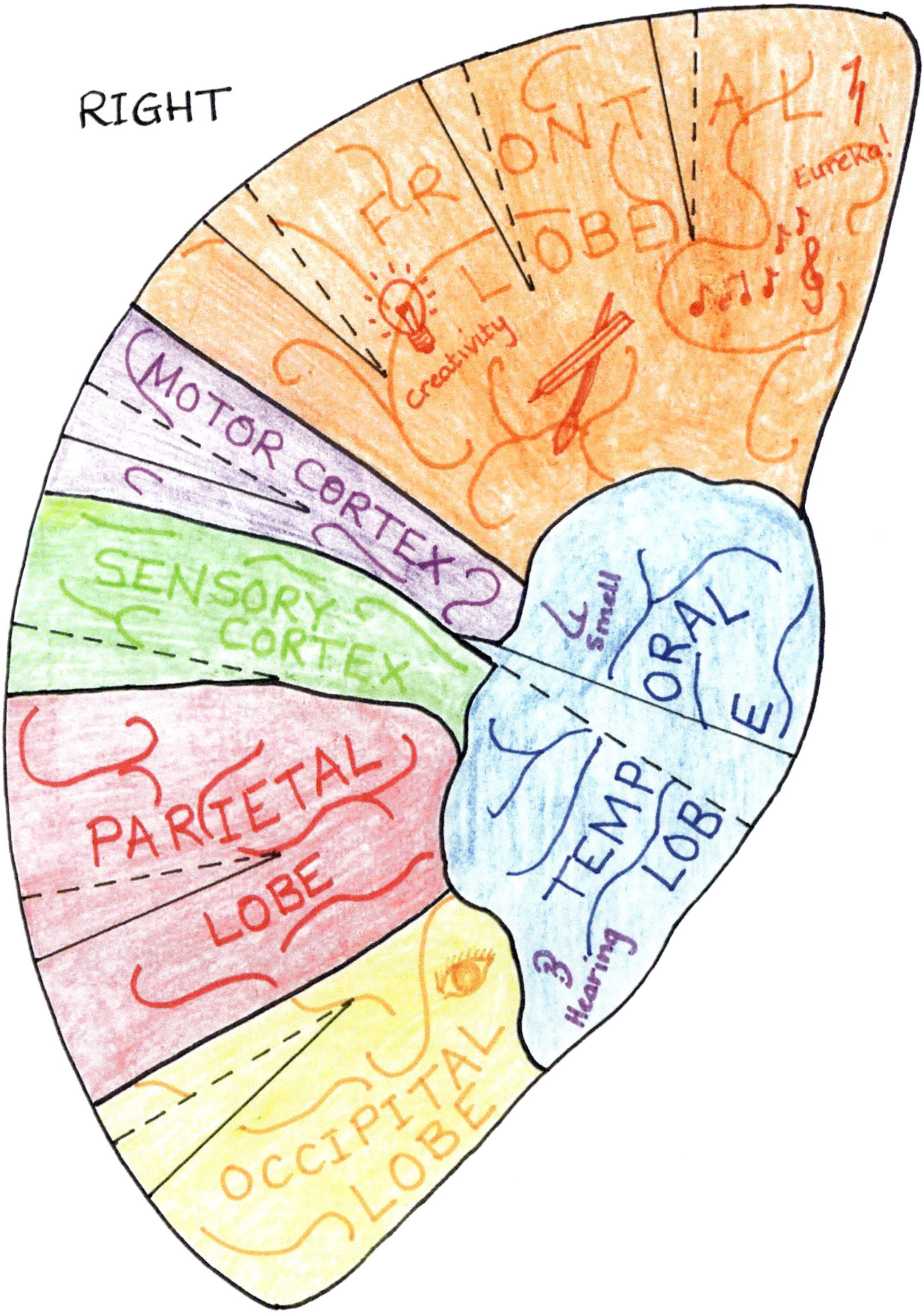
RIGHT
FRONTAL LOBE
Eureka!
creativity
MOTOR CORTEX
SENSORY CORTEX
PARIETAL LOBE
OCCIPITAL LOBE
TEMPORAL LOBE
smell
Hearing

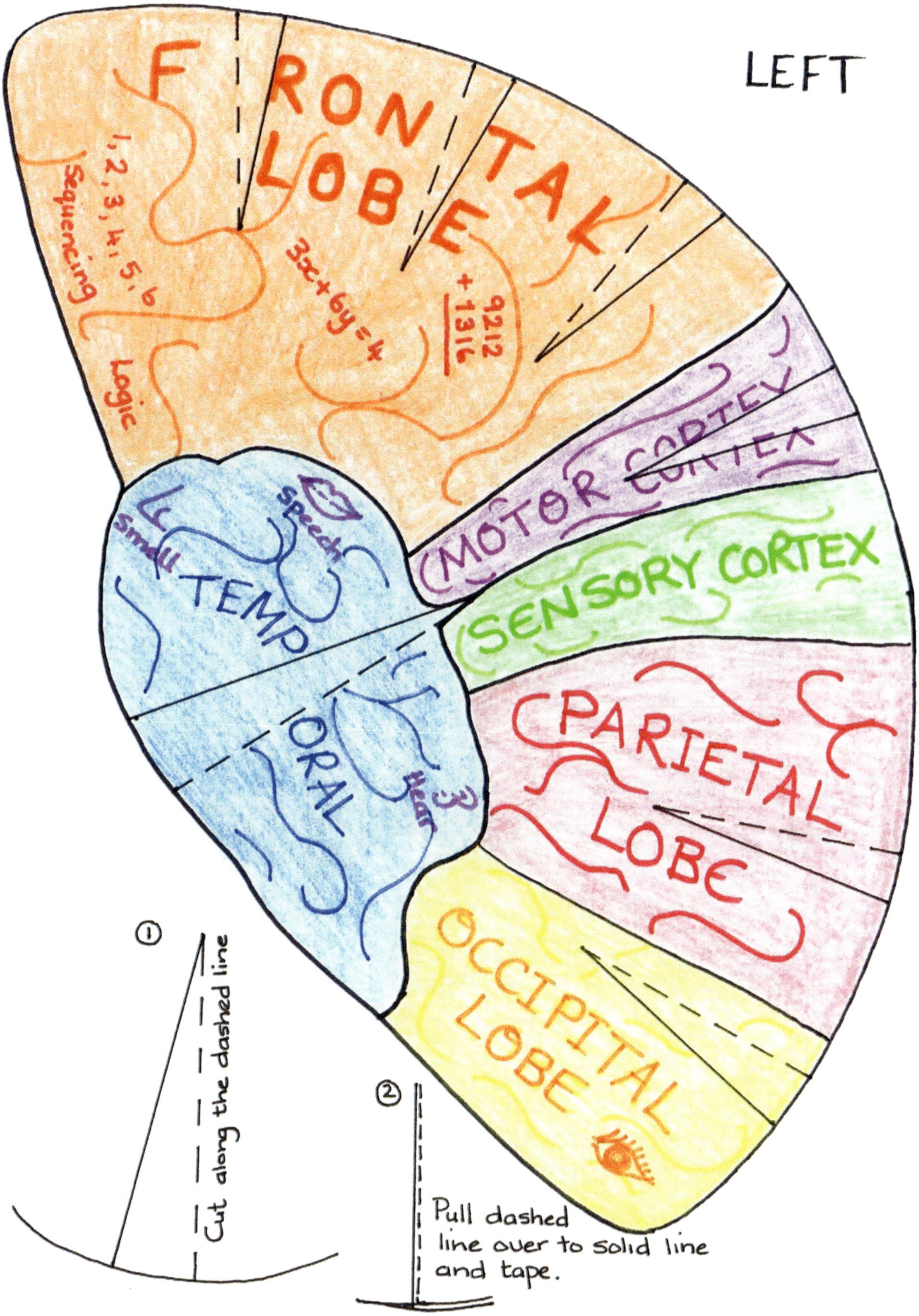
LEFT
FRONTAL LOBE
1, 2, 3, 4, 5, 6
Sequencing
Logic
3x + 6y = 4
9212
+ 1316
MOTOR CORTEX
SENSORY CORTEX
PARIETAL LOBE
OCCIPITAL LOBE
TEMPORAL
Speech
Smell
Hear
①
Cut along the dashed line
②
Pull dashed line over to solid line and tape.

The Brain

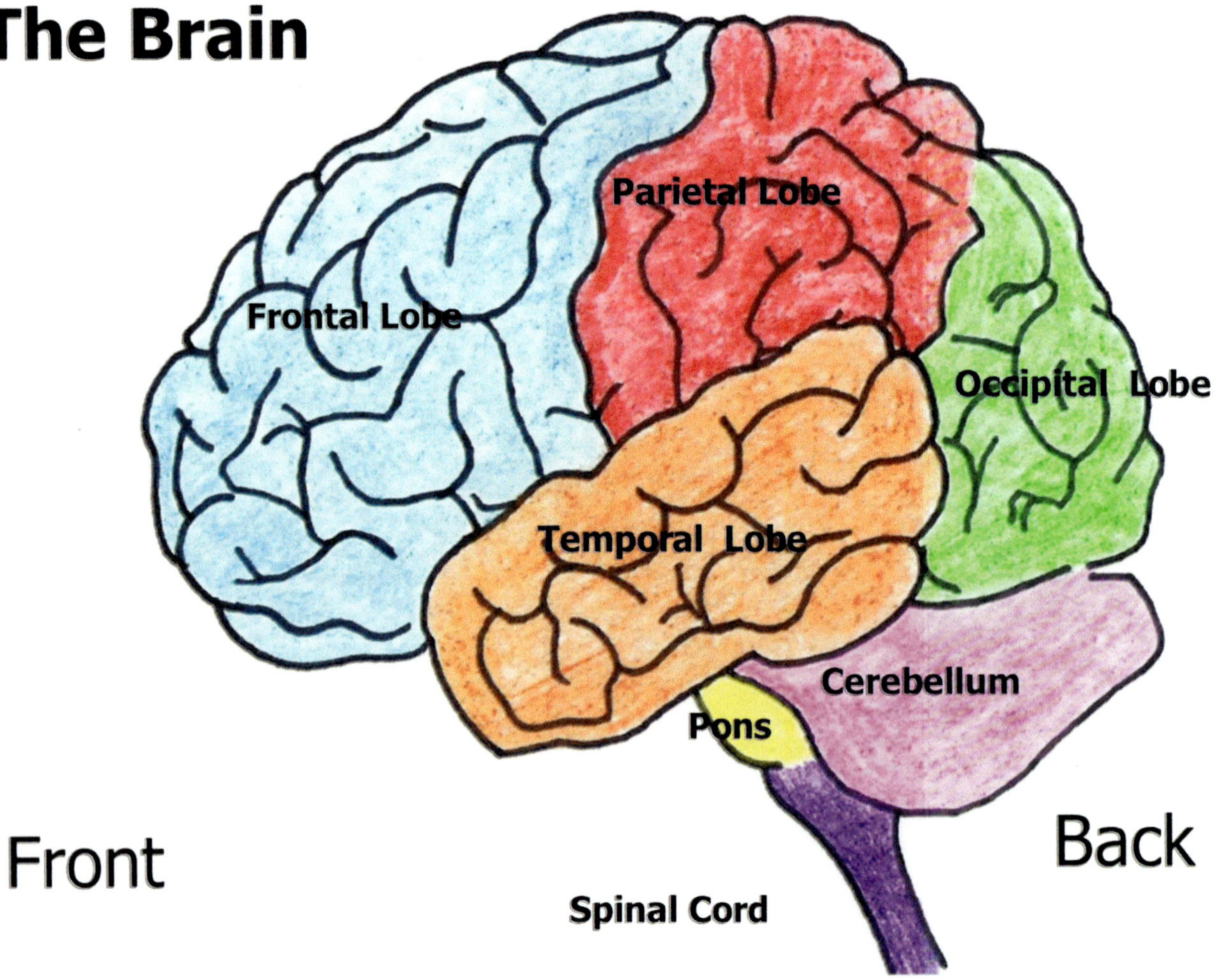
Parietal Lobe
Frontal Lobe
Occipital Lobe
Temporal Lobe
Cerebellum
Pons
Front
Back
Spinal Cord

Information about the Brain and Nervous System			
What I know about the brain and nervous system	What I want to know about the brain and nervous system	What I have learnt about the brain and nervous system	Thoughts and ideas

Cross Section of the Human Brain

Cerebrum (Cerebral Cortex)

Thinking, Learning, Remembering, Sensing, Speaking, Feeling emotions, Voluntary Movement (movements you choose to do) Planning, Decision Making, Reasoning

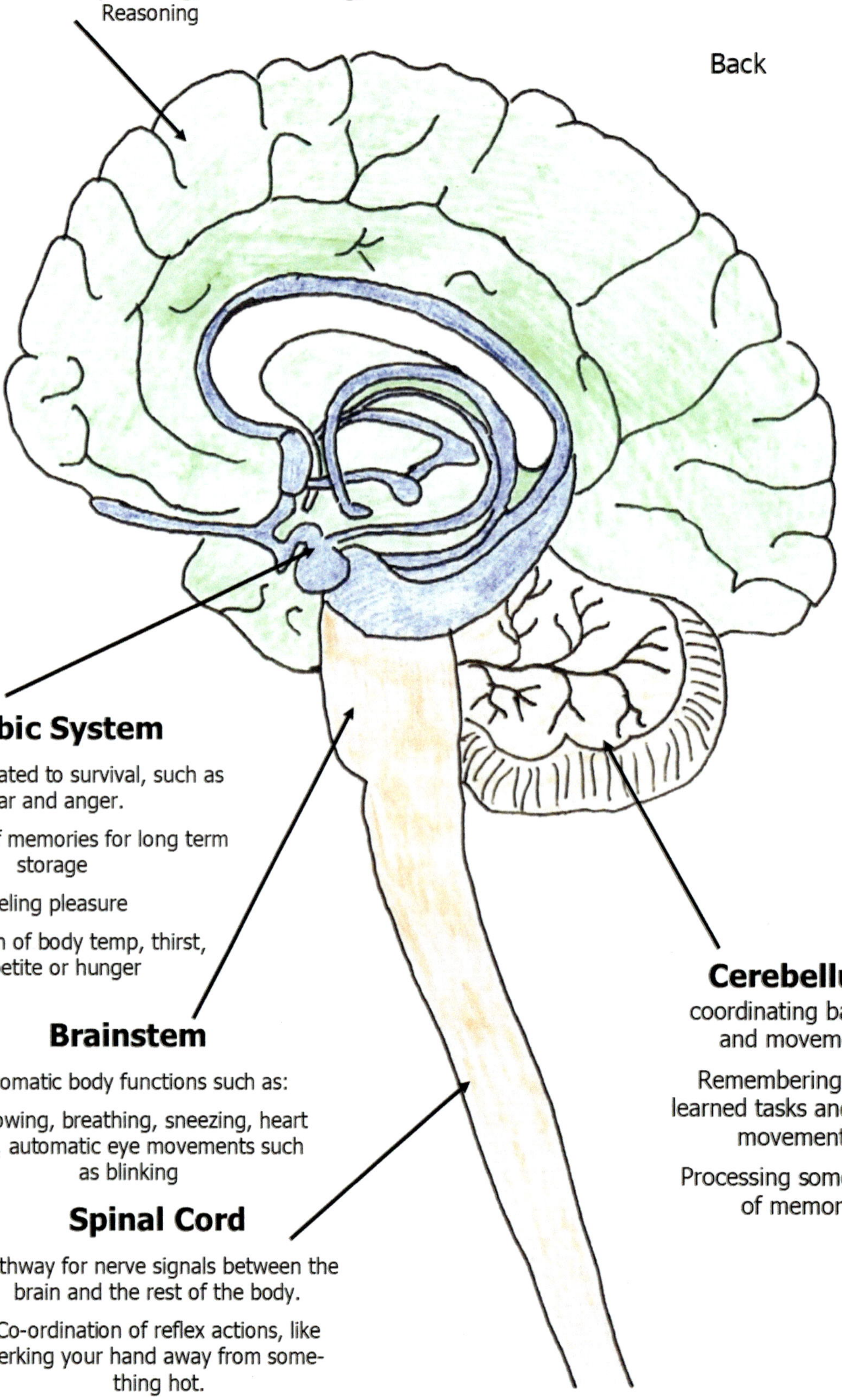

Limbic System

Emotions related to survival, such as fear and anger.

Processing of memories for long term storage

Feeling pleasure

Regulation of body temp, thirst, appetite or hunger

Brainstem

Automatic body functions such as:

Swallowing, breathing, sneezing, heart beat, automatic eye movements such as blinking

Spinal Cord

Pathway for nerve signals between the brain and the rest of the body.

Co-ordination of reflex actions, like jerking your hand away from something hot.

Cerebellum

coordinating balance and movement

Remembering well-learned tasks and skilled movements

Processing some types of memory

Lateral Surface of the Cerebrum showing areas of functional Localisation

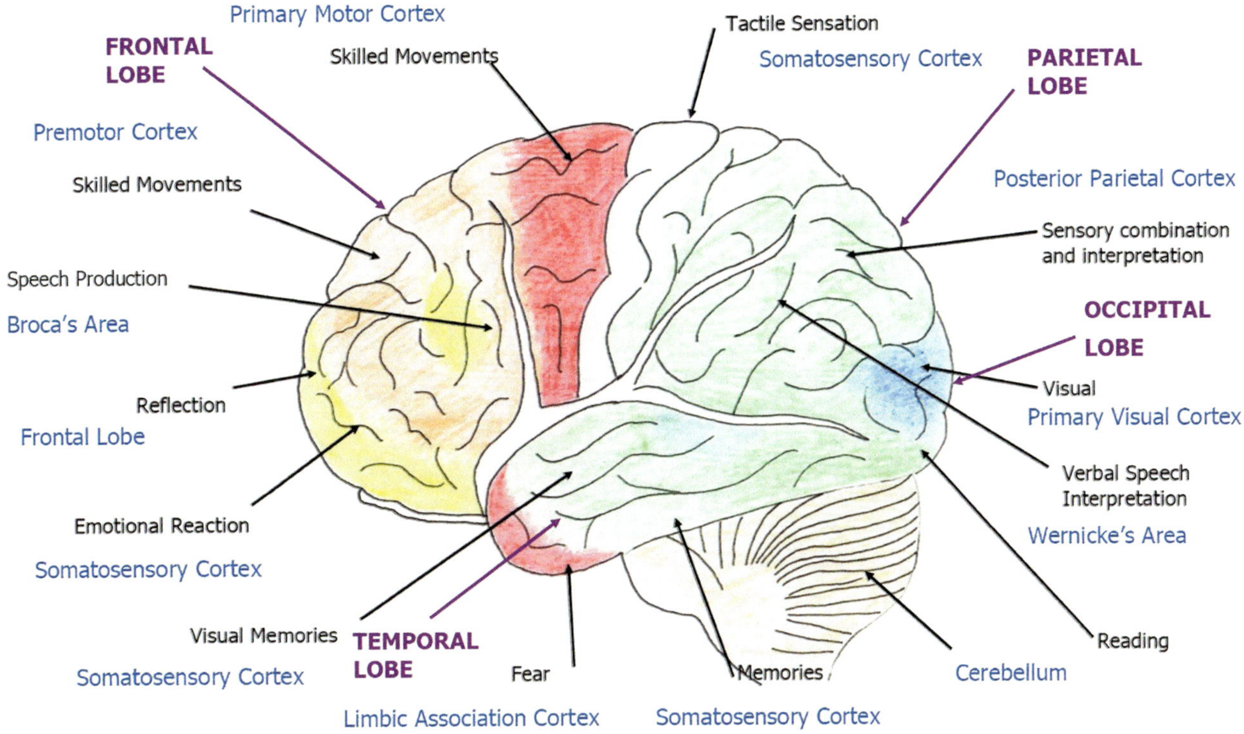

Lateral Surface of the Cerebrum showing areas of functional Localisation

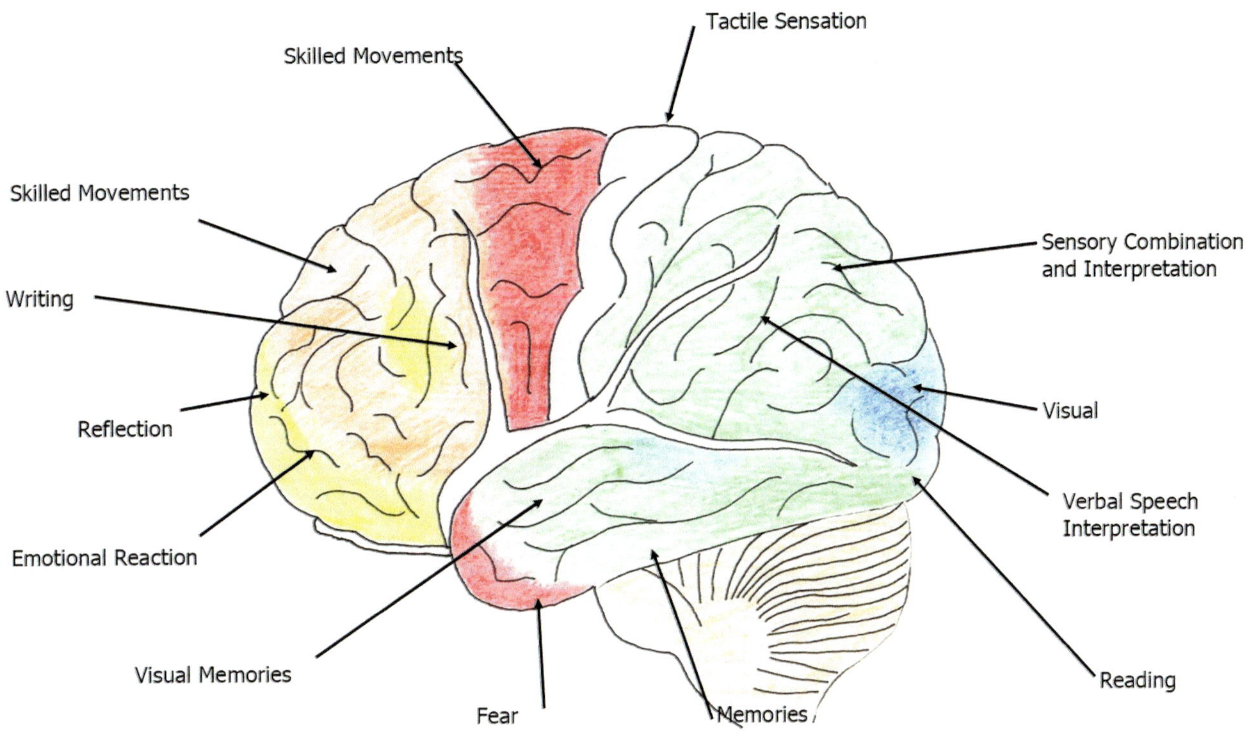

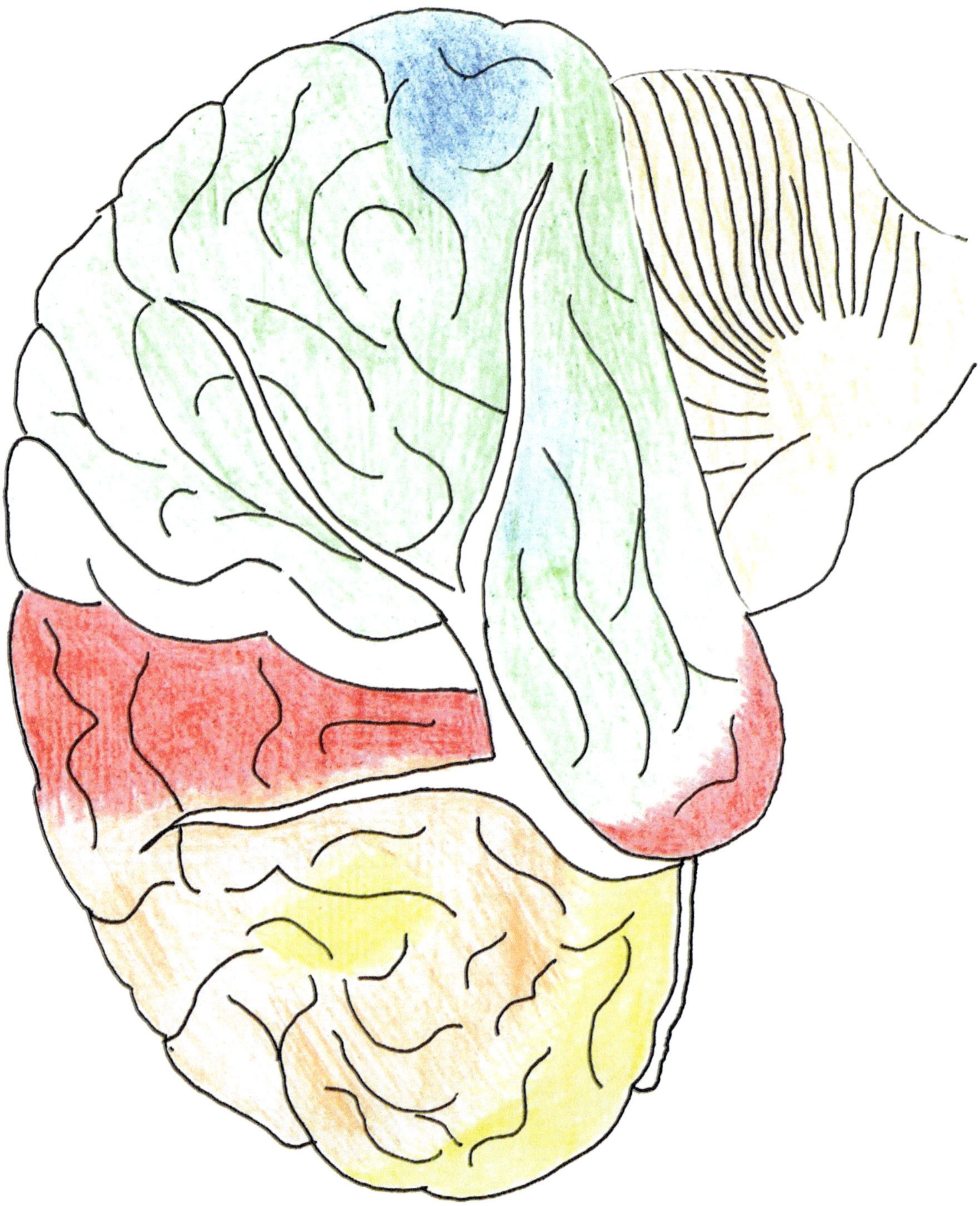

How the brain develops

1 2 3

SESSION OBJECTIVES

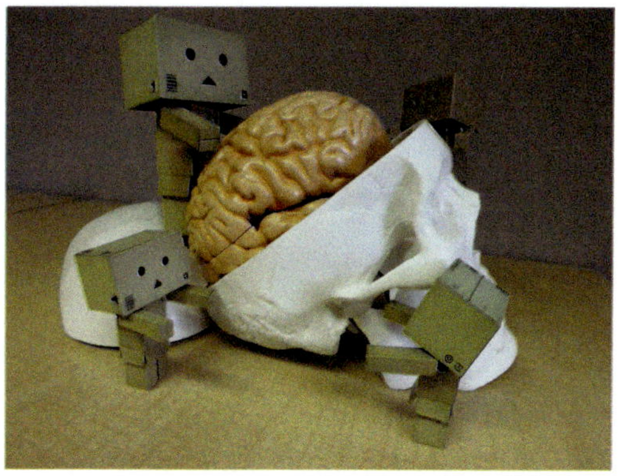

To understand how the human brain grows and develops both in the womb and also after birth.

SESSION OUTCOMES

✓ To be able to describe how a human baby's brain develops both in the womb and after birth.

✓ To be able to describe why what a mother does in pregnancy has an impact on the baby's development.

LESSON PLAN

➢ Ask the class to think about how much their class baby has changed since they have been observing them.

➢ Can they note the changes that they have seen?

➢ Ask the class baby's Mum to talk about pregnancy and what she did to keep the growing baby healthy.

For those classrooms not able to undertake the Circles for Learning Project, video clips or photographs can be used to support the discussion around the topic and stimulate thoughts and ideas from the children and young people.

Task

KS1: To make a postcard to show something that keeps us healthy.

KS2/KS3: To make a poster to help inform pregnant mothers how to keep healthy and support the growth of their baby.

KS1

1 Explain to the class that they are going to undertake a science experiment.

Give the class 5 flowers, separate them out and put them in 5 jam jars. Explain to the children that you have 5 different substances in each jar.

2 Place water and flower food in one jar, vinegar in another, soap and water in another, plain water and cola in the last one.

3 Ask the children what they think will happen and why.

4 Watch what happens over a few days and then discuss the result.

5 Help the children link this to staying healthy.

6 Ask the children to create a postcard to show how what they eat has an effect on their health.

KS2

1 Show the children a picture of the brain development of a baby in the womb.

2 Discuss the environment that the baby is growing in – the mother's body. What does this mean for the mother – that she needs to be careful what she puts into that environment. Explore how that might make her feel – happy that she has a baby growing inside her but also cross that she has to be careful what she eats and what she does.

3 Set up the flower experiment as for KS1 and discuss what they think will happen to the flower. Link this to the growth and development of the baby.

4 Ask one half of the children to research the things that are good for pregnant women and the other half things that they need to avoid.

5 Pair up the children, one from each of the groups and ask them to create a poster to demonstrate what and how a pregnant mother needs to do to keep the baby healthy.

6 Share the posters and discuss what they have learnt.

7 Remind the children that the baby's brain has not finished growing and developing when the baby is born and that the first 5 years of life are really important.

RESOURCES

1 Card, pens and paper

2 Flowers

3 Jam jars

4 Water, plant food, vinegar, washing-up liquid, cola

5 Internet access for research

6 Pictures to show the baby's developing brain in the womb

IMPORTANT POINTS

The baby grows in the mother's womb within her body and how she treats her body – what she puts into it and the things she does – has an effect on the growth and development of the baby.

LEARNING LINKS

Working together, research, thinking and learning, health awareness.

REFLECTION

Questions:

Positive comment from child:

Positive comment from adult:

LEARNING DIMENSIONS		SOCIAL & EMOTIONAL SKILLS	
Strategic awareness	(orange)	Emotional literacy	
Learning relationships	(orange)	Neuroscience	(green)
Curiosity	(orange)	Self-regulation	
Creativity		Self-development	
Meaning making	(orange)		
Changing & learning	(orange)		
Resilience			

The first 5 years

SESSION OBJECTIVES

To understand that the human brain continues to grow and develop after birth.

To understand that the environment impacts on brain development and growth.

SESSION OUTCOMES

✓ To create a road map to show milestones and what has been learnt over the first 5 years of life.

LESSON PLAN

➢ Ask the children to remember all the things their class baby has learnt since they have been observing them. Help them see how much the baby has learnt in only a small amount of time.

➢ Ask the children to think about the sort of environment that a baby needs to develop and thrive. What sort of things would they see in their home or in their room?

For those classrooms not able to undertake the Circles for Learning Project, video clips or photographs can be used to support the discussion around the topic and stimulate thoughts and ideas from the children and young people.

Task

KS1: Create a road map to show the first 5 years of their life and how they have changed.

KS2: Put a developmental timeline of achievements for a baby/young child in the correct order.

KS3: Create a developmental timeline for a baby/young child.

KS1

1 Share a range of photos of a young child learning to do things with the children.

2 Ask the children to help you put them in the order they were achieved.

3 Introduce the word 'milestones' and describe what it means.

4 Give the children the list of milestones and ask them to work in pairs and put them in order.

5 Get each pair to lay these out on their desk and then ask the children to walk around and see what the other children have done.

6 Discuss what they have created and show the milestones in the correct order on the board.

7 Ask the children to draw a road across a large sheet of paper.

8 Divide the road into 5 equal parts and label each one as 1 year.

9 Ask the children to draw a picture of themselves learning to do something in each year.

10 Share what they have done and explore what enabled them to do this – was it input from parents, copying older brothers or sisters, playing at nursery, a teacher or wanting to achieve something for themselves?

11 Highlight the many different forms of motivation there are and the many different people who have helped them.

KS2/KS3

1 Show a variety of photos of a baby learning to do things.

2 Ask the children to work in pairs and 'brain shower' all the things they think a baby can do by the age of 5. Write each one on a sticky note and put them in the order they think they happened.

3 Introduce the word 'milestones' and then work together to create a list of things that a baby learns by the age of 5.

4 Ask the children to create a timeline for themselves to show one thing they have learnt in each year of their life.

5 Ask the children to show 3 things that they are looking forward to being able to do this year. What do they need to be able to achieve them? e.g. learn to ride a bike – need a bike and an adult to help them know what to do and support them when they try this out or learn to do joined up writing – need lessons at school and lots of practice. Ask the children to think of 3 things they are looking forward to doing in the years ahead.

6 Share and discuss the different things that the children have come up with and think about what you need to achieve these goals.

RESOURCES

1 Large sheets of paper, pens and pencils

2 Milestone labels

3 Internet access

4 Sticky notes

5 Pictures of a baby doing a range of things

IMPORTANT POINTS

Our brain is continuously growing and developing; we are able to learn new things all the time.

LEARNING LINKS

Growing and learning, collaboration, working together, speaking and listening, planning and organisation.

REFLECTION

Questions:

Positive comment from child:

Positive comment from adult:

LEARNING DIMENSIONS		SOCIAL & EMOTIONAL SKILLS	
Strategic awareness		Emotional literacy	
Learning relationships		Neuroscience	■
Curiosity		Self-regulation	
Creativity		Self-development	
Meaning making			
Changing & learning			
Resilience			

Saying the word Dad	Crawling
Sucking	Walking
Holding a spoon	Rolling over
Sitting up	Recognising their Mum's face
Reading their name	Drawing a squiggle
Drawing a circle	Writing their name
Reading a sentence	Riding a bike
Eating solid foods	Using the toilet
Talking in sentences	Skipping
Uses thumb and finger to pick things up	Jumps with two feet
Throws a ball	Catches a ball
Expresses emotions	Laughs

Love grows brains

1 2 3

SESSION OBJECTIVES

To be able to describe the type of environment that enables brains to grow and children to thrive.

SESSION OUTCOMES

✓ To be able to describe the type of environment that enables brains to grow and children to thrive.

LESSON PLAN

- Ask the children to remember a time when their class baby and parent did something together. How did the baby respond to the focus and attention the parent gave it?
- Ask the children to describe a stimulating environment and a non-stimulating environment and the impact this might have on brain development. Ensure that human interaction is highlighted in the stimulating environment.

For those classrooms not able to undertake the Circles for Learning Project, video clips or photographs can be used to support the discussion around the topic and stimulate thoughts and ideas from the children and young people.

Task

KS1: To write a recipe for growing the brain.

KS2/KS3: Arguments for and against 'Love Grows Brains' and then debate.

KS1

1 Remind the children about how the mother's body gives the baby an environment in which to grow and the work they have previously done about how the mother can keep healthy during pregnancy. This includes what she eats and how she treats her body.

2 Ask the children to think about the environment that a baby needs to grow and develop in. Ask each child to think of one thing the baby needs – interaction, toys, food, a safe environment, etc.

3 Tell the children that they are going to write a recipe for growing brains. Share the language of recipes and write the sentence starters on the board – help the children identify the language of recipes – a pinch, a spoonful, a cup, a dash, a sprinkling, etc.

4 Give the children the recipe sheet and ask them to work in small groups or pairs and write a recipe for growing brains. This might include a loving parent who thinks you are the best, a bedroom with toys and games to play with, etc.

KS2/KS3

1 Share with the children brain scans of 2 children, one who has experienced severe deprivation and one who has experienced a caring and stimulating environment. See Resources section for link.

2 Discuss what the scan shows and why this difference in brain development has occurred.

3 Explain to the children that they are going to have a debate. The title for the debate is 'Does Love Grow Brains?'

4 Divide the children into two groups. One group will find evidence to show that love does grow brains; the other will find evidence to show that love has nothing to do with the growth of brains.

5 Ask each child to find 3 pieces of evidence. Write each piece of evidence on a sticky note. Collect the evidence for each point of view on large sheets of paper.

6 Ask the children to choose which side of the debate they would like to start on – yes, love grows brains or no, love doesn't impact on brain development. Set the room up with chairs on two sides facing each other. Put chairs across the bottom for those children who are undecided.

7 Ask the children to take their seats.

8 Explain the rules – if children wish to put forward a point of view, they have to put their hands up. When they have finished speaking, they choose the next person to talk. This person has to be on the opposite side. At intervals you will ask children if they wish to change and sit in a different place.

9 Set the time for the first part of the debate.

10 When you have reached the end, allow people to move sides.

11 Continue the debate and then remind people that you will be stopping. Ask for children to move and then count the number of children on each side. The winning side of the debate is the side with the most children.

12 You can allow the debate to be divided into two parts with a few days between so that children can talk about it with others and continue to research the topic.

RESOURCES

1 Brain scans of children from a deprived environment and a rich environment,

https://tinyurl.com/y5qanahq

2 Sticky notes

3 Large sheets of paper

4 Pens and pencils

5 Internet for research

6 Recipe sheet

7 A recipe with a variety of language for cooking

IMPORTANT POINTS

The environment in which we grow has an effect on how our brain develops.

LEARNING LINKS

Collaboration, speaking and listening, research, self-awareness.

REFLECTION

Questions:

Positive comment from child:

Positive comment from adult:

LEARNING DIMENSIONS		SOCIAL & EMOTIONAL SKILLS	
Strategic awareness		Emotional literacy	
Learning relationships		Neuroscience	
Curiosity		Self-regulation	
Creativity		Self-development	
Meaning making			
Changing & learning			
Resilience			

Recipe for a healthy brain

A cup of ....

Pour in a little ....

Mix in ....

A pinch of..........

A spoonful of ....

Add a little ....

A dollop of ....

A cup of ....

A dusting of ....

Add a little ....

Drizzle with ....

Mix in ....

Maintaining the brain

1 2 3

SESSION OBJECTIVES

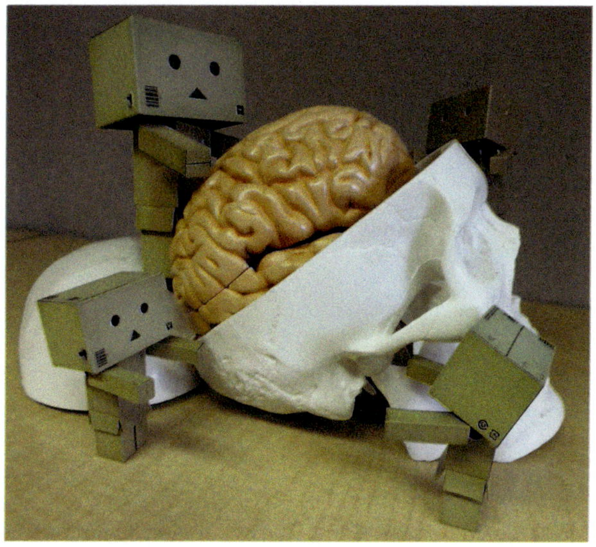

To understand that our brain is part of our body and is affected by what we eat and how we treat our body.

SESSION OUTCOMES

✓ To be able to describe how to keep healthy and look after our body and our brain.

LESSON PLAN

- Ask the children to describe the sorts of things a baby eats.
- What sort of diet has their class baby had?
- Was their baby breast fed or bottle fed?

For those classrooms not able to undertake the Circles for Learning Project, video clips or photographs can be used to support the discussion around the topic and stimulate thoughts and ideas from the children and young people.

Task

KS1: 'How to look after your brain' booklet.

KS2: 'How to look after your brain' advert.

KS3: Research that has informed us on what is good for the brain.

KS1

1 Ask the children to think of the things their brain needs to keep healthy.

2 Collect the ideas the children come up with and write them on the board.

3 Watch the 'Look after your brain' video, www.youtube.com/watch?v=12pbrkcfRDI

4 Was there anything you had forgotten? If so add it to the list.

5 Explain to the children that you want to make a 'Keep your brain healthy' leaflet as a class.

6 Ask each child to choose something that they would like to draw and write about which keeps their brain healthy.

7 Divide the different things up between the class – don't forget the front cover and the 'blurb' on the back cover.

8 Complete the booklet as a class and then share with another class or in assembly.

KS2

1 Ask the children to think of the things their brain needs to keep healthy.

2 Collect the ideas the children come up with and write them on the board.

3 Watch the 'Look after your brain' video, www.youtube.com/watch?v=12pbrkcfRDI

4 Was there anything you had forgotten? If so add it to the list.

5 Explain to the children that you would like them to make a 'Keep your brain healthy' poster.

6 Work together to decide the success criteria for the poster. Look at examples and decide why they do their job well.

- Clear information
- Easily read
- Pictures
- Eye-catching
- Ways to keep your brain healthy
- Why keeping your brain healthy is important

7 Allow the children to work in pairs or individually.

KS3

1 Ask the children to think of the things their brain needs to keep healthy.

2 Collect the ideas the children come up with and write them on the board.

3 Watch the 'Look after your brain' video, www.youtube.com/watch?v=12pbrkcfRDI

4 Discuss how we know these things – science has found them out.

5 Ask the children to find a piece of research about keeping the brain healthy. They will need to be able to share this with the group so may want to write notes or develop a drawing or poster of the information.

6 Find information about things that affect the brain in a negative way – this may be sugar or caffeine or drugs.

7 Share the information they have found.

8 How reliable is the evidence? Is it scientifically supported? How can we tell? Does the information come from a promotion site or is it valid?

9 Explore the evidence and agree 10 top tips for keeping the brain healthy.

RESOURCES

1 'Look after your brain – Brainsmart – BBC',

www.youtube.com/watch?v=12pbrkcfRDI

IMPORTANT POINTS

The brain is part of the body and so needs to have a healthy environment in which to grow and develop. Anything that the body experiences – this can be things that are bad for the body like sugar or caffeine drugs or alcohol – affects the brain.

LEARNING LINKS

Collaboration, speaking and listening, research bias, self-awareness, keeping healthy.

REFLECTION

Questions:

Positive comment from child:

Positive comment from adult:

LEARNING DIMENSIONS		SOCIAL & EMOTIONAL SKILLS	
Strategic awareness		Emotional literacy	
Learning relationships		Neuroscience	
Curiosity		Self-regulation	
Creativity		Self-development	
Meaning making			
Changing & learning			
Resilience			

Neurodiversity

1 2 3

SESSION OBJECTIVES

To understand that every brain is unique.

To be able to define what neurotypical and neurodiverse mean and give examples.

SESSION OUTCOMES

- ✓ To be able to draw a picture that represents their unique brain showing the things they enjoy and their interests.
- ✓ To be able to use the terms 'neurotypical' and 'neurodiverse' and explain what they mean.

LESSON PLAN

- ➢ Ask the children to describe how their class baby has developed since they have been observing them and to share how they are unique and individual.
- ➢ Ask the children to identify things that their class baby is interested in and how their parents have supported this interest. This could be colours linked to clothes, cartoons linked to films or lunchboxes.

For those classrooms not able to undertake the Circles for Learning Project, video clips or photographs can be used to support the discussion around the topic and stimulate thoughts and ideas from the children and young people.

Task

KS1: To create a brain picture that represents them showing the things they like and are interested in.

KS2: To create a neurodiversity poster.

KS3: To create a neurodiversity poster with information about different neurodiverse brains: ADHD, ASC, Dyspraxia, Dyslexia, etc.

KS1

1 Share a photo of a human brain with the children and ask them to share all the things they now know about the brain and what it can do as well as how it has grown and developed.

2 Share beautiful pictures of flowers and then use these to support the children's understanding that each brain has had a very different experience and so has grown and developed in its own very special way. Introduce the word UNIQUE and help them understand that every brain is one of a kind.

3 Explain to the children that you want them to draw a picture of their brain showing all the things that they love and are interested in.

4 Get them to think of one thing that the person on their right needs to put inside their picture.

5 Ask them for one thing the person on their left should have in their picture.

6 Ask them for one thing that they would want to put inside their picture.

7 Give the children a brain shape to fill in.

8 Cut different colour heads and shoulders out of sugar paper and stick the completed brain pictures inside. Create a display to show the UNIQUE brains of the children within the class.

9 Read the book *A Walk in the Rain with a Brain*. And discuss how all brains are equal and individual.

KS2

1 Share the 'What is Neurodiversity?' poster with the children.

2 Discuss and share thoughts and feelings.

3 What questions does it make them want to ask?

4 What thoughts do they have about different brains?

5 Ask the children to work in pairs and create a poster for their classroom about the benefits of being in a neurodiverse classroom.

6 Share the posters as they are being created and get feedback from the other children. Remember the feedback sandwich: I like . . . It would be good if you can expand or clarify . . . I think my favourite bit is . . . Because . . .

7 When completed, hold an exhibition to share the work.

8 Read the books *You're So Clumsy Charley* and *I have Bees in My Brain* and *The Higgledy-Piggledy Pigeon*.

KS3

1 Share the 'What is Neurodiversity?' poster with the children.

2 Discuss and share thoughts and feelings.

3 What questions does it make them want to ask?

4 What thoughts do they have about different brains?

5 Ask the children to choose which brain they would like to find out more information about. Ask them to research what the strengths and differences are for the different groups of brains – autism, dyslexia, dyspraxia, bipolar, epileptic, schizophrenic, ADHD, PTSD, Alzheimer's, OCD.

   Remind the children that it is not OK to pick on different groups of people and make them feel 'bad' for the way their brain is or the things they can or cannot do.

6 Ask the children to work in pairs and create a poster for their classroom about the benefits of being in a neurodiverse classroom.

7 Share the posters as they are being created and get feedback from the other children. Remember the feedback sandwich: I like . . . It would be good if you can expand or clarify . . . I think my favourite bit is . . . Because . .

8 When completed, hold an exhibition to share the work.

RESOURCES

1 'What is Neurodiversity?' poster

2 Internet for research

3 Large sheets of paper

4 Pens, pencils, etc

5 Brain outline

6 Sugar paper

7 Photo of the human brain

8 *I Have Bees in My Brain* by Trish Hammond

9 *A Walk in the Rain with a Brain* by Edward Hallowell

10 *You're So Clumsy Charley* by Jane Binnion

11 *The Higgledy-Piggledy Pigeon* by Don Winn

IMPORTANT POINTS

Each person has their own individual genetic makeup and this, linked with their different experiences, has helped to create a UNIQUE and different brain. Some brains are similar and so are grouped together and given different labels. Each person has a range of strengths and differences.

LEARNING LINKS

Speaking and listening, creativity, working together, self-development, self-awareness.

REFLECTION

Questions:

Positive comment from child:

Positive comment from adult:

LEARNING DIMENSIONS		SOCIAL & EMOTIONAL SKILLS	
Strategic awareness		Emotional literacy	
Learning relationships		Neuroscience	
Curiosity		Self-regulation	
Creativity		Self-development	
Meaning making			
Changing & learning			
Resilience			

What is Neurodiversity?

This is Sam

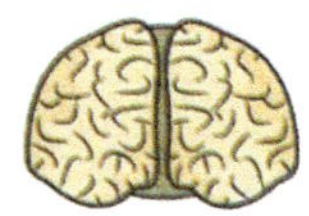

This is Sam's brain

These are Sam's friends. They all have brains too. No two brains are the same - This is NEURODIVERSITY. All brains are different and unique.

Sam and friends are happy with their individual differences. They support each other and value the strengths that they each bring to their group.

Some people's brains are similar and so they are labelled the same. Some of these labels are: typical, autistic, dyslexia, dyspraxic, bipolar. All of these labels except typical indicate NEURODIVERGENCE. This means that the brain is seen as different from societies expectation of normal. Not all neurodivergence is diagnosed, so that not all people who are perceived as neurotypical are. Neorodivergence is neither good nor bad. A person can be born with it or it can be acquired. It is up to each neurodiverse person to decide what support they would like.

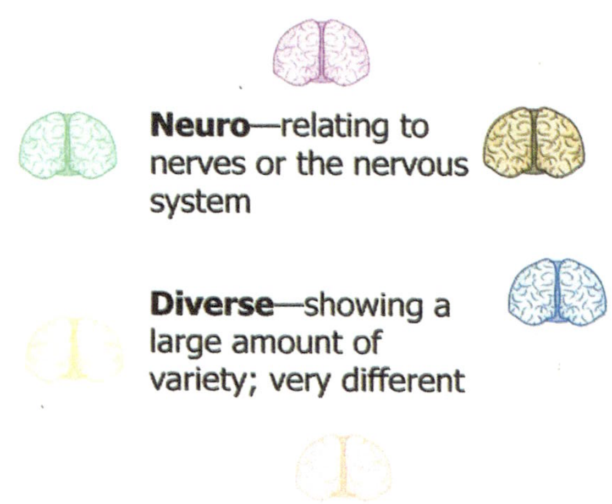

Neuro—relating to nerves or the nervous system

Diverse—showing a large amount of variety; very different

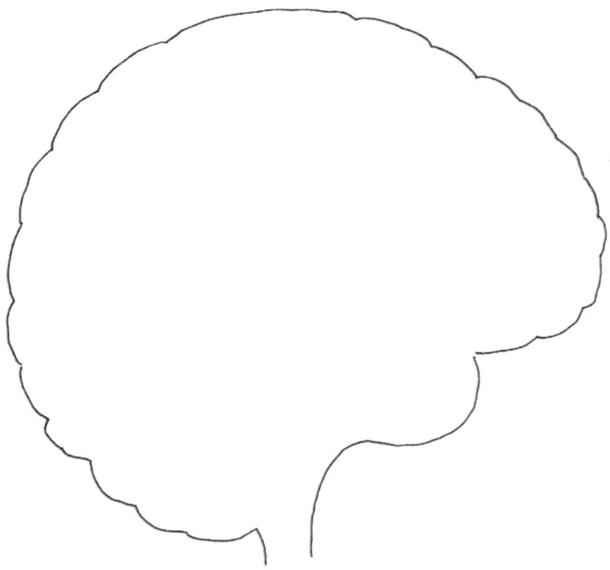

The nervous system

1 2 3

SESSION OBJECTIVES

To understand how messages are sent around the body through the nervous system.

SESSION OUTCOMES

✓ To be able to demonstrate how messages are transmitted around the body through the nervous system.

✓ To be able to describe a neuron and how it works.

LESSON PLAN

➢ Ask the children to remember a time when their class baby reacted to something. This may have been when they fell over, hit their hand or finger or hurt themselves.

➢ Ask them to think about how the brain knew what had happened. How was the message sent?

For those classrooms not able to undertake the Circles for Learning Project, video clips or photographs can be used to support the discussion around the topic and stimulate thoughts and ideas from the children and young people.

Task

KS1: How brain cells communicate.

KS2/KS3: Homeostasis and the body's need to balance.

KS1

1 Ask the children what happens if they hold their hand too close to a fire – they feel the heat and then pull it away very quickly.

2 Ask them to think about what is happening in the body: how does the message get to the brain about the heat and how does the brain know to tell the hand to move fast?

3 See if the children are able to identify the nervous system.

4 Show the children the picture of the nervous system inside the body. Explain that all the nerves lead to the brain and they send messages back and forwards.

5 Share the picture of a neuron with the children.

6 Ask the children to stand in 4 lines across the classroom (hall or playground are good to use as they have more space.) side by side. Explain that each of them is going to become a neuron – a special cell that makes up the nervous system.

7 Demonstrate the neuron:

- Their left hand is the dendrites of the neuron
- Their body is the cell body
- Their right arm is the axon
- Their right hand is the synaptic terminal.

8 Give each person in the line a small button or counter. They hold this in their synaptic terminal (right hand). Explain that this is the message that needs to go to the brain. Once it is received by their dendrite they can then send their own message to the next neuron (pass on their counter but keep the one they have been given).

9 When you say GO, the first person passes their neurotransmitter to the next persons dendrite (left hand) they keep the counter and then pass their counter (which is in their right hand) from their synaptic terminal to the next person's dendrite (left hand). This continues all the way down the line. This shows the 'signal' travelling all the way along the nerves to the brain.

10 Ask the children to make neurons and label them. They could use a variety of mediums to make them – pipe cleaners, clay, modelling clay, etc.

KS2/KS3

1 Ask the children what happens if they hold their hand too close to a fire – they feel the heat and then pull it away very quickly.

2 Ask them to think about what is happening in the body: how does the message get to the brain about the heat and how does the brain know to tell the hand to move fast?

3 See if the children are able to identify the nervous system.

4 Show the children the picture of the nervous system inside the body. Explain that all the nerves lead to the brain and they send messages back and forwards.

5 Share the picture of a neuron with the children.

6 Ask the children to stand in 4 lines across the classroom (hall or playground are good to use as they have more space.) side by side. Explain that each of them is going to become a neuron – a special cell that makes up the nervous system.

7 Demonstrate the neuron:

- Their left hand is the dendrites of the neuron
- Their body is the cell body
- Their right arm is the axon
- Their right hand is the synaptic terminal.

8 Give each person in the line a small button or counter. They hold this in their synaptic terminal (right hand). Explain that this is the message that needs to go to the brain. Once it is received by their dendrite they can then send their own message to the next neuron (pass on their counter but keep the one they have been given).

9 When you say GO the first person passes their neurotransmitter to the next person's dendrite (left hand), they keep the counter and then pass their counter (which is in their right hand) from their synaptic terminal to the next person's dendrite (left hand). This continues all the way down the line. This shows the 'signal' travelling all the way along the nerves to the brain.

Share with the children that messages are sent at speeds of 268 miles per hour through the nervous system

10 Ask the children to work in small groups and make:

- Neuron
- The spinal cord inside the vertebrae which protects it
- A diagram to show the nervous system
- A model to show how the neurons transmit signals to the brain.

RESOURCES

1 Picture of the nervous system

2 Picture of a neuron

3 Diagram to show how neurons fire

4 Clay, pipe cleaners or modelling clay for model neurons

5 Counters

6 Access to the internet

IMPORTANT POINTS

The nervous system transmits signals from the body to the brain and from the brain to the body. Neurons are special cells that make up the nervous system. Neurons use neurotransmitters to send messages across the synapse.

LEARNING LINKS

Collaboration, speaking and listening, research skills, creativity.

REFLECTION

Questions:

Positive comment from child:

Positive comment from adult:

LEARNING DIMENSIONS		SOCIAL & EMOTIONAL SKILLS	
Strategic awareness	(orange)	Emotional literacy	
Learning relationships		Neuroscience	(green)
Curiosity	(orange)	Self-regulation	
Creativity	(orange)	Self-development	
Meaning making	(orange)		
Changing & learning	(orange)		
Resilience			

Motor Neurons

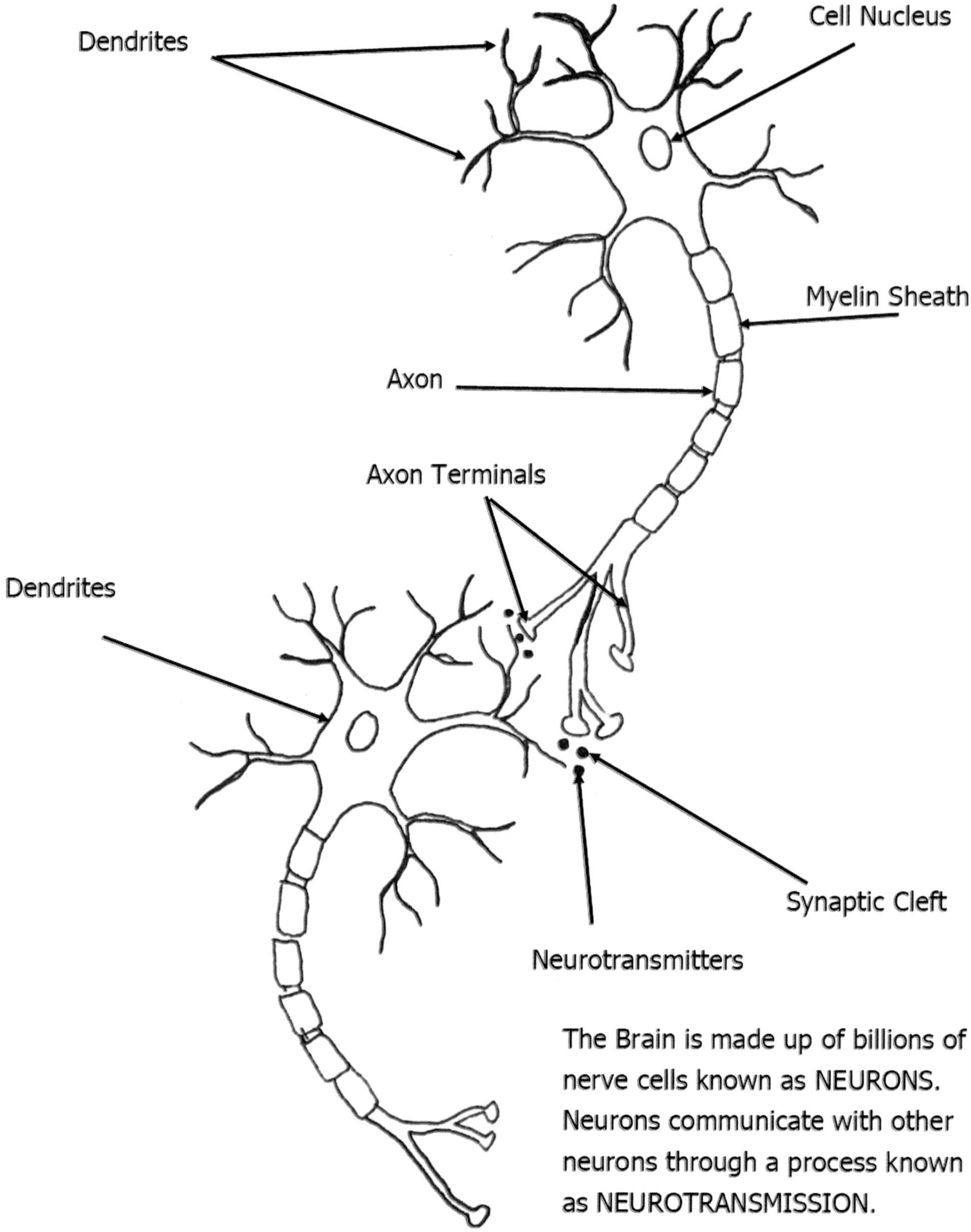

The Brain is made up of billions of nerve cells known as NEURONS. Neurons communicate with other neurons through a process known as NEUROTRANSMISSION.

Neurons Firing

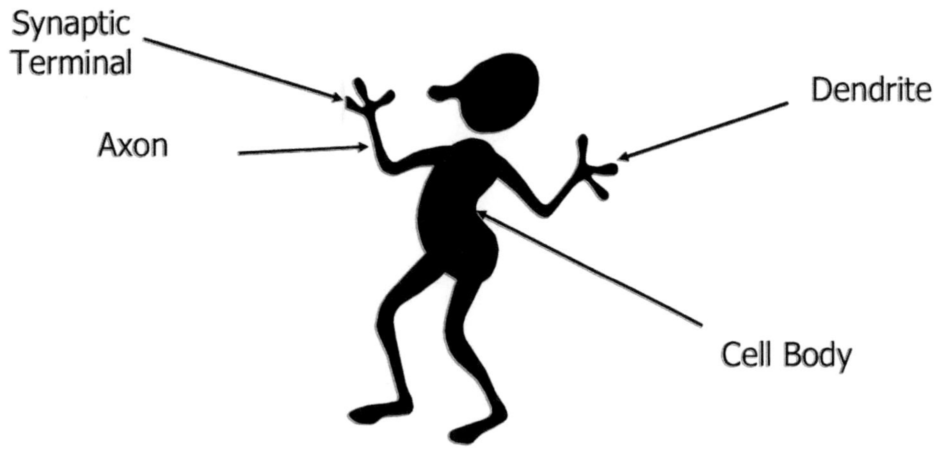

Sending Messages

How Neurons Communicate

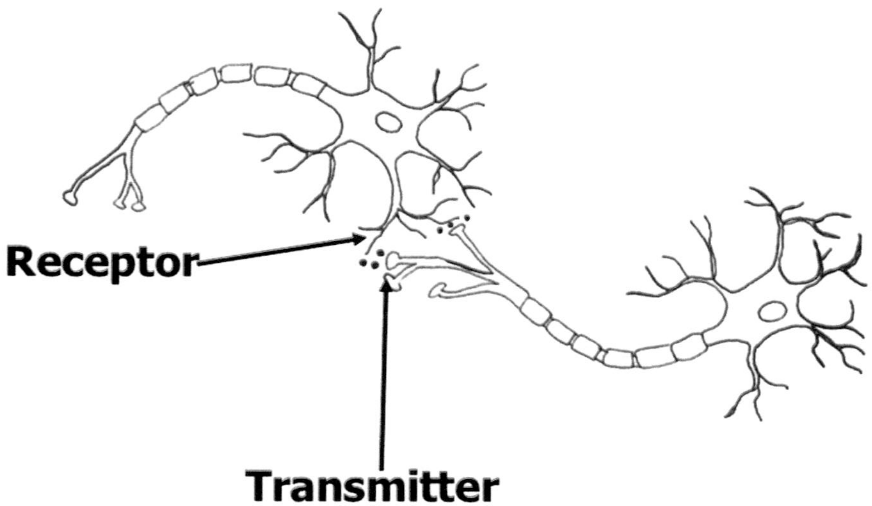

How People Communicate

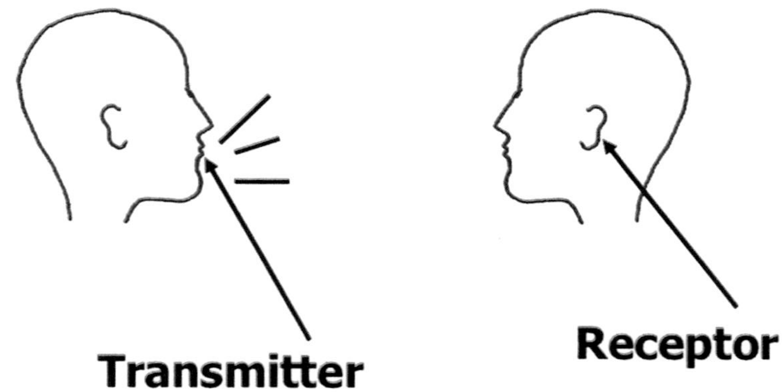

To send a message, a nerve cell releases a chemical (neurotransmitter) into the space separating two nerve cells, called the SYNAPSE. The NEUROTRANSMITTER crosses the synapse and attaches to proteins (receptors) on the receiving nerve cell. This causes the changes in the receiving nerve cell and the message is delivered.

The Nervous System: Nerves in the Body

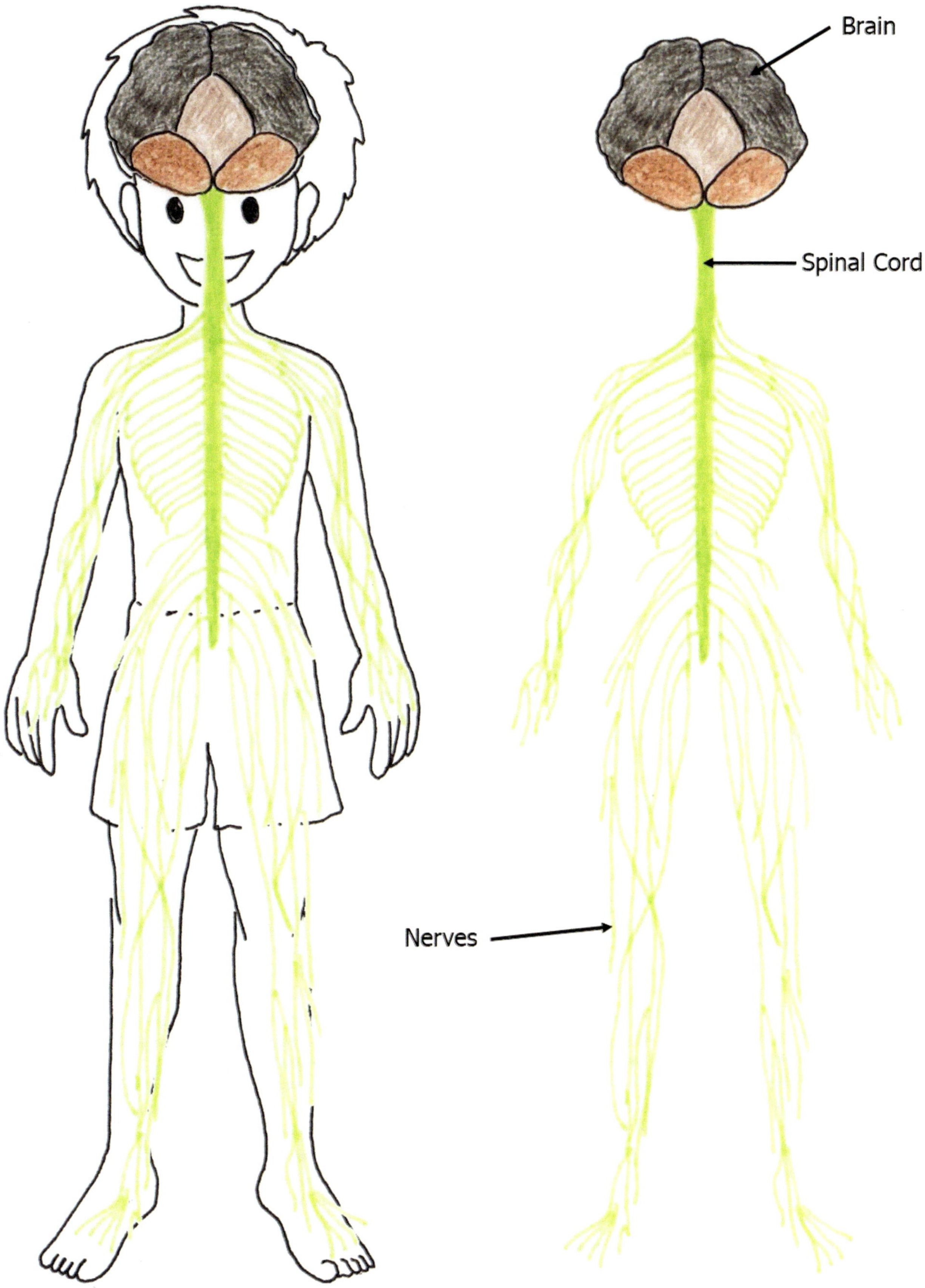

Addiction and the brain

SESSION OBJECTIVES

To understand why the brain likes certain substances and how addiction can occur because of this.

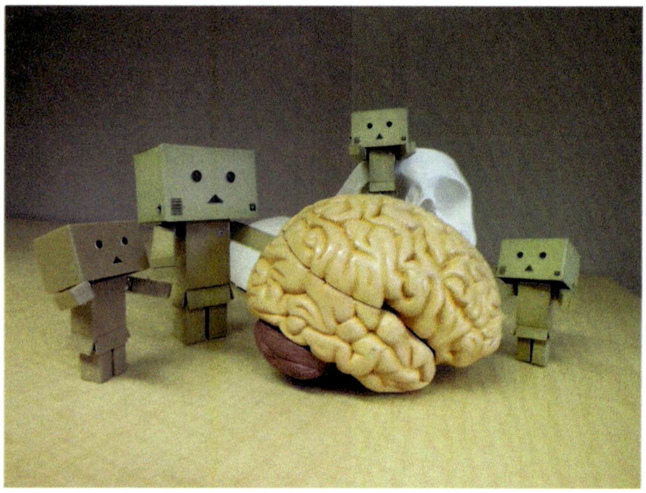

SESSION OUTCOMES

✓ To be able to share how the brain responds to certain substances and how addiction can occur.

✓ To understand what happens in the brain to make us feel happy.

LESSON PLAN

➢ Ask the children to remember a time when their class baby did something that made their Mum laugh.

➢ Ask them to think about what might have happened in her brain to make her feel this happy feeling?

For those classrooms not able to undertake the Circles for Learning Project, video clips or photographs can be used to support the discussion around the topic and stimulate thoughts and ideas from the children and young people.

Task

KS1: How brain cells communicate.

KS2: Homeostasis and the body's need to balance.

KS3: How addiction affects the brain.

KS1

1 Remind the children about how neurons send messages – one neuron receives a message and then sends their message from their synaptic terminal to the next neuron's dendrites.

2 Tell the children a joke and make them laugh. Explain that this feeling of happiness is caused by the neurons making a special substance called dopamine.

3 Teach the children how to play 'Synaptic Tag'.

KS2

1 Introduce the concept of **Homeostasis**. This is the state of steady internal conditions maintained by living things. Homeostasis is the dynamic state of equilibrium which enables optimal functioning for the organism. This state includes: body temperature pH of extracellular fluid, the concentrations of sodium, potassium and calcium ions, as well as that of the blood sugar level, all of which need to be regulated despite changes in the environment, diet or level of activity. Each of these variables is controlled by one or more regulators or homeostatic mechanisms, which together maintain life.

2 Show the children a balance and help them understand that the body likes to keep things in balance so that it can function at its best. When it moves out of balance several things are triggered with the aim of restoring the balance.

3 Share the sugar addiction cycle with the children and discuss what happens inside the body – remind them of the balance.

4 Ask the children what happens when they get too hot – they feel sweaty, they drink water, their faces become red, they remove excess clothes, look for cool fans or cold water – all these things cool the body and take it back to its optimum temperature. If the body stays at a very high temperature for too long its organs start to struggle and can become damaged. If we stay in the sun for too long, our skin burns and blisters.

5 Ask the children to work in pairs and show how temperature affects the body either when it gets too hot or too cold.

KS3

1 Ask the children to define addiction. Why do they think it happens? What things can the body become addicted to?

2 Fill in the sheet 'What I know, what I would like to know'.

3 Remind the children about how neurons work. They receive a chemical message into their dendrite and then send a neurotransmitter across the gap between itself and another neuron to the next neuron's dendrite. Many drugs interfere with the communication between the neurons.

4 Ask the children to work in pairs and find out how a variety of drugs affect the brain: coffee, nicotine, steroids, pain killers, sugar, Ecstasy, chocolate, alcohol, antidepressants, heroin, cannabis.

5 Ask the children to create a pop-up exhibition about their drug and how it affects the brain.

6 Ask the children what they have learnt about the different drugs and their effect on the brain.

7 In pairs, define addiction and explain how a drug creates this craving in the brain.

RESOURCES

1 'Synaptic Tag' instructions

2 Picture of a neuron

3 The sugar addiction cycle

4 Homeostasis worksheet

5 Balance

6 'What I know, what I would like to know' sheet

7 Internet access

IMPORTANT POINTS

The body tries to maintain its optimum conditions and so responds to any environment or internal change.

Chemical or drugs can affect the body in positive or negative ways by altering the balance of chemicals in the body or by stopping neurotransmitters to be produced, causing neurons to constantly fire or mimicking the effects of chemical messengers.

LEARNING LINKS

Self-awareness, working together, changing and learning, research.

REFLECTION

Questions:

Positive comment from child:

Positive comment from adult:

LEARNING DIMENSIONS		SOCIAL & EMOTIONAL SKILLS	
Strategic awareness		Emotional literacy	
Learning relationships		Neuroscience	
Curiosity		Self-regulation	
Creativity		Self-development	
Meaning making			
Changing & learning			
Resilience			

Sugar Addiction

1. You eat sugar

You like it. You want more of it.

It has addictive properties so you start to crave more sugar.

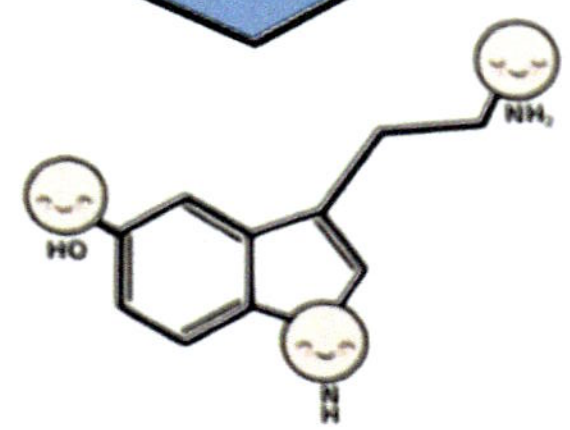

2. Your blood sugar levels go up

Dopamine is released in the brain–the body wants more.

ADDICTION

Mass insulin is secreted to drop the sugar levels.

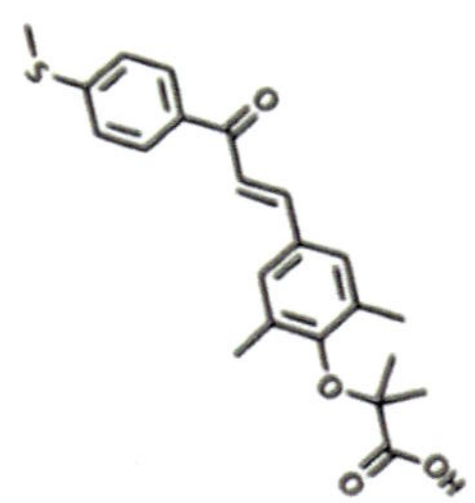

3. Blood sugar levels fall rapidly

High insulin levels cause immediate fat storage

The body craves the lost sugar high that it had experienced.

4. Hunger and cravings

Low blood sugar levels cause increased appetite and cravings.

Thus the cycle is repeated.

What I know about Drugs and Addiction

What I know about drugs and addiction	What I would like to know	What I have learnt	Thoughts and Ideas

The Body finds the Balance

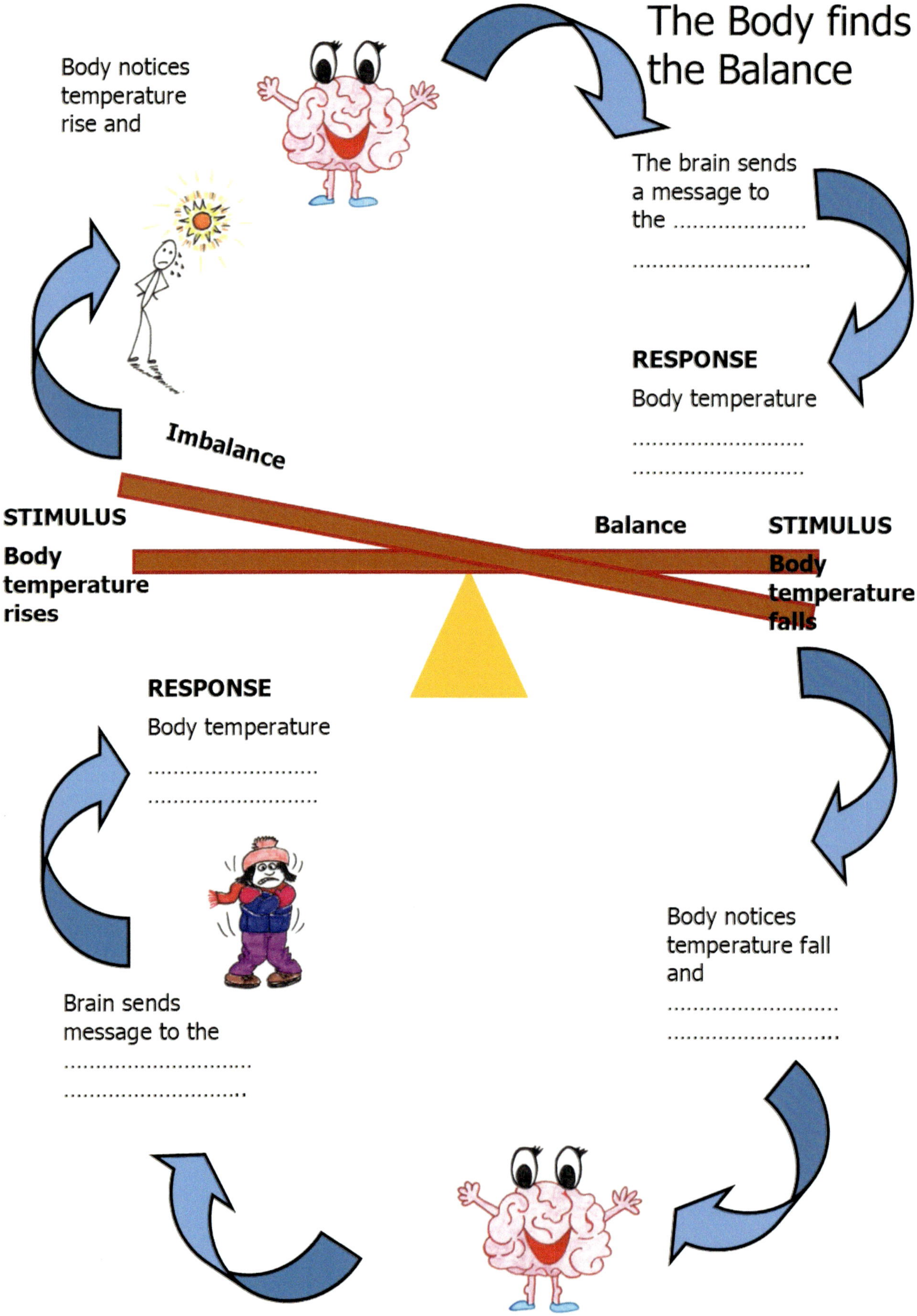

Synaptic Tag

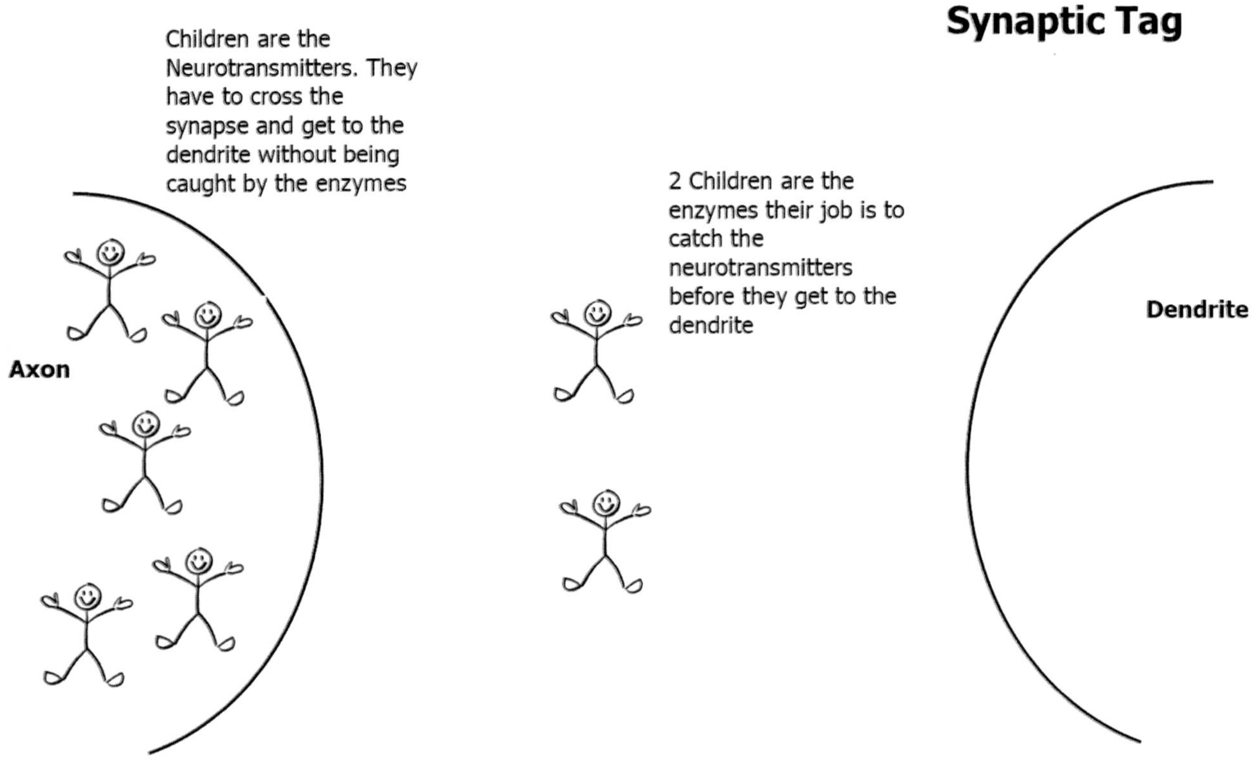

Chapter 2

How the brain works

What does the brain do?

SESSION OBJECTIVES

To help children understand that everyone's brain is different.

To help children understand the many things that the brain is able to do.

SESSION OUTCOMES

✓ To be able to describe the many different tasks the brain is able to undertake.

LESSON PLAN

➢ Ask the children to remember a time when they watched their class baby learn something new. Ask them to describe what they saw and how this learning developed – what happened before and then what happened after.

For those classrooms not able to undertake the Circles for Learning Project, video clips or photographs can be used to support the discussion around the topic and stimulate thoughts and ideas from the children and young people.

Task

KS1: To play the 'Find a person who can' game.

KS2: To play the 'Find a person who can' game and create a brain alphabet to show the things a brain can do.

KS3: To discuss and explore Brain v. Computer.

KS1/KS2

1 Ask the children to get into pairs. Give them the Brain Game 1 sheet. One person will be asking questions, the other will be writing names.

2 Share the record sheet with the children and explain that they are going to walk around the class asking each other the questions on the sheet such as do they forget things when

they are nervous? When they find someone who answers yes to the question, they write their name in the box. They can have more than one person.

3 When they have completed the sheet, they stop and sit down. It is not a race but a collection game.

4 Once everyone has finished, discuss what they have found.

5 Highlight that everyone has a different brain and they all work in different ways.

6 Write the alphabet on the board and see if as a class they can come up with an A–Z of things the brain can do. A – Answer questions, B – blink, etc.

7 For older children (KS2) you could ask them to work in pairs and fill in the alphabet sheet.

KS3

1 Ask the children to work in pairs and think of three things that make the brain similar to a computer and three things that make it different.

2 Share the similarities and differences and make a list of them on the board.

3 Ask the children to work together to come up with as many similarities and differences as they can when comparing a computer with the brain.

4 Watch the video clips and then discuss what you have found out.

RESOURCES

1 'Find a person who can' games

2 Alphabet sheet

3 Brain v. Computer

4 YouTube: 'Are brains like computers?,

https://www.youtube.com/watch?v=rjnRiEaudOY

5 YouTube: 'Brain vs Computer',

https://www.youtube.com/watch?v=TIUK69Wsk6g

IMPORTANT POINTS

Each brain is different and can do many different things. Some things we are aware/conscious of – such as scratching our head or other things it does without our awareness, such as breathing, keeping our temperature at the correct level.

LEARNING LINKS

Working together, talking and listening, research, creativity, meaning making.

REFLECTION

Questions:

Positive comment from child:

Positive comment from adult:

LEARNING DIMENSIONS		SOCIAL & EMOTIONAL SKILLS	
Strategic awareness		Emotional literacy	
Learning relationships		Neuroscience	
Curiosity		Self-regulation	
Creativity		Self-development	
Meaning making			
Changing & learning			
Resilience			

The BRAIN Game 1

Find a person who:

1. forgets things when she/he is nervous	2. likes to be challenged to solve a problem		
3. has pictures in his or her head, likes day dreaming	4. likes to put things neatly in order	5. enjoys word games, writing or reading	6. loves music, rhythm, singing / playing an instrument
7. notices small things even when nervous	8. feels that colours are important, likes colourful things	9. reads the end of the book first before reading the rest	10. likes black and white pictures more than colour paintings
11. likes cosy rooms and cuddly things	12. can solve problems and answer questions even when nervous		

and write their name in the box.

A	
B	
C	
D	
E	
F	
G	
H	
I	
J	
K	
L	
M	

N	
O	
P	
Q	
R	
S	
T	
U	
V	
W	
X	
Y	
Z	

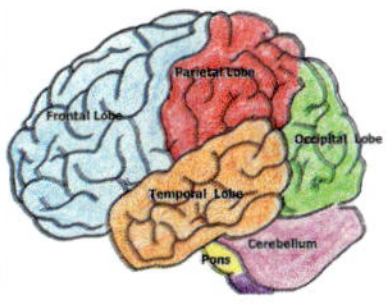

Brain V Computer

Similarities	Differences

Parts of the brain

1 2 3

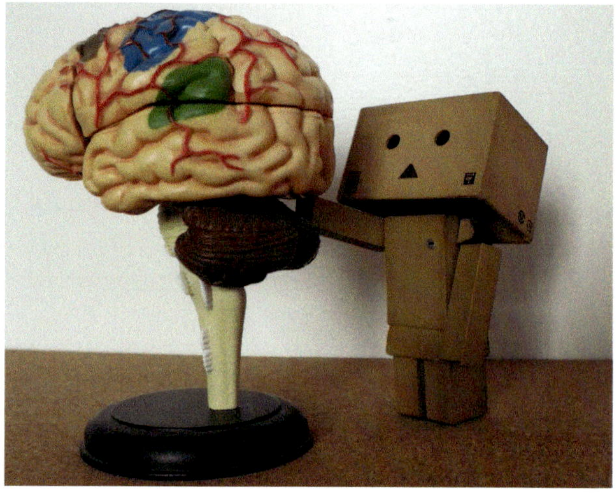

SESSION OBJECTIVES

To be able to describe the different parts of the brain and what they do.

SESSION OUTCOMES

✓ To be able to discuss the different part of the brain and explain what they do.

LESSON PLAN

➢ Ask the children to think about all the things their class baby has learnt to do. Explore with them the different experiences they have had which have then caused their brain to grow and develop in a unique way. Just coming to see them has caused the brain to grown and learn things!

For those classrooms not able to undertake the Circles for Learning Project, video clips or photographs can be used to support the discussion around the topic and stimulate thoughts and ideas from the children and young people.

Task

KS1: Create a brain hat.

KS2: Create a lift-the-flap poster to show the different areas of the brain and what they do.

KS3: Create a class PowerPoint showing different parts of the brain and what they do.

KS1: To create a clay brain puzzle showing the different parts of the brain.

KS2: To create a short sketch giving the audience a guided tour around the brain explaining what each part does.

KS3: Create a news 'round-up' show from around the brain. Each part of the brain has a reporter who tells the story of what happened there today.

KS1

1 Recap with the children the different parts of the brain – they can get out their brain hats to remind them.

2 List the main parts of the brain on the board.

3 Remind the children what they do.

Cerebellum: The cerebellum receives information from the sensory systems: spinal cord, and other parts of the brain and then regulates motor movements. The cerebellum coordinates the voluntary movements of posture, balance, coordination, and speech, resulting in smooth co-ordinated muscular activity.

Frontal Lobe: The frontal lobe is the part of the brain that controls cognitive skills in people, including emotional expression, problem solving, memory, language, judgment, and sexual behaviours. It is the "control panel" of our personality and allows us the ability to communicate.

Sensory Cortex: The somatosensory cortex receives all the sensory input from the body. The specialised Cells that form the brain or nerves that extend into the body are called neurons. The neurons sense feelings in our skin, pain, visual, or auditory stimuli, and then send information to the somatosensory cortex for processing.

Parietal Lobe: The parietal lobe is at the back of the brain and is divided into two hemispheres. It functions in processing sensory information regarding the location of parts of the body as well as interpreting visual information and processing language and mathematics.

Temporal Lobe: The temporal lobe is involved in auditory perception, such as hearing, and holds the primary auditory cortex. The primary auditory cortex receives sensory information from the ears and process the information into meaningful units such as speech and words.

Occipital Lobe: The occipital lobe is one of the four major lobes of the cerebral cortex in the brain of mammals. It is the visual processing centre of the mammalian brain and contains most of the anatomical region of the visual cortex.

Spinal Cord: The brain and spinal cord are your body's central nervous system. The brain is the command centre for your body, and the spinal cord is the pathway for messages sent by the brain to the body and from the body to the brain.

Limbic System: A group of areas inside the brain that is responsible for emotions and memories.

4 Give the children the brain diagram showing the different areas and ask them to work in pairs to create a clay jigsaw of the areas that can be moved and fitted back together.

5 Once the pieces are made, allow to dry and then paint with different colours and label with a marker pen.

KS2

1 Remind the children about each part of the brain and what they do.

2 Share the book *The Adventures of Your Brain*.

3 Watch the video on YouTube: 'How to learn major parts of the brain quickly',

www.youtube.com/watch?v=FczvTGluHKM

4 Explore the limbic system, explaining that it is made up of several different parts

5 Watch the video: 'What is the limbic system in the brain? Definition, functions & parts',

https://tinyurl.com/y3mklph9

The limbic system is made up of:

Amygdala: The amygdala is part of the limbic system of the brain, which is involved with emotions The amygdala is a processing centre that is wired up to receive incoming messages from both our senses and our internal organs. It is highly involved with different emotional responses.

Hippocampus: The hippocampus is associated mainly with memory, especially long-term memory. This part of the brain also plays an important role in spatial navigation.

Thalamus: The thalamus's job is to send sensory impulses from receptors in different parts of the body such as the skin to the cerebral cortex. These sensory impulses then travels from the body surface to the thalamus. The Thalamus receives these as sensations. These sensations are then passed on to the cerebral cortex which interprets them as touch, pain or temperature.

Hypothalamus: The hypothalamus is part of the brain that controls body temperature, hunger, and important aspects of parenting and attachment behaviours. It is also responsible for thirst, fatigue, sleep and circadian rhythms.

Basal Ganglia: The basal ganglia are parts of the brain which are associated with a variety of functions. These include the control of voluntary motor movements, procedural learning, habit learning, eye movements, cognition, and emotion.

Cingulate Gyrus: A component of the limbic system, it is involved in processing emotions and behaviour regulation. It also helps to regulate autonomic motor function.

6 Divide the class into small groups (you need 13 groups) and ask each group to choose a part of the brain that they are going to describe and share with the other members of the group. This can be done by writing the different parts of the brain on paper and then folding them up and asking the children to choose.

7 Ask each group to research their part of the brain and write a script for what they will say during the tour of the brain. They could make props to help people remember what they do, or a rap to say what their part does, or a rhyme of the name of their part of the brain a bit like a cheer leader's chant. Be creative and have fun.

8 Draw the outline of the brain on the playground or in the hall using chalk (so that it comes off!!) and then make sure each group knows where their correct spot is. Start the tour (it is useful to have a tour guide – a child who is able to walk around the brain and introduce the different parts).

9 Video the brain tour and share with other classes.

10 Share the book *Silly Limbic* by Naomi Harvey.

KS3

1 Remind the children about each part of the brain and what they do.

2 Watch the video on YouTube: 'How to learn major parts of the brain quickly',

https://www.youtube.com/watch?v=FczvTGIuHKM

3 Explore the limbic system, explaining that it is made up of several different parts.

4 Watch the video: 'What is the limbic system in the brain? Definition, functions & parts',

https://tinyurl.com/y3mklph9

5 Explain to the children that you are going to create a news 'round-up'-programme that hears different stories from around the brain. Ask for 2 people to present the programme – they are the hosts and will direct the audience to the different parts of the brain to hear their stories.

6 Divide the class into 13 small groups and give each one a part of the brain.

7 Ask each group to write a story for the programme that describes what happened in that part of the brain today, e.g. 'Let's go and hear from the spinal cord – hi spinal cord, what's the news from your area today?' 'Well we've had a really busy day today with messages racing around from and to the brain. A few near misses when messages got a

bit muddled and our human put the milk in the oven and the rice pudding in the fridge. We also had a huge amount of messages to deal with this afternoon as our human was learning to drive the car – nightmare stuff with having to deal with messages for both feet and the hands and eyes all at the same time. We are exhausted and hoping for a calm night.'

8 Once the stories have all been written, create your news round-up and video to share with others or put on an assembly or news round-up special with another class.

RESOURCES

1 Brain hats from Chapter 1

2 Clay

3 Diagram of the brain from Chapter 1

4 Video camera

5 YouTube: 'How to learn major parts of the brain quickly',

https://www.youtube.com/watch?v=FczvTGIuHKM

6 'What is the limbic system in the brain? Definition, functions & parts',

https://tinyurl.com/y3mklph9

7 Model brain

8 Chalk

9 *The Adventures of Your Brain* by Dan Green

10 *Silly Limbic* by Naomi Harvey

IMPORTANT POINTS

The brain has many different areas; each area is responsible for a range of things.

LEARNING LINKS

Collaboration, research, knowledge and understanding, speaking and listening, understanding ourselves.

REFLECTION

Questions:

Positive comment from child:

Positive comment from adult:

LEARNING DIMENSIONS		SOCIAL & EMOTIONAL SKILLS	
Strategic awareness		Emotional literacy	
Learning relationships		Neuroscience	
Curiosity		Self-regulation	
Creativity		Self-development	
Meaning making			
Changing & learning			
Resilience			

The Limbic System

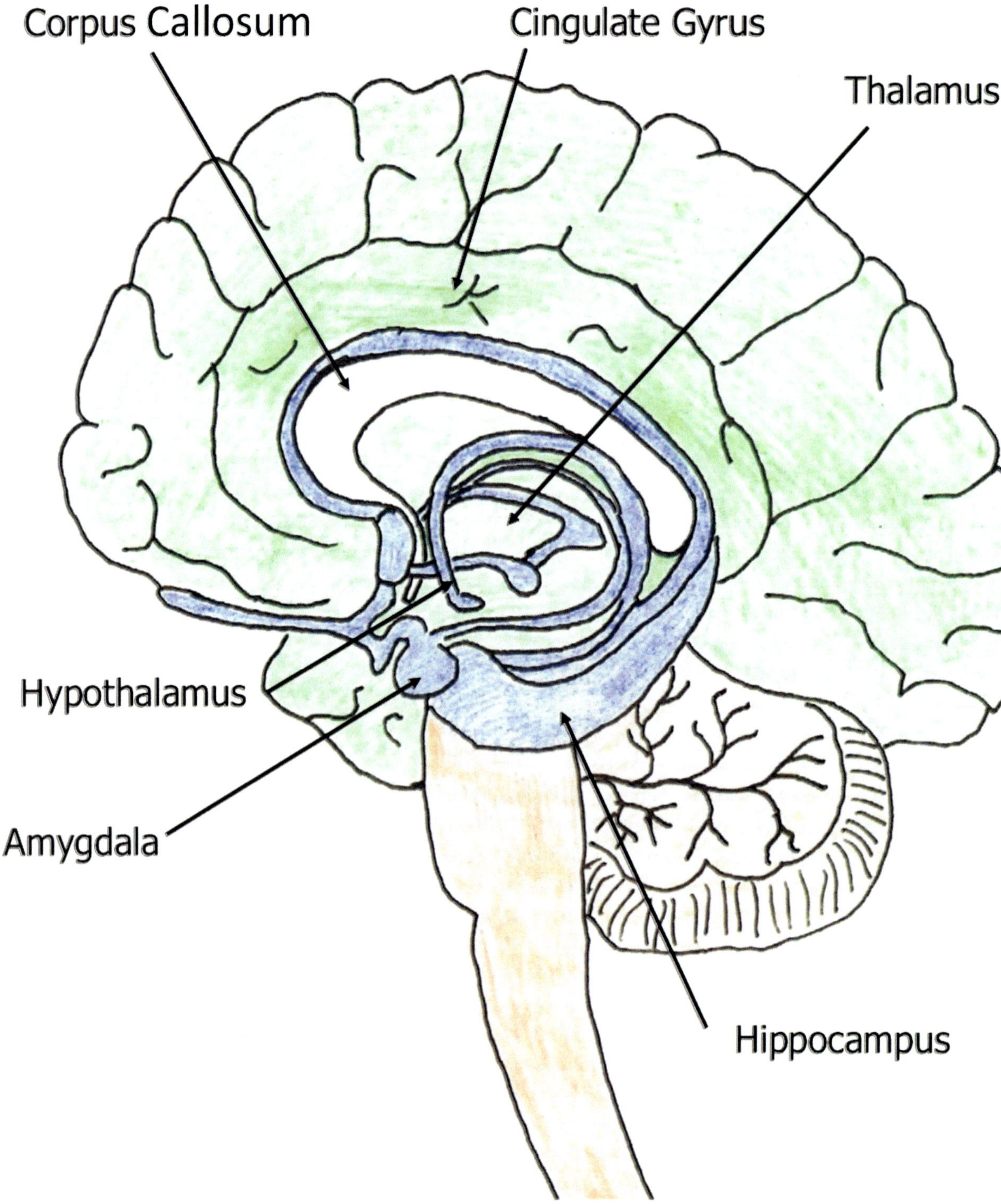

What is a thought?

1 2 3

SESSION OBJECTIVES

To come up with a creative idea about how a thought is born and how it develops.

SESSION OUTCOMES

✓ To draw a picture of a thought.

LESSON PLAN

➢ Ask the children to remember a time when they watched their class baby think about something. Describe their expression and what had caused the thought and then what the result of the thought was.

For those classrooms not able to undertake the Circles for Learning Project, video clips or photographs can be used to support the discussion around the topic and stimulate thoughts and ideas from the children and young people.

Task

KS1: To draw a thought and share how they believe it happens.
KS2/KS3: To show thoughts within the brain using a variety of media.

KS1

1 Ask the children to think a happy thought.

2 Wait for all the children to find a happy thought and then ask them what their thought is. Share some of the thoughts the children have had.

3 Now ask the children to think about something they would like to do but haven't done yet which would make them happy.

4 Give the children the brain outline and ask them to draw how a thought is born and how it becomes a thought that they can describe.

5 Ask them to be as creative as they like.

6 Once the pictures have been finished, get the children to mount them and then display them in the classroom.

7 Set up a thought exhibition to show the different ways they think thoughts may be created.

8 Share the book *Henry Finch* and explore the thought that he had and how it developed and grew.

KS2/KS3

1 Explain to the children that you would like them to come up with a really creative drawing of what a thought is and how it is born, grows and develops into an idea.

2 Ask the children to work in pairs. They are going to act as a coach for each other and help each other come up with a drawing, painting or sculpture that shows a thought being born and growing.

3 Share other artwork that has focused on thoughts or thinking and discuss or use as inspiration.

4 Give them a brain outline to draw their thought inside – they could do a series of pictures to show the thought beginning and growing into the idea or a fully formed thought.

5 They can use the internet to see what science says about how thoughts are created or they might like to look at artwork that has been created about thoughts.

6 Ask each child to create their rough sketch/idea and then share this with their coach. It is the coach's job to help the person think about how the picture/art piece will look, what it will be made of or the type of paint used.

7 Once the artworks have been created, ask the children to write the title and a short description about the artwork, how it came about and the thinking behind it.

8 Ask each child to find a quote about thinking that they like or that means something to them.

9 Share the Tibetan saying:

'Thoughts and feelings come and go like writing on water.'

Help the children explore and discuss this and what it might mean.

10 Thoughts are not facts but they are very powerful – they can impact on how we feel, how we behave and how we then think.

11 Divide the children into small groups and give each group 2 situation scenarios. Ask the group to discuss the thoughts that arose for each of them and the consequences of these thoughts.

12 Share and discuss

13 Create an exhibition of thoughts and quotes about thinking.

RESOURCES

1 Henry Finch

2 Artwork: *Birth of a Thought 1,*

http://collections.vam.ac.uk/item/O138457/birth-of-a-thought-1-print-aldworth-susan/ (accessed 17 September 2019)

3 Artwork: *Through Thought,*

https://wakeupscreaming.com/laura-scull-through-thought/ (accessed 17 September 2019)

4 Artwork: *Thought Forms,*

https://publicdomainreview.org/2014/03/19/victorian-occultism-and-the-art-of-synesthesia/ (accessed 17 September 2019)

Artwork: *Many Thoughts,*

https://www.artmajeur.com/en/artdenoe/artworks/9941416/many-thoughts (accessed 17 September 2019)

5 Paper

6 Pens, paint, clay or other media

7 Card for quotes

8 'Thoughts are not facts' scenario sheet

IMPORTANT POINTS

Thoughts are personal and private but can be keep to ourselves or shared with others through behaviour, speech or art work

LEARNING LINKS

Creativity, collaboration, speaking and listening.

REFLECTION

Questions:

Positive comment from child:

Positive comment from adult:

LEARNING DIMENSIONS		SOCIAL & EMOTIONAL SKILLS	
Strategic awareness	■	Emotional literacy	
Learning relationships		Neuroscience	■
Curiosity	■	Self-regulation	
Creativity	■	Self-development	■
Meaning making	■		
Changing & learning			
Resilience			

Thoughts Are Not Facts Scenarios

You have just met a new friend whilst at a concert. You swap numbers and say you will keep in touch.	You text them the next day and receive nothing back What do you think? CONSEQUENCE
You go out with a group of people to a funfair. One of your friends isn't able to come. You put a couple of photos on Instagram of you all having fun.	You meet up with them at school on Monday and they are really quiet. What do you think? CONSEQUENCE
You meet up with a group of friends to go to the cinema. You then go on to get something to eat. One of your friends has had a row with their parents; they are fed up. You ignore them when they try to talk about it as you don't want to spoil the evening.	The next day they don't meet up with you and the others for lunch. What do you think? CONSEQUENCE
You put some photos of you having fun at your birthday BBQ with your friends.	At school on Monday two of your friends seem to be avoiding you. What do you think? CONSEQUENCE
You get a great mark in your science test and are really pleased.	During the next lesson, one of the group of people you sit with starts taking the micky out of you for being brainy and a swot. What do you think? CONSEQUENCE
You audition for the school production. The teacher hints that you would be really good in one of the main parts as you have a great voice and can sing. You are really excited and tell your friend what the teacher said.	Your friends becomes very quiet and doesn't seem interested. What do you think? CONSEQUENCE
One of the girls on the bus keeps looking at you and sending you messages on your phone.	The next day you see her with one of your friends and they tell you they are off to the cinema. What do you think? CONSEQUENCE

Chemicals you produce

1 2 3

SESSION OBJECTIVES:

To understand that the brain releases chemicals which have an effect on how we feel.

SESSION OUTCOMES

✓ To be able to describe how the chemicals released by the brain affect how we feel.

LESSON PLAN

➢ Ask the children to describe all the different emotions they have watched their class baby experience and what happened to cause them.

For those classrooms not able to undertake the Circles for Learning Project, video clips or photographs can be used to support the discussion around the topic and stimulate thoughts and ideas from the children and young people.

Task

KS1: Draw a neuron releasing dopamine as something nice has happened.
KS2/KS3: Show how neurons release a range of neurotransmitters depending on what information has been transmitted by the senses.

KS1/KS2:

1 Ask the children to indicate on a line what they feel– happy being one end, OK in the middle and sad at the other end.

2 Read them a sad story – *Sad, the Dog* by Sandy Fussell.

3 At the saddest part ask the children to indicate on their line where they feel now.

4 Read the children a funny book – *The Wonky Donkey* by Craig Smith.

5 Ask the children to mark on their line where they are now.

6 Discuss what happened in their body. The brain listened to the story and felt sad – it sent out chemicals to tell the rest of the body it was sad. The story that made them laugh also made their brain laugh and so it sent out happy chemicals in the body.

7 Pose the question for the children – does this mean we can change how we feel by thinking different thoughts?

8 Ask the children to draw happy cartoon neurons. The chemical that is produced to make them feel happy is dopamine. Ask them to draw sad cartoon neurons. When we don't produce enough dopamine or serotonin we can feel sad.

KS2/KS3

1 Share the pictures of neurons with the children and recap on what they do. Remind the children about the neurotransmitters, the chemicals produced by the neurons to send messages to the other neurons.

2 Divide the children into small groups (6 groups) and give each group the information sheet on one of the chemicals. Each group needs to share with the rest of the class information about their chemical. They need to include in their presentation:

- A picture to show how the neurotransmitters are produced and sent from one neuron and received by another.
- A description about what the chemical does and how it affects the human being.
- 3 ways that this chemical could be prevented from causing the effect it is designed for, or ways to moderate the effect.
- A postcard showing the chemical and a brief description about what it does that can be photocopied for the other groups.
- A short video to show how it works.

3 When the groups have completed the tasks, gather everyone together and share what they have found.

4 Discuss the impact of what they have found by asking, 'What will you take away from this?'

5 Photocopy each group's postcard of information so that each group has information on the different neurotransmitters.

RESOURCES

1 *The Wonky Donkey* by Craig Smith

2 *Sad, the Dog* by Sandy Fussell

3 Paper

4 Pens

5 Felt tips or pencil crayons

6 'Neurons firing' picture sheet

7 'Chemicals produced by the body' information sheet

IMPORTANT POINTS

The brain produces chemicals and it is these chemicals that affect how we feel.

LEARNING LINKS

Collaboration, creativity, research, knowledge and understanding, speaking and listening, learning to learn skills.

REFLECTION

Questions:

Positive comment from child:

Positive comment from adult:

LEARNING DIMENSIONS		SOCIAL & EMOTIONAL SKILLS	
Strategic awareness		Emotional literacy	
Learning relationships		Neuroscience	■
Curiosity		Self-regulation	
Creativity		Self-development	
Meaning making			
Changing & learning			
Resilience			

Chemicals produced by the body	
Serotonin 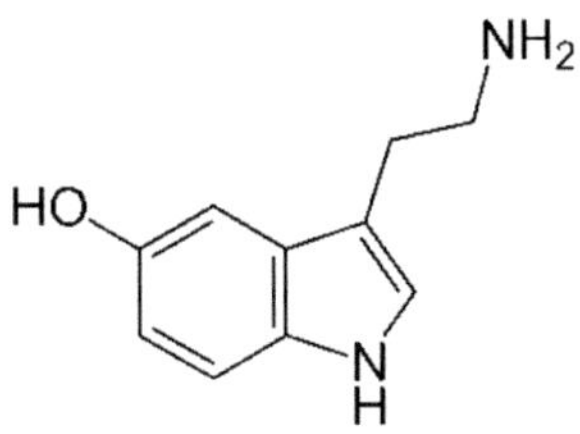	**Where found:** Serotonin is found mainly in the digestive system and throughout the central nervous system. **What does it do?:** Serotonin is considered to be a natural mood stabilizer. It aids sleeping, eating and digestion. It has been found to reduce depression, regulate anxiety, heal wounds, stimulate nausea and maintain bone health. Medical practitioners have found that low levels of the chemical have been associated with depression. **What can boost serotonin levels?:** Exposure to bright light or sunshine, exercise, a healthy diet. Some foods can increase serotonin levels, e.g. eggs, cheese, turkey, nuts, salmon, tofu and pineapple. Meditation has been found to help relieve stress, which can greatly boost serotonin levels.
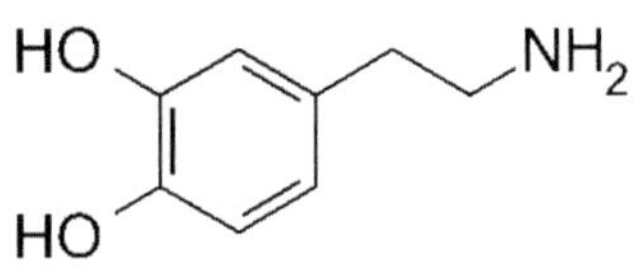	**What does it do?:** Dopamine is associated with feelings of happiness, bliss, motivation, and concentration. It plays an important role in a range of body systems and functions, including movement, sleep, learning, mood, memory and attention. If dopamine levels become unbalanced then this can be linked to depression. Too little dopamine can also lead to Parkinson's disease. Dopamine helps to control the flow of information through the brain, particularly supporting working memory, a part of the memory that provides short-term recall. When working memory isn't working well, it can cause a problem with concentration, following instructions and the ability to stay on task. Dopamine is needed by a specific part of the brain, the basal ganglia, which regulates movement. **How does dopamine get released?:** The brain releases dopamine when it experiences pleasure, e.g. while eating or drinking something we love. This 'feel-good' factor, however, can cause some people problems as several illegal recreational drugs stimulate its release and increase the amount of dopamine in the brain. The increased feelings of pleasure that result from these drugs make users susceptible to addiction.

Chemicals produced by the body	
Oxytocin 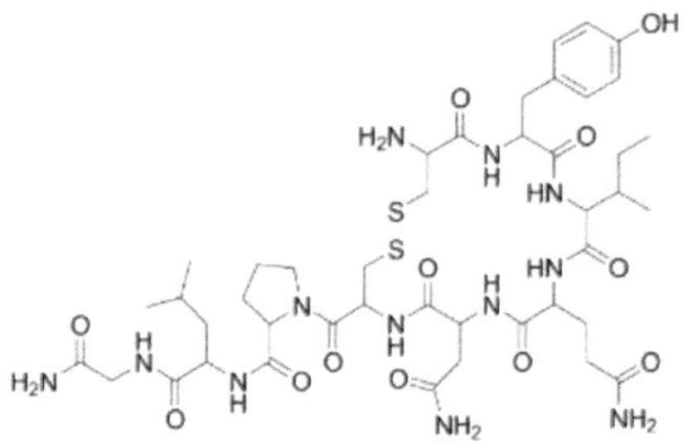	**What does it do?:** Oxytocin, is released when you're attracted to another person and is often called the love hormone. When your brain releases dopamine, your serotonin levels increase, and oxytocin is produced. The release of oxytocin causes a positive feeling. Research suggests that oxytocin has a positive impact on social behaviours as it makes us relax and trust. The hormone has also been shown to decrease stress and anxiety levels when released into certain parts of the brain. **Benefits:** Oxytocin is really important to parents, especially mothers. It signals the uterus to contract, beginning labour. After delivery, it helps the uterus return to its previous size. It supports the ability to breastfeed – when a baby latches on to its mother's breast, it triggers a release of oxytocin. This signals the body to let down milk for the baby. Human and animal studies on the effects of oxytocin on the mother-child bond have shown that mothers with higher levels of this hormone are more likely to engage in affectionate parenting behaviours such as: touch, singing or speaking to baby in certain way, grooming and bathing behaviours. There is now evidence that parenthood causes oxytocin to be released in fathers too. Research has demonstrated that specific types of interaction between father and baby led to higher oxytocin levels.
Endorphins 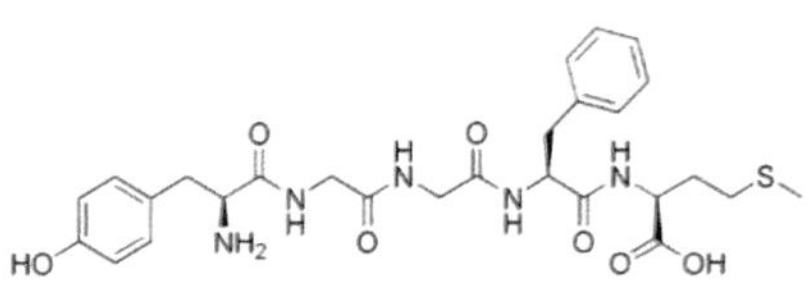	**What does it do?** After exercise tiny neurochemicals are released by your body. These are called endorphins. Endorphins are linked to our natural reward circuits and are related to important activities like eating, drinking, physical fitness, and sexual intercourse. They minimise discomfort and pain and maximise pleasure. This has the effect of helping us to continue functioning despite injury or stress. From an evolutionary standpoint, this helps ensure survival. **Benefits:** Endorphins have been found to alleviate depression, reduce stress and anxiety, boost self-esteem, reduce weight by regulating appetite and help manage pain during childbirth.

Chemicals produced by the body	
Glutamate 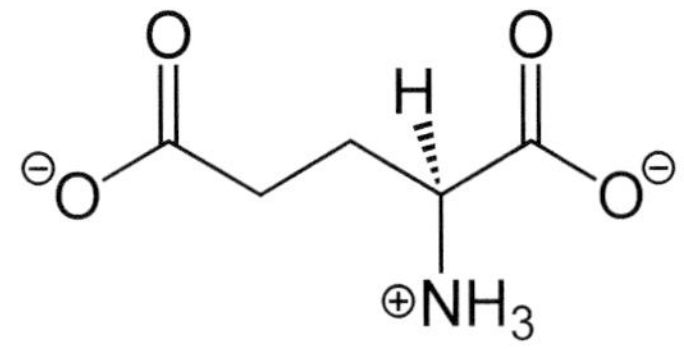	**What does it do?:** Glutamate is a powerful excitatory neurotransmitter that is released by nerve cells in the brain. Its role is linked to sending signals between nerve cells, and it plays an important role in learning and memory. It acts as the brain's 'on switch'. It is often referred to as the 'excitatory neurotransmitter'. This is because, wherever it finds a receptor to dock with, it causes the hosting neuron to become excited. An excited neuron is more likely to 'fire', resulting in the release of its own unique mix of neurotransmitters. **Benefits and disadvantages:** Glutamate can be damaging to nerve cells and the brain. If there is too much glutamate, this can lead to over-excitation of the receiving nerve cell. Or the receptors for glutamate on the receiving nerve cell can be oversensitive, so much so that fewer glutamate molecules are necessary to excite that cell. In both these examples, cells activated by glutamate become overexcited, which can lead to effects that can cause cell damage and/or death.
Norepinephrine 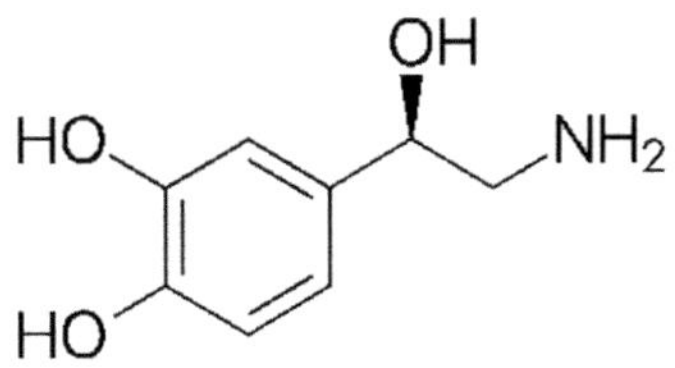	**What does it do?:** Norepinephrine is a chemical neurotransmitter released from the sympathetic nervous system in response to stress. However, because the release of norepinephrine affects other organs of the body, it is also referred to as a stress hormone. When the body senses danger, the sympathetic nervous system triggers a response that is commonly referred to as our 'fight or flight' response. To ensure our body works as efficiently as possible in times of danger/stress, norepinephrine causes several changes in body function. These include: an increase in the amount of oxygen going to our brain – which enables us to think clearer and faster; an increase in our heart rate – this enables our heart to pump more blood around the body, which helps our muscles work faster and more efficiently; an increase in release of glucose – which provides energy for the muscles; an increase in breathing rate to enable more oxygen to be delivered to the brain and the body; a shutting down of metabolic processes such as digestion, which allows for the blood and energy used by these to be re-directed to muscles and brain. Norepinephrine helps people pay attention and focus in the course of their normal day. Low levels of this chemical in the brain can make it harder to focus.

Chemicals produced by the brain

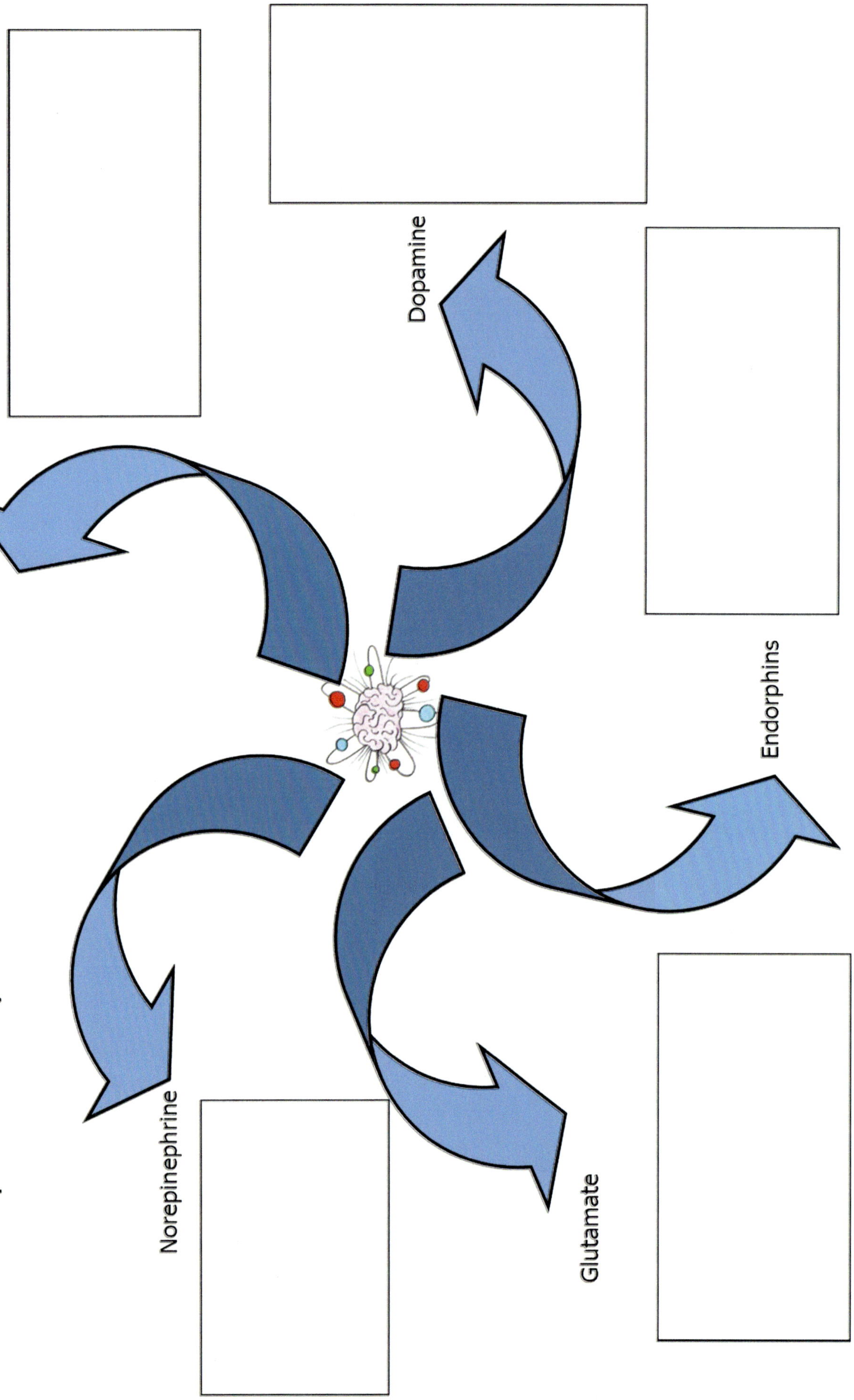

Cortisol and the brain

1 2 3

SESSION OBJECTIVES

To understand how stress can affect the brain.

SESSION OUTCOMES

✓ To be able to describe what happens when a person becomes stressed and ways that can be used to de-stress.

LESSON PLAN

➢ Ask the children to describe a time when their class baby became stressed. How did they know? What happened? What did their parent do to help the baby?

For those classrooms not able to undertake the Circles for Learning Project, video clips or photographs can be used to support the discussion around the topic and stimulate thoughts and ideas from the children and young people.

Task

KS1: To show what happens to the body when it is feeling stressed and to share ways to de-stress.

KS2/KS3: To create a cartoon drawing to show how and why cortisol is produced and what it can do.

To create a stress toolkit to manage stress.

KS1

1 Remind the children about how the body needs to be in balance. Temperature, nutrients, water. When the body feels out of balance it does something.

Temperature – Too hot – sweats

Too cold – shivers

2 Ask the children to think of something that makes them happy. Give them time to feel this and then comment on what you can see – smiles, bright shiny eyes, flushed faces, etc. Remind them that just by thinking about something the body responds.

3 Introduce the word STRESS and ask the children for a definition.

4 Ask them to think of times when they have seen people stressed and get them to describe what they have seen.

5 Remind the children that the body likes to feel balanced. Does stress affect the balance? The answer is yes. Stress makes the body feel unbalanced and under threat. It thinks something bad might happen so it has to get ready for this. It is like it has to pack its first aid box to deal with anything that might happen.

6 When the body feels under threat it hasn't got time to think about what to do so a part of the body called the sympathetic nervous system takes over and gets things ready.

7 Ask the children if there is anything that makes them stressed. List the things on the board and help the children see that different things affect different people.

8 Ask the children what their body feels when they get stressed and write these down as a list.

9 Ask the children to work in pairs to complete the 'Stress Busting' sheet.

10 When finished, come back together and share thoughts and ideas.

11 At the end, explain to the children that as a class you are going to try out some of their stress-busting ideas over the next few weeks so that if and when they experience stress, they have some tools to deal with it.

Stress-busting ideas:

1 Slow focused breathing – star breathing or hand breathing

See star breathing chart

2 Guided relaxation

See guided relaxation sheets

3 5 4 3 2 1

Ask the children to sit still and breathe in and out three times. Then ask them to look around and find 5 things they can see, 4 things they can hear, 3 things they can feel, 2 things they can smell and 1 thing they can taste.

4 Surround Sounds

Ask the children to sit still and breathe in and out 3 times. Then ask them to focus on what they can hear, counting the different sounds that are around them. Do this for 1 minute and then share. Gradually increase until the children can focus and concentrate on the sounds around them for 2 minutes.

5 My Favourite Place

Ask the children to think of their favourite place – the place they love to be – this might be at home in bed, snuggled up on the settee with Mum or Dad, in their tree house, snuggled up to their dog, etc. Ask them to fill in the 'My Favourite Place' sheet. Ask them to draw themselves in their favourite place first and then think of 4 things that they can see, smell, hear and feel and fill in the bubbles. Then ask the children to close their eyes and imagine that they are in their favourite place. They can feel it, smell it, see the things they can see from it and feel the things they can feel when they are in it. Get them to practise this on regular occasions so that when they need it they can visualise it straightaway.

KS2/KS3

1 Start the lesson with a short roleplay by yourself and another member of staff if you have one.

2 Show how stressed you are and get them to add to this by doing things that annoy you. Describe how you are feeling – I am so stressed, I've got so much to do, I've got to mark these books, sort out and assembly, finish making the Easter Display and I haven't got any food in the house so I must go shopping . . .

3 When you have finished, ask the children about what might be happening in your body? Remind them of homeostasis and the fact that the body likes to feel balanced. When your body is stressed is it in balance?

4 Ask the children to work in small groups. Give each group the Chain Reaction sheet and ask them to cut out the cards and put them in the correct order to show what is happening when the body believes it is in danger or under attack – stressed

5 Ask the children to share what they have created, explaining why they have put things in the order they have.

6 Discuss how stress affects the body, introduce the term TOXIC STRESS and share the impact this can have.

7 Ask the question – If we know stress is not good for us, how can we manage it so that our bodies don't become flooded with all the stress chemicals and go to high alert all the time?

8 Collect ways to combat stress.

9 Ask the children to create a cartoon character or group of characters, THE STRESS BUSTERS, who have a range of powers to combat stress. These could be linked to the stress-busting ideas from the KS1 lesson or the balancing strategies listed below.

10 Explore and share these with the children, discussing how they each feel and which ones they like best. Create a display 'How to help the body keep in balance'.

Balancing strategies:
Positive thinking

Gratitude

Reframing

Meditation

RESOURCES

1 Stress-busting strategies

2 Balancing strategies

3 Chain reaction

4 Toxic stress description

5 Balance

6 Homeostasis description from Chapter 1

IMPORTANT POINTS

When the body feels as if it is under attack or threatened emotionally, psychologically or physically, it tries to manage this. The way it manages this is to put the body on high alert. There are ways we can support the body so that it doesn't have to become overwhelmed.

LEARNING LINKS

Speaking and listening, working collaboratively, emotional literacy, self-awareness.

REFLECTION

Questions:

Positive comment from child:

Positive comment from adult:

LEARNING DIMENSIONS		SOCIAL & EMOTIONAL SKILLS	
Strategic awareness		Emotional literacy	
Learning relationships		Neuroscience	
Curiosity		Self-regulation	
Creativity		Self-development	
Meaning making			
Changing & learning			
Resilience			

MAGIC CARPET RELAXATION

Take in a deep breath and close your eyes. I'm going to count down from 5 to 1 and when I get to 1, your whole body will feel floppy and heavy and very relaxed. In fact you will feel so relaxed that you will not even want to move . . . but just stay still and enjoy the wonderful calm feeling that begins to flow into your body.

5 . . . Start to feel the calm relaxation flow into your arms and legs

4 . . . Your legs are starting to feel floppy and heavy. Your arms start to feel the same too

3 . . . Your whole body now feels calm and relaxed. It feels heavier and heavier and more relaxed and comfortable . . .

2 . . . With every breath you take in and out you feel more and more relaxed. As I count down the numbers you feel more and more floppy and your body feels like it is floating on air.

As I say 1 . . . now, your whole body is very heavy . . .

Now I want you to imagine that you are lying on a beautiful, colourful carpet. It is a very special carpet. It is a magic carpet. I want you to put out your hand and feel it soft and smooth underneath you.

This magic carpet is the most beautiful carpet in the world. It is made of the softest wool and has the most beautiful colours woven into it. The patterns are bright and beautifully woken by very skilled and artistic people.

The people who made the carpet took enormous care when they worked. They loved making the carpet and you can feel that love and care around you gently holding you. They made this very special magical carpet just for you. It is the only one in the whole world quite like this; it is unique and very special.

I want you to put out your hands and find the special tassels that hang down at each of the front corners of the carpet. As you touch them, the tassels become hard and strong and stick straight up like handles . . . you feel perfectly safe.

The magic carpet gently moves; it is getting ready to take you on a very special journey. You feel safe and curious about where you will go and what you will see. Gently it moves, slowly at first because it doesn't want to frighten you. You feel safe and comfortable. You know the magic carpet is strong and will look after you but you are also keen to start your adventure. The magic carpet gently sways and flies up; it makes you giggle with delight and excitement! What an adventure! It takes you up into the sky, higher and higher, up to the soft fluffy white clouds that surround you like the softest of cotton wool. It's wonderful to be here . . . feeling free and completely relaxed. You can breathe clearly here. You inhale deeply and exhale slowly. You love the feel of floating in the clouds. Your body feels light and full of calm. You gently float along watching the white clouds gently bump and play around you. They make you smile. You look down and see the beautiful green patches below you; the fields and the hedges are tiny and stretch out below like a big green carpet. The trees seem to wave at you while the wind gently blows their branches back and forth. You can see fields and woods, ponds and rivers, mountains and hills all passing slowly below you. As you watch, you see houses that look quite tiny from all the way up here.

As you float gently along, all your worries seem to leave you, soaking into the clouds all around you soaked up like blotting paper. All problems and difficult thoughts you had seem to disappear and your mind feels calm, relaxed and as if it has a big smile inside. As you are gently blown along by the breeze, all the worries and problems are left far, far behind you. This is a beautiful carpet ride. You are now ready for the carpet to play. First it swoops and turns . . . then it twirls and flies up and down. You can feel laughter growing inside you as you swirl and turn up and down like your very own magical roller-coaster. You love the feeling of the wind in your hair and the clouds gently touching your hands. You laugh again and the laughter makes the clouds wobble as if they are laughing too. You can go as fast as you want or as slow as you would like. You play, one minute going fast and the next minute going slow. You are in full control – up down and around you steer it. Faster and faster, higher and higher, then down and down. Slower, faster – you choose . . . What an amazing ride up in the sky.

It is time to slow down and gradually stop. Now, take in a deep breath and glide your magic carpet back down on the ground. Gently it lands on the ground and comes to a stop when you're ready. As you land think of all the wonderful, happy feelings you have and bring them back with you. When you are ready, open your eyes. Breathe in deeply and breathe out. Do this a couple of times. You've done a fantastic job of using your imagination!

RELAXATION: FLYING HIGH LIKE A BUTTERFLY

Close your eyes and take in a nice deep breath. Breathe in through your nose and out through your mouth. Breathe in again and feel the wonderful air flow into your lungs.
Allow your tummy to fill up like a balloon, and then exhale slowly. Do this 5 times to really relax your whole body completely.

(Pause for breathing.)

Your body begins to feel deeply relaxed and you can feel it grow heavy as the calmness flows through your arms, legs and body. It feels good, like warm sunshine flowing through you.
Your legs begin to feel very heavy. Your arms begin to feel heavy and relaxed. You enjoy every moment as your body continues to relax with each word I say.

Now as your body relaxes, imagine you're a beautiful butterfly gently resting on a flower in a wonderful garden. Around you, you can hear the gentle humming of bees and the breeze gently flowing through the branches of the trees. The sunshine is filling the garden with warmth and yellow light. Around you birds are singing and you can hear a lawnmower in the distance cutting the grass. You watch as a small brown bird flies above you. You remember you have beautiful wings folded up and decide that you would like to fly in the breeze and see the garden from above. You flap your wings and gracefully rise into the air, fluttering up into the sky.

As you look down, you can see the green fields and hedges below you like a huge patchwork quilt. You can see the lovely green valley below you with lots of colourful flowers, just waiting for you to enjoy.

You feel the wind blow against your delicate wings.

As the wind gently touches your beautiful wings, it gently blows away any worries, any stress you feel. You feel them blow away into the sky; it feels wonderful to be free of them. Your mind is clear and calm. It feels as though it is full of sunshine and smiles. The worries are now left far behind you. You feel relaxed and happy as you gracefully fly in the sky. Happiness flows through your body making your wings strong and beautiful.

The sun gently touches your body and warms you. Big, white fluffy clouds float above you in the blue sky gently bumping into each other and playing hide and seek. Their silliness and happiness makes you giggle. You are warm, and relaxed as you fly in the breeze watching the green fields and trees below you. A ribbon of silver twists across the green below as you notice a river sparkling in the sunlight it looks wonderful. You are enjoying each moment here in the sky, gliding along feeling calm and peaceful. You spread your wings far and stretch.

It feels so good. Your body is calm and your mind is peaceful.

Five Four Three Two One

5 Things you can see

4 Things you can hear

3 Things you can feel

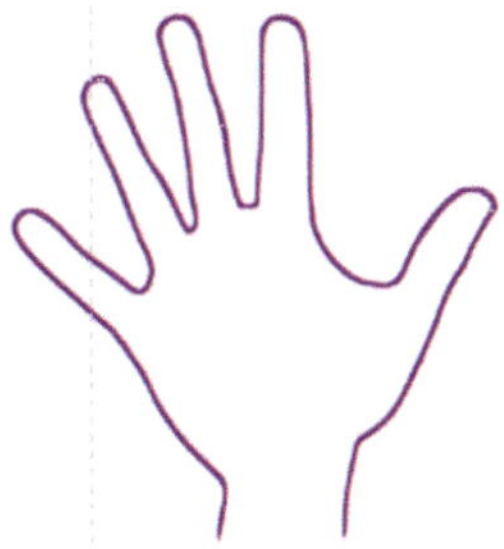

2 Things you can smell

1 Thing you can taste

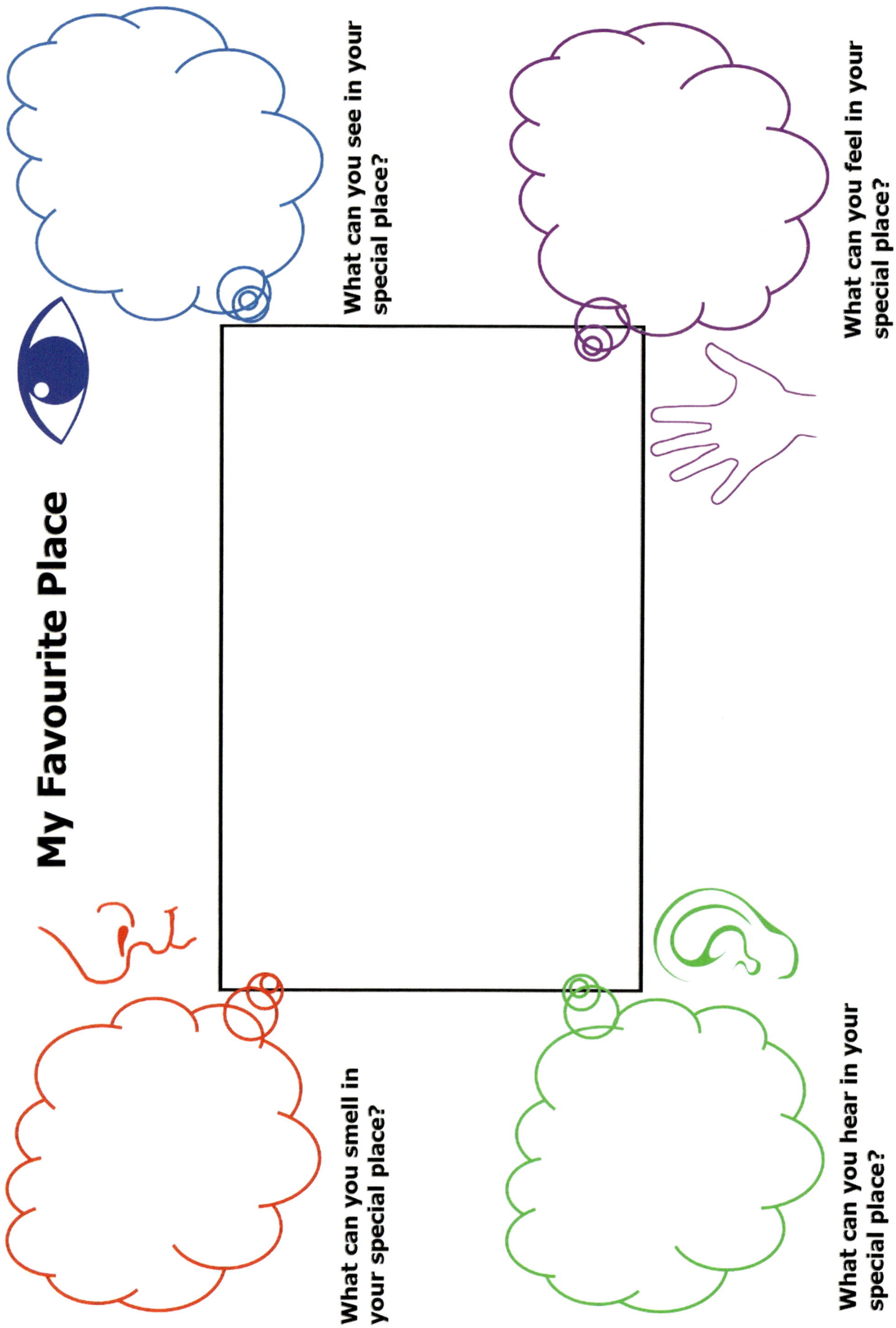

My Favourite Place
What can you see in your special place?
What can you feel in your special place?
What can you smell in your special place?
What can you hear in your special place?

Star Breathing

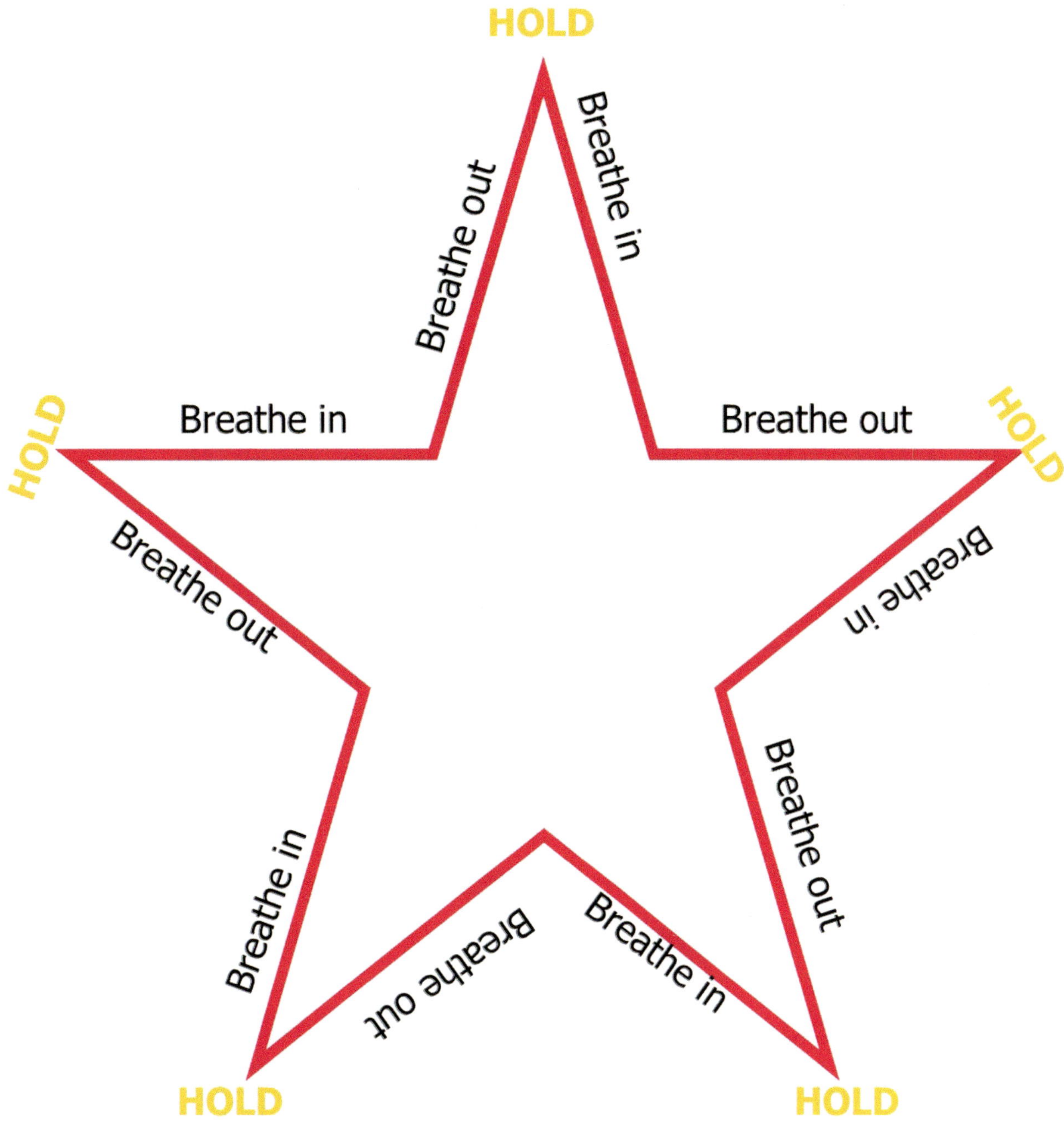

Get your finger ready to trace around the star. Place it on any of the 'Breathe in' places. Breathe in and then hold your breath and count to three, then breathe out. Keep going until you have been all around the star.

Gratitude Jar

Our science teacher chose not to give us homework today.

Mum is going to her evening class to-night so we've got pizza for tea

The school bus was late so I missed having to go to assembly

Today was a GREAT Day

Today I was grateful for....	Today I was happy because....
....	....
....	....
....	....

The best part of my day....	I laughed today because....
....	....
....	....
....	....
....	....

A good thing happened to-day	Today I smiled because....
....	....
....	....
....	....
....	....

Train your brain to see the world in a more positive way

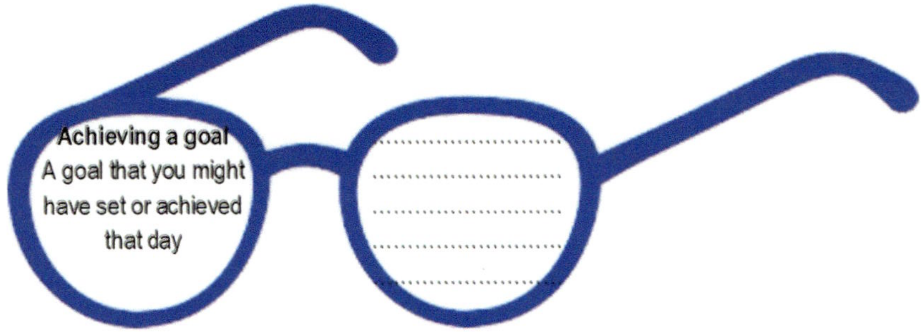

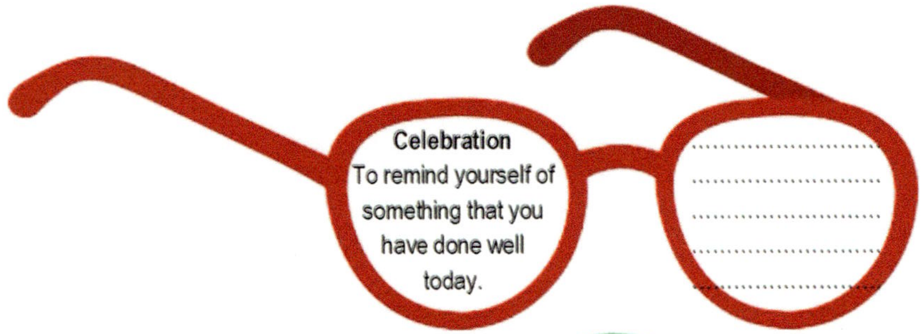

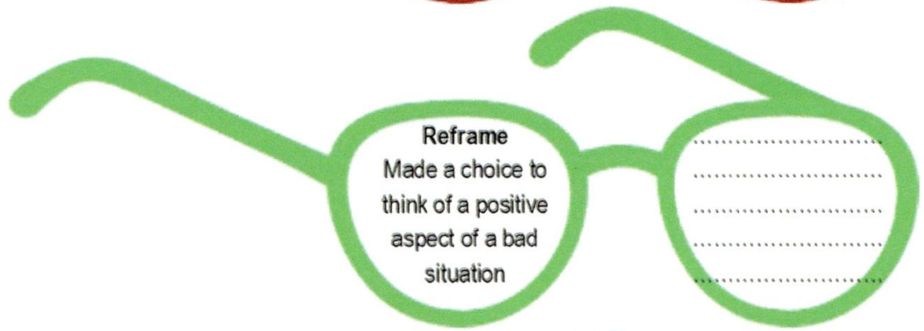

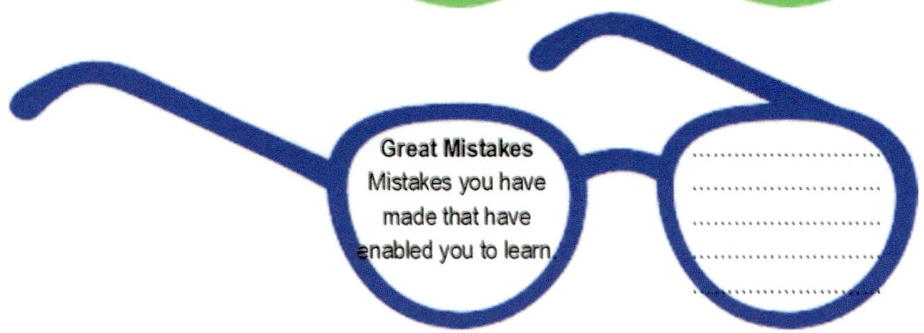

FOLLOW THE LEADER

This meditation works best for children in KS1 and KS2.

1 Ask the children to picture their best friend or a sibling. It needs to be someone that they enjoy doing things with.

2 Ask them which one usually leads. Usually one child is the one who decides things – the one who is more of the leader; the other one is the friend who usually follows the leader. Ask them which they would like to be today.

3 If they are the leader, you can tell them to picture themselves as the breath.

4 If they are the follower, you can ask them to picture themselves as the mind.

5 Start by saying 'So you and your friend/sibling do everything together. Let's imagine that your breath and your mind are best friends, too. And that you are just like the mind – the follower or just like the breath – the leader.'

6 Sit down comfortably and close your eyes.

7 Bring all of your attention to your breath and slow it down, breathing in deeply and slowly exhaling.

8 Let's have the mind follow the breath – no matter what. Picture yourself as your mind, the one that's following your friend/sibling, your breath. Try to focus your mind on the breath and follow as the breath inhales and exhales.

9 Count to 10 at the end of every exhale. Don't let the mind jump in and count; make sure that it stays as the follower.

Neurotransmitters 2 3

SESSION OBJECTIVES

To understand how neurons send messages to other neurons using neurotransmitters.

SESSION OUTCOMES

✓ To be able to describe the sequence of events that a neuron goes through in sending a message to another neuron using neurotransmitters.

LESSON PLAN

➢ Ask the children to describe a time when they watched their class baby respond to something. This may have been when they were frightened by a noise, hurt themselves by falling over or became frustrated at not being able to do something.

➢ Ask the children to describe the order of events.

For those classrooms not able to undertake the Circles for Learning Project, video clips or photographs can be used to support the discussion around the topic and stimulate thoughts and ideas from the children and young people.

Task

KS2/KS3: To play the neurotransmitters game.

KS2/KS3

1 Watch the YouTube video: 'Neurotransmitters - What are neurotransmitters and what do they do in the body?',

www.youtube.com/watch?v=Mz3PIvyu3ew
YouTube: 'The chemical mind - Crash Course Psychology #3',
www.youtube.com/watch?v=W4N-7AIzK7s

2 Ask the children to work in pairs.

3 Give the children the neurotransmitter cards (9 cards in the sequence) and ask them to put the cards in the order of the sequence of events.

4 Share the sequence and discuss.

5 Introduce the game. The purpose of the game is to acquire 3 or more cards in a neurotransmitter sequence.

- You need one set of cards per player. The sets of cards are shuffled and then dealt. Each player receives 5 cards. The other cards are placed in a pile in the centre of the table.
- The first player is the player on the left of the dealer. Each player begins their turn by picking up a card from the pile.
- Sets of 3 or more cards in sequence can be laid down at any time during a players turn, including after a card has been drawn from the pile. Players may add cards to their existing runs, but only when it is their turn.
- Only one' Choice Card' may be included in any run. Once the 'Choice Card' has been used, it is not allowed to be moved to another position.
- If a player has no cards left in their hand at the end of their turn they draw another card from the pile.
- The game continues until all the cards have been drawn from the pile and no player is able to lay down or add to any runs.
- The score for each player is the number of cards they have laid down in the runs minus the number of cards they have in their hand.

RESOURCES

1 Cards

2 YouTube video: 'Neurotransmitters – What are neurotransmitters and what do they do in the body?',

www.youtube.com/watch?v=Mz3Plvyu3ew

3 YouTube: 'The chemical mind – Crash Course Psychology #3',

www.youtube.com/watch?v=W4N-7AlzK7s

IMPORTANT POINTS

Neurotransmitters are the chemicals released by the neurons which take a message to the next neuron.

LEARNING LINKS

Speaking and listening, collaboration, knowledge and learning, creativity.

REFLECTION

Questions:

Positive comment from child:

Positive comment from adult:

LEARNING DIMENSIONS		SOCIAL & EMOTIONAL SKILLS	
Strategic awareness		Emotional literacy	
Learning relationships		Neuroscience	
Curiosity		Self-regulation	
Creativity		Self-development	
Meaning making			
Changing & learning			
Resilience			

Neurons, neurotransmitters and sending messages

Message Received

Messages are received on dendrites or on the cell body.

Neuron Fires

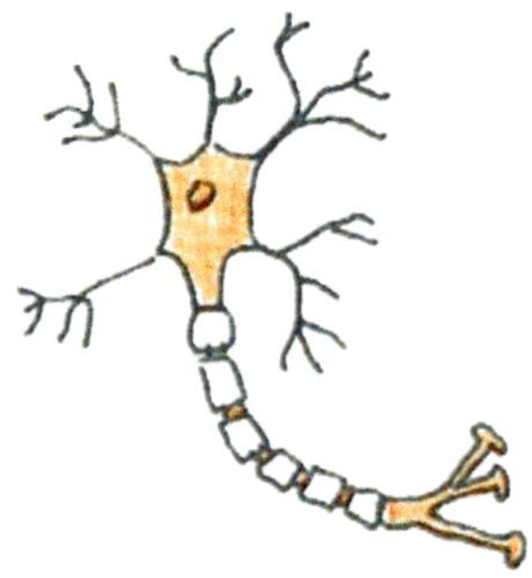

The combined messages generate an electrical impulse.

Axon

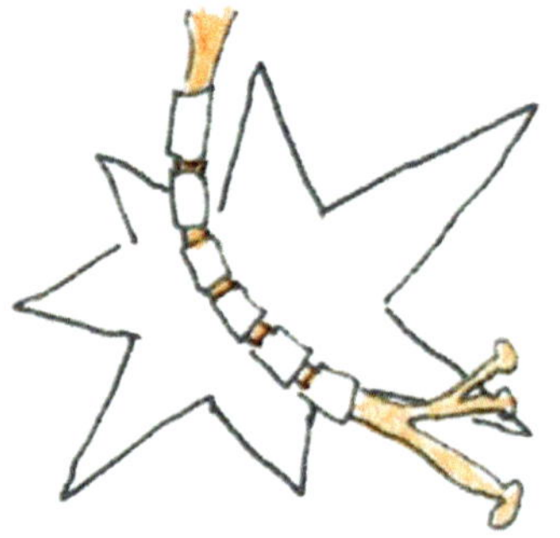

The impulse travels down the neuron to the end of the axon.

Neurotransmitters

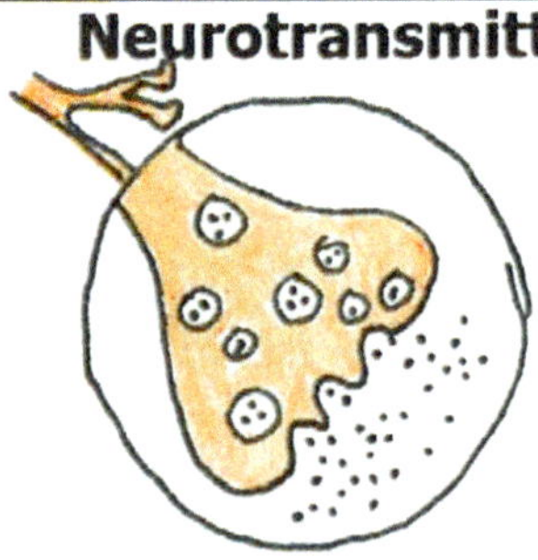

The electrical impulse causes neurotransmitters to be released from the axon.

Synapse

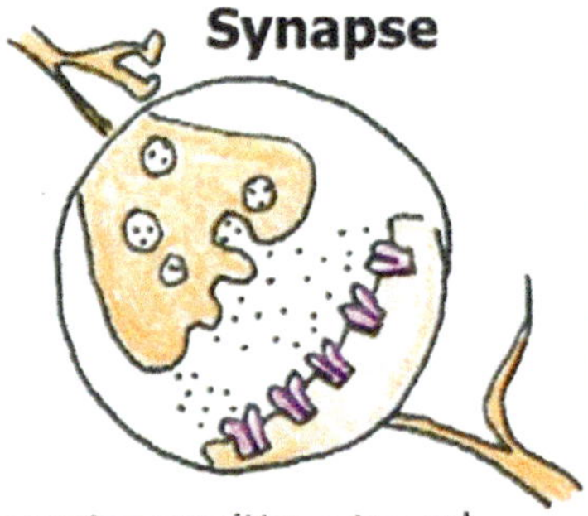

Neurotransmitters travel across the gap (synaptic cleft) between the neurons

Receptor

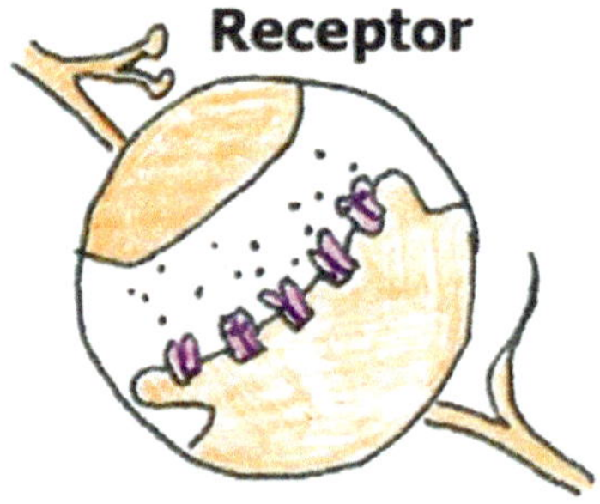

Some neurotransmitters attach to special receptors on the receiving neuron.

New Message

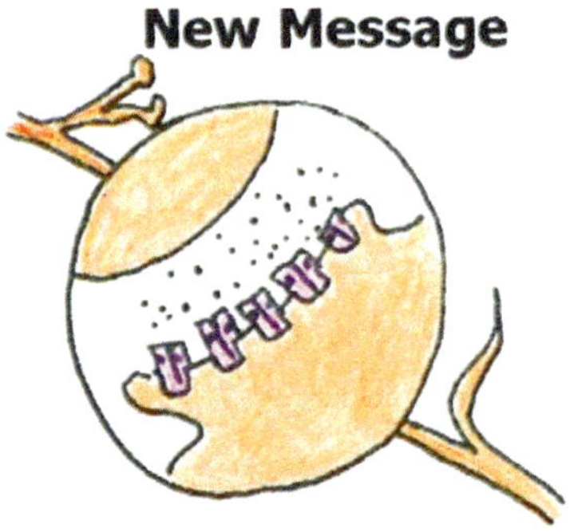

When the neurotransmitters attach to the receptors then can cause a new impulse to start in the receiving neuron.

Recycle

Neurotransmitters are cleared from receptor sites and the synapse.

Choice Card

Two Neurons

Reticular Activating System (RAS)

1 2 3

SESSION OBJECTIVES

To understand the job of the Reticular Activating System (RAS)

SESSION OUTCOMES

✓ To be able to describe how the RAS filters information that comes into the brain and focus on what is important.

LESSON PLAN

➢ Ask children to think about all the information that their class baby is processing each time they visit their class.

➢ Make a list of all the information that they have coming into their brain; circle the important information in red.

For those classrooms not able to undertake the Circles for Learning Project, video clips or photographs can be used to support the discussion around the topic and stimulate thoughts and ideas from the children and young people.

Task

KS1: To be able to describe how the RAS filters information from the senses.

KS2/KS3: To be able to describe how the RAS works and how to train it.

KS1

1 Share with the children where the RAS is within the brain. The Reticular Activating System (RAS) is located at the top of the spinal column in the brain. The RAS is approximately the size of your little finger. It is a filter for your brain, sifting through the millions of bits of information your brain encounters to determine what is important versus what you can ignore.

2 Ask the children to sit quietly for 1 minute and become aware of all the information that their senses are collecting. Collect the information in columns: what they can see, what they can hear, what they can smell, what they can taste, what they can feel.

3 Show the children a colander. Put a mixture of gravel and rice in a container and explain to the children this represents the information coming into the brain from all the senses. The gravel represents unimportant pieces of information like the birds singing outside, the hum of the computer or the smell of lunch from the dining hall and the feel of their socks against their feet. The rice represents the important information – the teacher's voice explaining something, the noise of someone sitting next to them, the writing on the whiteboard.

4 Ask what they think will happen when you pour this in the colander.

5 Demonstrate that the rice is able to pass through – like the important information and the less important information is held back.

6 Ask the children why they think this is an important for the RAS to do this for their brain? Help them understand that the brain would be flooded with information if it was not for the RAS and then it wouldn't be able to do anything except sort out information.

7 Support the children in identifying when their brain loses focus and gets distracted and help them bring it back to what it is supposed to be doing. Create a 'Tips to focus' list of things that the children identify as being a good way to focus and ignore the stones.

KS2/KS3

1 Share with the children where the RAS is within the brain. The Reticular Activating System (RAS) is located at the top of the spinal column in the brain. The RAS is approximately the size of your little finger. It is a filter for your brain, sifting through the millions of bits of information your brain encounters to determine what is important versus what you can ignore.

2 Ask the children to sit quietly for 1 minute and become aware of all the information that their senses are collecting. Collect the information in columns: what they can see, what they can hear, what they can smell, what they can taste, what they can feel.

3 Show the children a colander. Put a mixture of gravel and rice in a container and explain to the children this represents the information coming into the brain from all the senses. The gravel represents unimportant pieces of information like the birds singing outside, the hum of the computer or the smell of lunch from the dining hall and the feel of their socks against their feet. The rice represents the important information – the teacher's voice explaining something, the noise of someone sitting next to them, the writing on the whiteboard.

4 Ask what they think will happen when you pour this in the colander.

5 Demonstrate that the rice is able to pass through – like the important information and the less important information is held back.

6 Ask the children why they think this it is important for the RAS to do this for their brain. Help them understand that the brain would be flooded with information if it was not for the RAS and then it wouldn't be able to do anything except sort out information.

7 Support the children in developing mindful ways of developing their senses with a range of challenges.

Mindful listening

Ask the children to work in teams and listen to a range of sounds. Working together, list what they think the sounds are.

YouTube: 'Guess the sound game',

www.youtube.com/watch?v=lZsssS_I_2Y

Mindful observation

Working in small groups or teams, ask the children to observe an object for 2 minutes. Ask them to write as many details as they can down.

Objects might include ceramic vases with painted designs, carved boxes, artwork, a flower, an illustrated book, old kitchen equipment, toys, etc

Mindful smelling

Working in small groups, give the children a collection of pots with holes punched in the lids. Each pot should hold an object that has a smell. Ask the groups to list the different smells that they can identify.

8 Discuss why focusing and being able to concentrate is a useful skill to have.

9 What strategies have the children developed to support them being able to direct their focus where they want it to be? What activities do they find easy to focus on? Which ones are difficult? Why do they think there is a difference?

RESOURCES

1 YouTube: 'Guess the sound game',

   https://www.youtube.com/watch?v=lZsssS_I_2Y

2 Small pots or containers with a hole punched in the lid for smelling game

3 Variety of objects that smell – oranges, onions, coffee, lavender, toothpaste, crushed strawberries, vanilla, etc.

IMPORTANT POINTS

Our RAS helps the brain filter out information that is important.

LEARNING LINKS

Speaking and listening, collaboration, self-awareness, skills for learning.

REFLECTION

Questions:

Positive comment from child:

Positive comment from adult:

LEARNING DIMENSIONS		SOCIAL & EMOTIONAL SKILLS	
Strategic awareness		Emotional literacy	
Learning relationships		Neuroscience	
Curiosity		Self-regulation	
Creativity		Self-development	
Meaning making			
Changing & learning			
Resilience			

Chapter 3

The brain and learning

The brain and learning

SESSION OBJECTIVES

To develop an understanding about how the brain likes to learn and the many different ways that support learning.

SESSION OUTCOMES

✓ To be able to describe how they have learnt to do something and the different stages you go through.

LESSON PLAN

➢ Ask the children to think of a time when they watched their class baby learn to do something. Describe what they saw and the process involved.

For those classrooms not able to undertake the Circles for Learning Project, video clips or photographs can be used to support the discussion around the topic and stimulate thoughts and ideas from the children and young people.

Task

KS1: To become a learning coach and support each other in developing skills for learning.

KS2: To create a learning profile for themselves.

KS3: To create their own personal learning profile and then to use a learning log to support their development.

KS1

1 Ask the children what they think makes a good learner in the classroom. Collect all the ideas and write them on the board under the headings:

   self-regulation (thinking before doing something), manage emotions (staying calm and managing frustration), flexibility (being able to move from one task to another), focus and concentration (being able to keep themselves focused for a length of time), planning (being able to organise how they want or need to do a task), organisation (getting all the things they need to do a task and then working through it in the correct order), time management (getting the task done in the time they have), and reflection (thinking about how the task went and what they needed to change as they did it).

2 Ask the children to write their name in the middle of the sheet of paper and then draw themselves doing each of the activities. Put a tick by the ones that they would like to get better at.

3 Ask the children to walk around and look at each person's profile sheet. Ask them to put a counter on each one showing which area they think the person is best at.

4 Put the class in groups – each group with skilled people in (the children who feel that this is their strongest area).

5 Ask each group to make a badge for the team to show their strength.

6 Pair up the children with a coach or mentor for the skill they would like to develop most.

7 Set a piece of work for the class to do and at each stage pull out the coaches for that area.

E.g. The challenge is to make a card for a special person

- Put one of the Planning coaches on each of the tables and ask them to help the table create a task sheet to show what they need to do and in what order.
- Ask one of the Organising coaches to work on each table and ask them to help the tables write a list of the things they need.
- Ask the Time coaches to work out with each table how long they need for each part of the task and then to support a member of the table in watching the time and reminding each other how long there is to go.
- Ask the Self-regulation coaches to support children in coming up with a list of ways that people could move or take a break – cards with ideas on – go to the loo, have a drink, stretch, look at someone else's work, etc.
- Ask the Focus and Concentration coaches to monitor the noise and remind people how well they are doing or that they may need a break.
- Celebrate the end result and the fact that people have helped each other.

KS2

1 Ask the children to fill in the 'Executive Function' sheet. Explain that it is for them and they can share it if they wish, but they do not have to.

2 Once the profile is filled in, ask them to add up their scores for each section.

3 Ask them to share their strongest section but not give the score.

4 List the children under each section – to show the strongest in each section.

5 Ask the children to choose out of the 3 lowest areas which one they would like to work on and improve.

6 Write their names in another colour under the headings.

7 Explain that they are the apprentice – explore whether the children know the meaning of this word. Those people who are strong in a particular area are the coaches. Their role is to support the apprentices in developing this area.

8 When working on class activities, highlight the different areas and ask the coaches to explain how they may do something – use different coaches so the children can understand that there may be different ways of being organised or planning.

9 Get the organisers and the planners to come together to create a task sheet template that could be used by children to support their learning.

10 Ask the Time caches to help structure the lesson and help people think how long they have for each part of the task – some will need longer to write and less time to draw as drawing is their strength. Help children to understand that they plan around their strengths.

11 Discuss with the children what they feel has been important to them from the lesson.

KS3

1 Ask the children to fill in the 'Executive Function' sheet. Explain that it is for them and they can share it if they wish, but they do not have to.

2 Once the profile is filled in, ask them to add up their scores for each section.

3 Ask them to share their strongest section but not give the score.

4 List the children under each section – to show the strongest in each section.

5 Ask the children to choose out of the 3 lowest areas which one they would like to work on and improve.

6 Write their names in another colour under the headings.

7 Ask the children to focus on their learning and to complete a Learning Log after each lesson for a week.

8 Discuss what they find at the end of each lesson and how the class could support them in developing their skills for learning.

RESOURCES

1 Example task sheet

2 'Executive Function' questionnaire

3 Labels

4 Personal learning log

IMPORTANT POINTS

We have all got strengths and areas we can work on. When we want to improve, one way of doing this is to find a person who is really good in that area, watch and observe how they work, and then try this out.

LEARNING LINKS

Collaboration, self-awareness, self-development, coaching, supporting others, skills for learning, knowledge and understanding.

REFLECTION

Questions:

Positive comment from child:

Positive comment from adult:

LEARNING DIMENSIONS		SOCIAL & EMOTIONAL SKILLS	
Strategic awareness		Emotional literacy	
Learning relationships		Neuroscience	
Curiosity		Self-regulation	
Creativity		Self-development	
Meaning making			
Changing & learning			
Resilience			

Task Planner

The Task: Measure the area of shapes

What do I need?

What do I need to do?

Measure the area of the quadrilateral shapes

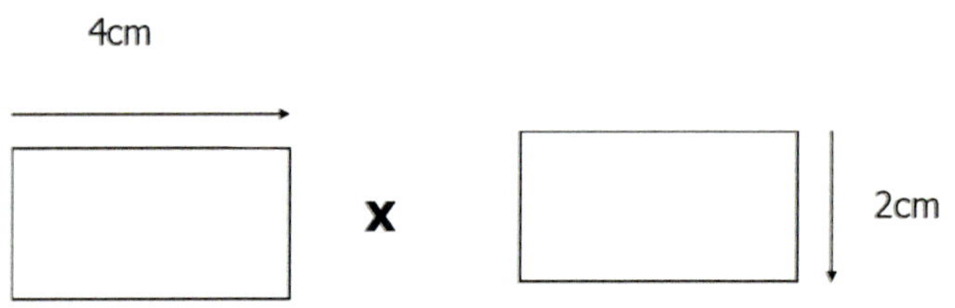

4cm x 2cm = 8cm2

What do I do next?

Choose 4 different quadrilaterals and work out the area.

Reflection

EXECUTIVE FUNCTIONING SELF-ASSESSMENT QUESTIONNAIRE							
Executive Function	Not at all 0	1	2	3	4	5	Very much 6
Response Inhibition is the capacity to think before acting. Weaknesses in RI include:							
Act without thinking							
Interrupt others							
Blurt out answers							
Talk too loudly							
Act inappropriately							
Emotional Control is the ability to manage emotions in order to achieve goals and complete tasks. Weaknesses in EC include:							
Over/under react							
Are easily overwhelmed							
Have low frustration tolerance							
Flexibility is the ability to adapt to changing conditions. Weaknesses in flexibility include:							
Are upset by changes							
Have difficulty transitioning between activities							
Have difficulty developing multiple solutions							
Working Memory is the ability to hold and manipulate information in memory when performing complex tasks. Children with WM weaknesses:							
Forget directions							
Get lost in a problem							
Work ineffectively							
Task Initiation is the ability to begin tasks in a timely manner. TI Weaknesses include:							
Put off doing the work							

EXECUTIVE FUNCTIONING SELF-ASSESSMENT QUESTIONNAIRE							
Executive Function	Not at all 0	1	2	3	4	5	Very much 6
Hand in assignments late							
Are disruptive in class							
Sustained Attention is the capacity to maintain focus in spite of distractions, tiredness and/or boredom. SA weaknesses include:							
Not being able to do the work							
Being unable to complete multiple assignments at once							
Planning is the ability to create a roadmap to reach a goal or complete a task. When children have planning weaknesses:							
Work does not get done							
Parts of assignments are completed out of order							
They miss steps to the assignment							
Organisation is the ability to create and maintain a system to keep track of information. Weaknesses in this area include:							
Being unable to find necessary materials for a task							
Having messy books							
Time Management is the ability to handle their time effectively. Weaknesses in TM include:							
Wasting time in class							
Being late for class							
Poor estimate of time							
Failing to meet deadlines							
Goal Directed Persistence is the capacity to follow through to the completion of a goal. GDP weaknesses include:							

EXECUTIVE FUNCTIONING SELF-ASSESSMENT QUESTIONNAIRE							
Executive Function	Not at all 0	1	2	3	4	5	Very much 6
Failure to meet goals							
Tendency to quit easily							
Frequently changing plans							
Metacognition is the ability to monitor, and be reflective about one's own thinking. Metacognition weaknesses include:							
Making the same mistakes over and over							
Lacking insight							
Poor problem-solving skills							

Self-regulation Coach	Thinking before doing something
Managing Emotions Coach	Staying calm and manage frustration
Flexibility Coach	Being able to move from one task to another
Focus and Concentration Coach	Being able to keep themselves focused for a length of time
Planning Coach	Being able to organise how they want or need to do a task
Organisation Coach	Getting all the things they need to do a task and then working through it in the correct order
Managing Time Coach	Getting the task done in the time they have
Reflection Coach	Thinking about how the task went and what they needed to change as they do it.

My Personal Learning Log

I was very interested in...

I found this fact surprising.....

1 thing I will remember

I want to find out more about

What I liked most about the lesson was

I am not sure/didn't understand ......

The most useful thing about the lesson

I might have learnt more if ....

Learning and stress

1 2 3

SESSION OBJECTIVES

To understand how stress can impact on learning.

SESSION OUTCOMES

✓ To be able to use a range of techniques to avoid becoming stressed over learning.

LESSON PLAN

➢ Ask the children to remember a time when their class baby became overwhelmed with emotions when they were trying to do something. Explore the language that the children use to discuss and describe this.

➢ Ask the children how it feels when we cannot do something that we are being asked to do. It becomes frustrating and then this becomes stressful.

For those classrooms not able to undertake the Circles for Learning Project, video clips or photographs can be used to support the discussion around the topic and stimulate thoughts and ideas from the children and young people.

Task

KS1: To create a poster to show what you can do when you don't know what to do.

KS2/KS3: To create a 'stress-busting' cartoon to show different ways to defeat stress.

KS1

1 Share the 'When I get stuck with my learning' poster with the children and let them know that you are all going to create a poster display to show what to do when you get stuck in learning.

2 Ask the children what they could do for each section.

3 Collect the ideas and then ask children to draw them for the display.

4 Photocopy the 'When I get stuck with my learning' poster onto A3 and put it in the middle of a display board. Put the pictures around it with a piece of string leading to the section it is describing.

When I forget I could – ask a friend, etc.

5 Once the display is up at the end of each session, ask the children which strategy they have used and discuss if it helped, or if they have found a new one.

KS2/KS3

1 Share with the children the Learning Zone and talk about how the stress levels go up as we move out of our comfort zone.

2 Share the stress cycle with the children and discuss what happens when the body becomes stressed.

3 Discuss how stress impacts on learning:

High cortisol has a negative impact on memory. The stress hormones divert glucose to muscles in case the subject has to run or fight. Therefore less goes to the hippocampus. This creates an energy crisis in the hippocampus which means it is not able to create any new memories.

Cortisol interferes with the function of neurotransmitters – the chemicals used by the cells to communicate with each other. This results in people struggling to think or being able to access long term memories (which might help them know what to do) so they feel confused and befuddled and their mind goes blank.

Speech can also be affected, with people struggling to say what they want or what they need.

4 Ask the children to draw or write a description for a stress-busting cartoon character.

5 This character must have a variety of secret weapons to defeat stress – some might like to draw a cartoon character for stress and then show a battle between them.

6 Discuss with the children what strategies they use to beat stress. List them on the board and discuss when they can be used and how.

These could include:

Counting backwards from 100 in 3s

Soles of the feet meditation

Breathing exercises 7:11 or star breathing

Going for a walk

Visualisation

7 Get the children to weave these into their story/character description or cartoon plus any others they think about.

8 Can they come up with a song to the tune of 'Ghostbusters' – Stress Busters!!

9 When the cartoons have been created – have a stress-busting afternoon trying out the different techniques.

RESOURCES

1 Learning zones

2 The body's stress response

3 'When I get stuck with my learning' poster

4 Paper

5 Pens, crayons and felt-tip pens

6 String

7 Soles of the feet meditation

IMPORTANT POINTS

Stress impacts in a negative way on learning. If we can manage stress, then we will improve our ability to learn and achieve.

LEARNING LINKS

Speaking and listening, knowledge and understanding, self-awareness, self-development, self-regulation, learning.

REFLECTION

Questions:

Positive comment from child:

Positive comment from adult:

LEARNING DIMENSIONS		SOCIAL & EMOTIONAL SKILLS	
Strategic awareness		Emotional literacy	
Learning relationships		Neuroscience	
Curiosity		Self-regulation	
Creativity		Self-development	
Meaning making			
Changing & learning			
Resilience			

When I get stuck with my learning I

When I forget I can......

When I feel stupid I can.......................

When I don't understand I can..........

When I feel frustrated I can.........

When I don't know I can...........

When I am confused I can ....

When I get frightened of making a mistake I can.....

When I get overwhelmed I can.......

Learning Zones

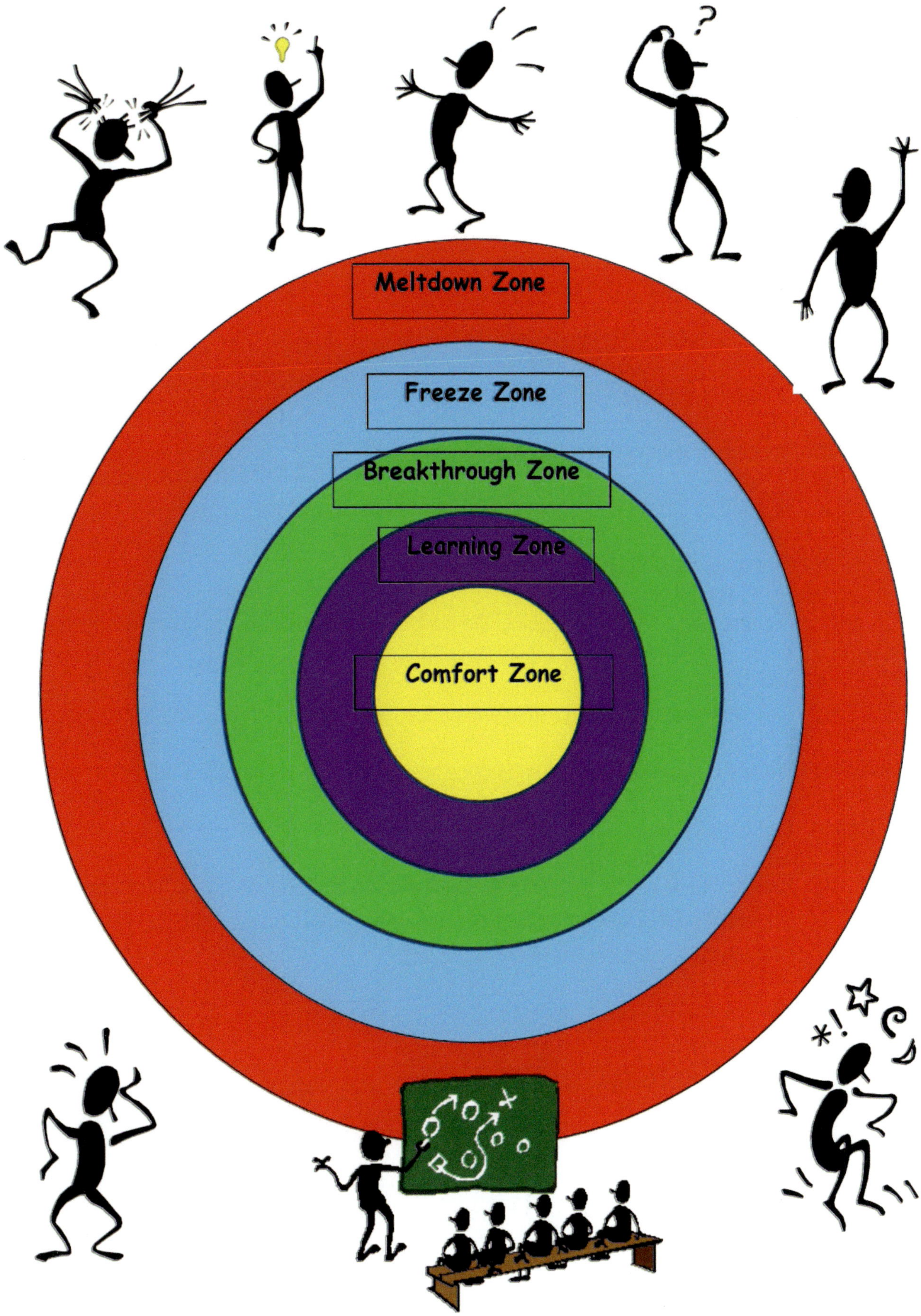

SOLES OF THE FEET MEDITATION

1. If you are standing, stand in a natural relaxed posture with your arms hanging by your sides and your knees slightly bent and with the soles of your feet flat on the floor.
2. If you are sitting, sit comfortably with the soles of your feet flat on the floor.
3. Breathe naturally, and do nothing.
4. Now, shift all your attention to the soles of your feet.
5. Slowly, move your toes.
6. Feel your shoes covering your feet, feel the texture of your socks or tights.
7. Notice the temperature of your feet – warm or cool.
8. Notice how light or heavy they feel.
9. Now notice the connection with the surface beneath your feet.
10. Take a moment and focus on how your feet feel.
11. Feel the heels of your feet against the back of your shoes. If you do not have shoes on, feel the floor or carpet with the soles of your feet.
12. Slow down your breathing a little and notice it as it enters and flows into your lungs.
13. Breathe out in a slow breath and notice how it leaves your lungs, flowing out of your nose.
14. Do this three times.
15. Now, gradually let yourself think and see the room in which you are in. Think about your whole body, when you are ready give your hands a shake and then notice how you feel in comparison to how you felt when you started.

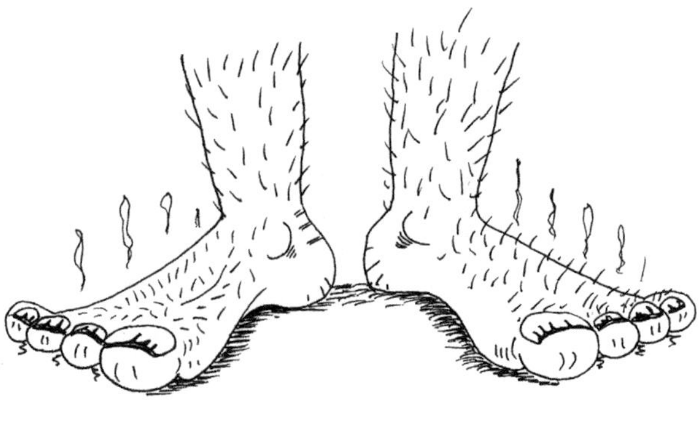

Less reactive, more reflective

1 2 3

SESSION OBJECTIVES

To be able to calm and self-soothe the stress system.

SESSION OUTCOMES

✓ To be able to share how they know they are becoming stressed and ways that they can soothe their stress system.

LESSON PLAN

➢ Ask the children to remember a time when their class baby became very overwhelmed and needed their parent to help them calm down.

➢ Ask them to describe how their class baby behaved and how they knew that they were not coping on their own.

➢ Ask them to describe what their class baby's mum did to help them calm. Did the baby try anything – a dummy, cuddly toy?

For those classrooms not able to undertake the Circles for Learning Project, video clips or photographs can be used to support the discussion around the topic and stimulate thoughts and ideas from the children and young people.

Task

KS1: To be able to describe things that make them calm.

KS2: To be able to describe how they know they are feeling overwhelmed and going to have a melt down and ways that they can sooth their stress system. To play the Stress System card game.

KS3: To be able to explore how to organise, plan and carry out revision and what they can do to self-soothe if they become anxious.

KS1

1 Ask the children to share a time when they had a meltdown.

2 Collect words about how they felt – hot, twitchy, itchy, couldn't sit or stand still, heart racing, couldn't find words to explain, etc.

3 Help the children understand that a 'thought' caused their body to think it was in danger and to send chemical messengers to get the body ready to deal with the danger. The brain's most important job is to ensure the body survives.

4 Help the children to understand that the body's chemicals cause the whole body and all of its systems to be on high alert.

5 When the body gets to high alert it has to be helped to soothe itself and calm down. Ask the children to talk in pairs and come up with 3 ways that they calm their system.

6 Share the strategies the children come up with.

7 Ask the children to draw pictures around the alarm system to show what they can do.

8 Ask them to put warning signs on the poster to show what to look out for.

9 Ask them to show 3 things that their friends could do to help them.

10 Share the stories *Silly Limbic* and *Rosie's Brain* with the children.

KS2

1 Explore with the children what they think and know about stress. How does the body feel when it is stressed? What is the trigger to stress? What happens in the body and why? How do they switch off their stress system and calm it down after the event?

2 Ask the children to think and share what happens when their body sees a threat?

3 Create a Mind Map on the board.

4 Divide the class into small groups and give each group a set of cards. Ask them to show the stress system cycle.

5 Share the order of what happens and discuss. Ask the question – can the cycle be stopped once it has started and if so how?

6 Help the children understand that the stress system was triggered by a thought – the senses sent information that was interpreted by the amygdala as being of danger to the body so the ALARM system was initiated.

7 Ask the children to share ways of calming or soothing their system. This can include: breathing, having a hot bath, drinking hot chocolate, going for a walk, thinking about good and happy memories, cuddling the dog, listening to music, having a hug, etc.

8 Ask them to create their own self-soothing first aid box.

9 Share the different ways of soothing the body and helping restore calm. Explain that many different strategies are needed to cope in different situations. You can't have a bath in the middle of an audition!!

10 Read *Rosie's Brain* and *Silly Limbic* to the children and discuss.

11 Play the Stress Response card game:

Give each child a set of cards and then ask them to get into groups of 4 or 5.

Get the group to shuffle the cards and give each person 10 cards.

The aim of the game is to get rid of all your cards. You can lay 3 or more cards down to show the stress response. The cards have to be in the correct order. So you could lay cards 1, 2, 3, 4 or you could lay cards 6, 7, 8, etc.

The person to the left of the dealer starts. They ask the person on their left for a card. If that person has the card, they have to hand it over. If they don't have the card, they say 'STRESS' and it is then their go.

The next person takes their go and asks for a card from the person on their left.

If that person doesn't have the card they say 'STRESS' and then the go passes on to the next person.

At any point people can lay down a run of cards (has to be 3 or more cards).

When it is your go you can also lay cards down on other people's runs. So if you have card 4 and someone has laid cards 1, 2, 3 down, you can now get rid of your card 3 on their run.

The winner is the person who gets rid of all their cards first.

KS3

1 Explore with the children things that have made them feel stressed.

2 Collect them on the board.

3 Share the stress response and explain that the body believes it is in danger and therefore sends chemical messages to put the body and its systems on high alert.

4 Explore how their body feels and why.

5 Ask the children to work in small groups, give each group a set of cards and ask them to set them out to show the stress system and what happens.

6 Discuss ways they use to calm the system and self-soothe.

7 Explore how the children feel about exams and how stressed this makes them.

8 Together, look at ways to make this manageable.

9 Create a list of things to do:

- Make a calm place to revise
- Put a revision plan in place weeks before the exams
- When revising, work for 30 minutes and then take a 10-minute break
- Practise relaxation
- When revising, only revise what you don't already know
- Before each session, sit down and plan what you want to achieve and how you will know you have achieved it
- Make sure you reward yourself after each session
- Make a plan for what will happen after the exams – take a picture and put it where you can see it so that it helps you stay motivated
- Make sure that you use a range of techniques that suit how you need to learn things. DON'T just read the book.

10 Share good revision strategies and revision methods or resources, so the children can see what you mean and how to make things.

11 Play the Stress Response card game with the children.

RESOURCES

1 Alarm sheet: 'Ways to soothe myself'

2 Self-soothing first aid box

3 How the body feels when the stress system is triggered

4 The Stress System game

5 *Silly Limbic* by Naomi Harvey

6 *Rosie's Brain* by Linda Ryden

IMPORTANT POINTS

Stress is the body's way of getting ready for danger; it is a survival system. When the body has been stressed, it is important to calm the system. This can be done in a variety of ways.

LEARNING LINKS

Speaking and listening, collaborative working, knowledge and understanding, skills for learning, self-awareness, emotional literacy.

REFLECTION

Questions:

Positive comment from child:

Positive comment from adult:

LEARNING DIMENSIONS		SOCIAL & EMOTIONAL SKILLS	
Strategic awareness		Emotional literacy	
Learning relationships	■	Neuroscience	■
Curiosity		Self-regulation	
Creativity	■	Self-development	■
Meaning making			
Changing & learning	■		
Resilience			

My Self-Soothing First Aid Box

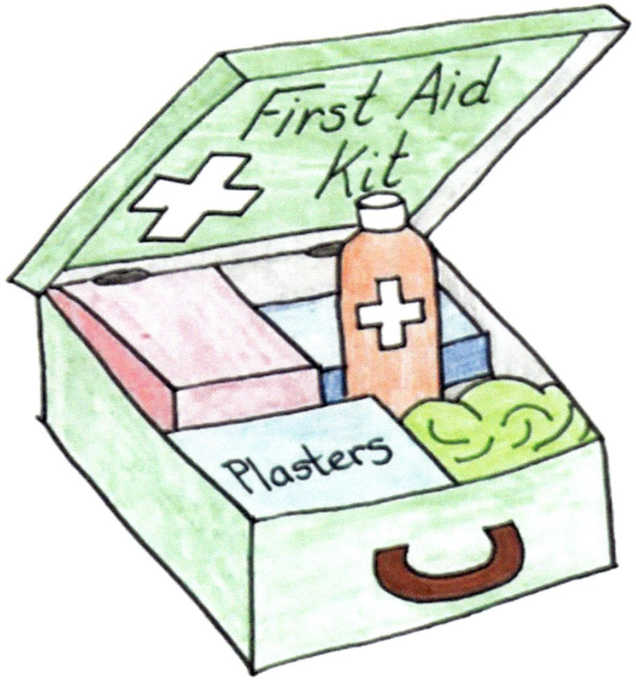

Ways to Soothe Myself

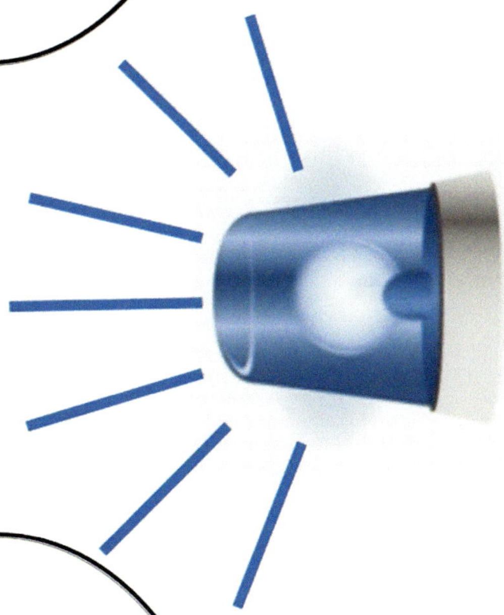

THE STRESS RESPONSE: WHAT HAPPENS INSIDE OUR BODY?

Stress is both a biological and psychological response that the body experiences when it believes it is under a threat which we believe we do not have the skills or abilities to deal with.

A stressor is the stimulus (or threat) that causes stress response within the body e.g. exam, moving school, loss of a friend, separation from a loved one.

Sudden and severe stress causes these effects in the body:

- Increased heart rate
- Increase in breathing, which often becomes shallow and fast (lungs dilate)
- Decrease in digestive activity, which is often why we feel butterflies in our tummy (don't feel hungry)
- Liver releases glucose for energy – so we become fidgety and can't sit still

When something happens our body looks at the information it has and decides whether or not it is stressful. This decision is made based on sensory information (i.e. the things we see and hear in the situation) and also on our memories (i.e. what happened the last time we were in a similar situation).

If the brain decides that the situation is stressful, the hypothalamus (at the base of the brain) is activated.

The hypothalamus in the brain is in charge of the stress response. When a stress response is triggered, it sends signals to two other structures: the **pituitary gland**, and the **adrenal medulla**.

These short term responses are produced by **The Fight or Flight Response** via the Sympathomedullary Pathway (SAM). Long term stress is regulated by the Hypothalamic Pituitary-Adrenal (HPA) system.

The Hypothalamic Pituitary-Adrenal (HPA) System

1. The Hypothalamic Pituitary Axis (HPA) is activated by the stressor
2. The hypothalamus stimulates the pituitary gland
3. The pituitary gland secretes adrenocorticotropic hormone (ACTH)
4. ACTH stimulates the adrenal glands to produce the hormone corticosteroid
5. Cortisol enables the body to keep a steady supply of blood sugar

A steady supply of blood sugar helps the body to cope with stress that goes on for a long time and then helps the body to return to normal.

The adrenal glands release stress hormones called cortisol. The hormone cortisol has a number of functions: it releases stored glucose from the liver (for energy) and controls any swelling that may have been created. To enable the body to focus on reducing swelling and making sure the body has enough sugar the immune system stops working at its full capacity.

Sympathomedullary Pathway (SAM)

Once a stressor is identified the hypothalamus also activates the adrenal medulla. The adrenal medulla is part of the autonomic nervous system (ANS).

The ANS is the part the nervous system that acts as a control system, maintaining homeostasis in the body. Homeostasis is how the body keeps conditions inside it the same. It is the maintenance of a constant internal environment.

Two examples of things that the body keeps the same are:

body temperature at 37°C
the amount of water inside our body

These activities are generally performed without conscious control.

The adrenal medulla secretes the hormone adrenaline. This hormone gets the body ready for a fight or flight response. Physiological reaction includes increased heart rate, dry mouth, quickening of breathing.

Adrenaline causes the sympathetic nervous system to become aroused and this reduces the activity in the parasympathetic nervous system.

Adrenaline creates changes in the body such as decreases (in digestion) and increases (sweating, increased pulse and blood pressure).

Once the 'threat' is over the parasympathetic branch takes control and brings the body back into a balanced state.

No ill effects are experienced from the short-term response to stress and it further has survival value in an evolutionary context.

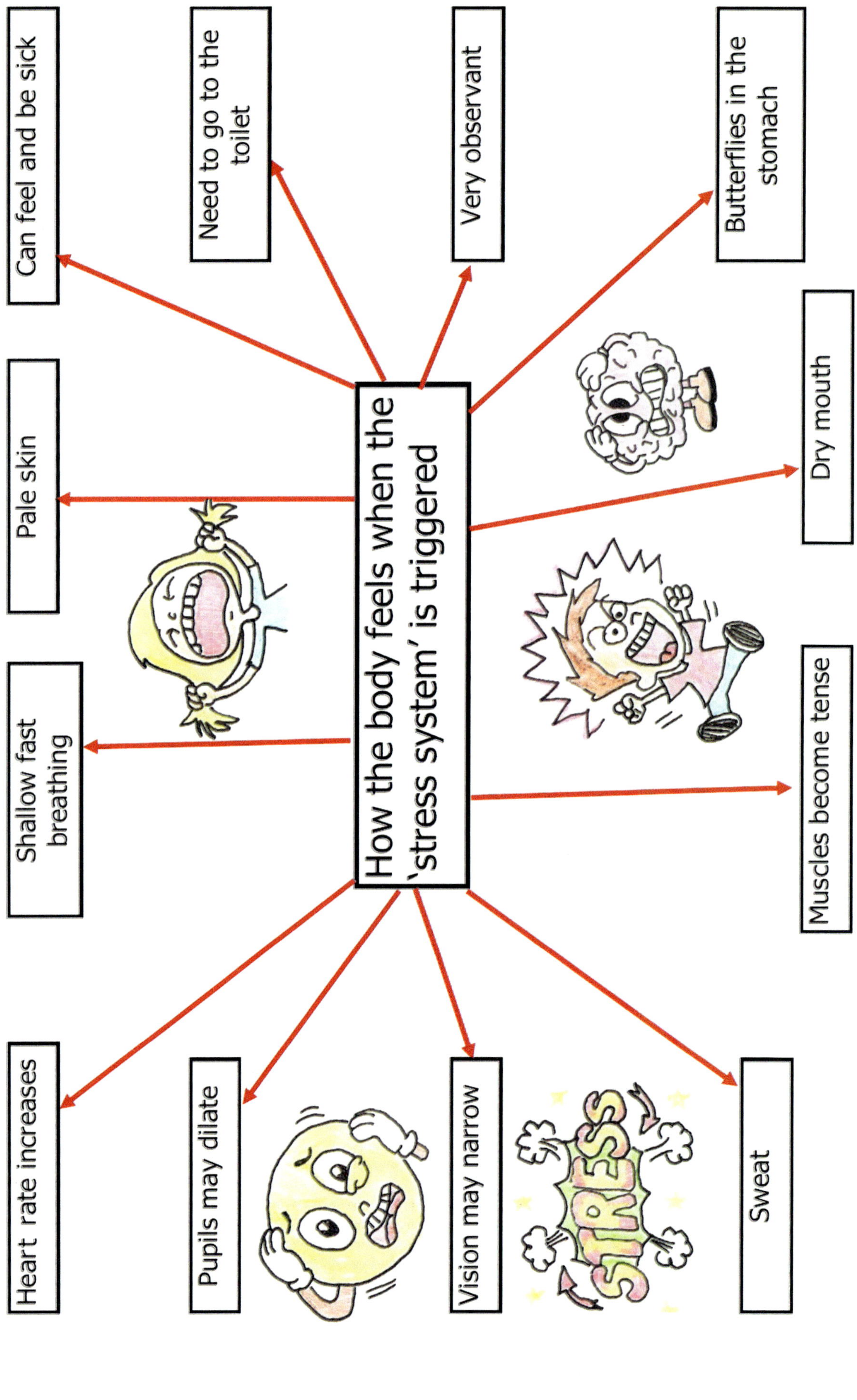
How the body feels when the 'stress system' is triggered
Heart rate increases
Shallow fast breathing
Pale skin
Can feel and be sick
Pupils may dilate
Need to go to the toilet
Vision may narrow
Very observant
STRESS
Sweat
Muscles become tense
Dry mouth
Butterflies in the stomach

1. The Senses send information to the brain

2. The Amygdala senses a potential threat and send a distress signal to the Hypothalamus

3. The Hypothalamus sends a message to the adrenal glands

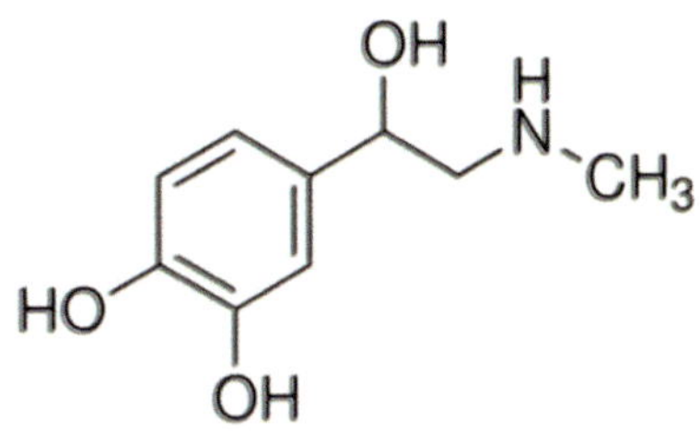

4. The Adrenal Glands secrete Adrenaline into the bloodstream.

5. The Adrenaline activates the Sympathetic Nervous System and this triggers the Fight or Flight Response providing the body with energy.

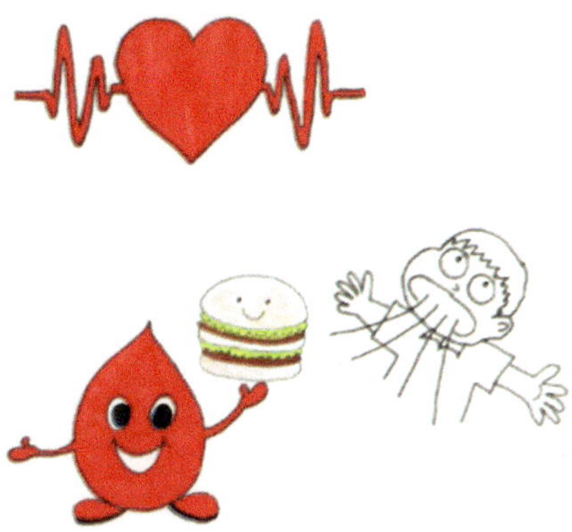

6. Adrenaline also causes: increases heartrate, increases breathing, causes more oxygen to be sent to the brain, causes glucose to be released into the blood to supply the body with energy.

7. The second part of the Stress Response System is activated, the Hypothalamus, Pituitary Gland and the Adrenal Glands (HPA Axis) This keeps the Sympathetic Nervous System (SNS) activated

8. If the brain continues to perceive danger then the Hypothalamus releases Corticotrophin

9. Corticotrophin causes the Pituitary Gland to release Adrenocorticotropic Hormone which makes the Adrenal Glands release Cortisol which keeps the body on high alert.

10. When the threat passes the cortisol levels fall and the Parasympathetic Nervous System takes over and dampens the Stress Response.

Memory

1 2 3

SESSION OBJECTIVES

To explore some of the strategies we can use to memorise information.

SESSION OUTCOMES

✓ To be able to explain and discuss strategies that support the memorisation of information.

LESSON PLAN

➢ Ask the children to describe how their class baby's vocabulary has developed. What were their first words? How many words do they know now? How have they learnt nursery rhymes or songs?

For those classrooms not able to undertake the Circles for Learning Project, video clips or photographs can be used to support the discussion around the topic and stimulate thoughts and ideas from the children and young people.

Task

KS1: To play Kim's Game and discuss how we remember things. Create a mnemonic for 5 tricky words.

KS2: To memorise a short play.

KS3: To explore memorising information for a test.

KS1

1 Ask the children how they remember something. If they have a message from a teacher for their parents or need to bring something to school, how do they make sure they remember?

2 Share and discuss some of the strategies they use.

3 Play Kim's Game with the children:

Put 10–15 items on a tray (these can be things in the classroom – pen, rubber, counter, pencil sharpener, etc.).

Tell the children that they will be given 2 minutes to look at the objects and then you will cover them up.

When the tray is covered, you will ask them to name as many objects as they can remember.

When you have finished, discuss the ways the children used to remember things – might be colours or positions or linking them together in a story or another way.

4 Divide the class up into small groups and give each group a set of words (one for each child) to remember how to spell. These can be linked to a topic or project that the children are doing. The groups need to be organised in ways that mean that children can have words that they have a good chance of being able to learn to spell.

5 Explain to the children that they are going to have a week to learn how to remember to spell their word. During the week you could share a variety of ways about how to remember to spell a word – mnemonic, visualisation, saying the letters of the word in the right order out loud again and again, writing them down, etc.

6 At the end of the week get the children to share the different ways they have used to remember how to spell their word.

7 Collect the different ways and discuss how each one works.

8 Ask the children to choose a new word and use a different method of remembering how to spell their new word.

9 The following week, discuss how they have got on and how they found the new strategy.

KS2

1 Ask the children to share what they know about how the memory works. Put all the information on a large Mind Map on the board. As you go along, write questions that the children raise that you would like to know the answer to on one side of the board.

2 When you have written up as much as possible, ask the children to work in pairs and research some of the questions that they have raised.

3 Come back together and share what you have found.

4 Help the children understand the different types of memory – automatic, short-term and long-term memory.

5 Divide the children into groups and explain that you have a group task for them. You want then to learn a short play together over the following week.

6 At the end of the week you are going to ask people to recite their play either in front of the class or just in front of you. Explain that you will also be asking them to describe the strategies that they have used and how the journey went.

7 Make sure you give time to practise during the week and also allow them to practise at break and play-time.

8 At the end of the week have a performance where each of the groups can share their play.

KS3

1 Ask the children how they remember things. Collect different strategies that the children use and give examples. How do they remember phone numbers, jobs that they have to do, homework, people's names, how to do something on the computer or phone?

2 Create a Mind Map on the board to show all the things the children know about memory. Write questions that come up in another colour at the side of the board.

3 When complete, divide up the questions to the children and ask their to research the answer and then share what you have found.

4 Look at the 3 parts of the brain which are used in memory storage – amygdala, hippocampus and frontal cortex.

Watch the YouTube video 'Where are memories stored?'.

Amygdala – measures the emotion attached to the memory. Memories with high levels of emotion are often the strongest. The amygdala is better at tagging negative memories than positive ones.

Hippocampus – has a central role in remembering. It decides what information goes where with the tagged information from the amygdala.

Frontal cortex – is involved with planning, evaluating consequences and determining goals. It neatly organises memory into a temporal, logical and meaningful story.

5 Explain to the children that 50 per cent of learning from books or lessons is forgotten within days. If, however, you review the information a week or so later, your ability to remember will improve.

6 Ask the children to work in groups and devise an experiment to see if this hypothesis is true.

7 Ensure that the experiment is safe and ethical (the experiment cannot hurt anyone or put them at risk psychologically, emotionally or physically and has to be moral).

8 Discuss as a group how you might set up your experiment to test how they as students can remember information for a test.

9 Allow each group to present what they wish to do and how to the rest of the class – this enables the other young people to act as the ethics committee and make sure the experiment is moral and safe.

10 Allow the children to try out their experiment and share what they find in relation to remembering information.

RESOURCES

1 TES, 'Fairy tales as play scripts',

www.tes.com/teaching-resource/fairy-tales-as-play-scripts-6233715

2 YouTube: 'Where are memories stored?,

www.youtube.com/watch?v=R0wbTR95VEs

3 YouTube: 'How to memorize fast and easily',

www.youtube.com/watch?v=0nFkQ4cQhME

4 Tray

5 Cloth

6 Items for Kim's Game

IMPORTANT POINTS

There are strategies that can support us remembering information.

LEARNING LINKS

Collaboration, self-awareness, skills for learning, knowledge and understanding.

REFLECTION

Questions:

Positive comment from child:

Positive comment from adult:

LEARNING DIMENSIONS		SOCIAL & EMOTIONAL SKILLS	
Strategic awareness		Emotional literacy	
Learning relationships		Neuroscience	■
Curiosity		Self-regulation	
Creativity		Self-development	
Meaning making			
Changing & learning			
Resilience			

WHAT IS MEMORY?

Do you have difficulties remembering facts, historical dates, people's names or how to spell words for a spelling test?

Your memory is a bit like a computer database. You can only find information/facts/dates or spellings that are in its database – the information needs to have been put in the database first and then saved.

Your memory is really clever: it can store facts, sounds, tastes, smells, touch sensations, what you see, and even your feelings.

Using your memory is a bit like you storing files in different folders on your computer so that you can find them more easily when you need them. If you don't file things properly or you put them in the wrong folder or you can't remember your password, then you could be in trouble!

Your memory has three parts: Automatic, Short term and Long term

Automatic memory is the memory that you don't even think about. It is the part of your brain that runs all of your body's systems – your heart for pumping blood around your body, your lungs which enable you to breathe, digestion and keeping your body at the right temperature.

Short-term memory is like the files that you are working on at the moment or the ones you use a lot.

Long-term memory is like the stuff you save on your computer. You don't need to use it all the time but you know you can find it when you need it - well that is if you can remember where you put it of course!

Improving your memory

You can exercise your memory and label the information you want to save in such a way that you can find it when you need it. Your amazing brain does a whole heap of this without you even noticing when and what it is doing.

How many times have you been able to recognising a smell or a sound automatically? Not only this but sometimes when you hear or smell something another memory floats into your mind of where you heard or smelt that before. It could be the scent of camp fires that leads to the memory of one particular time in your life. It may be a song that reminds you of someone who sang it to you or the place where you heard it. Sometimes memories can flood into your mind without you having to think "where and when did I hear or smell that?"

So, if your mind can produce several memories all at once with just one trigger, then why can't you remember how to spell 'because' or 'helicopter', or which witch is which?

Well, the trick is to give your memory more than one way of remembering. You can do this by using more than one sense, (touch, sight, hearing, taste and smell) or by using visualisation

How to get your memory fit and ready for action

Here are 5 good techniques for remembering:

1 Visualisation

This is seeing something in your mind so that you will remember it - like when you take your PE kit out of your bag and put it on the floor under the coat rack. Think about the PE kit and how it is hiding under the coat rack and make a picture in your mind about something really silly like your football kit running and playing hide and seek. It will help you to remember where you left it when you are packing your schoolbag later.

2 Linking

This is like visualisation, but you link several things together.

Suppose you had to remember a list of things that your Mum wanted you to get from the shop. Maybe she wanted baked beans, bread, milk and cat food.

In your mind, 'link' them together in a funny way so that you can remember. How about little baked bean people chasing the cat trying to make it eat a bread sandwich and a glass of milk!! The sillier the picture, the easier it is to remember what you need.

3 Link to a place

This method was used by the Romans hundreds of years ago as a way to remember a list.

They would think of each object in a certain place and then imagine going to that place to pick it up.

For instance, if you needed to remember a list of things you needed to take on holiday then you could imagine one object in each of the rooms of your house. Toothpaste, toothbrush, hairbrush, swimming costume, phone charger, book, coat, wellingtons. Then imagine walking in your front door and walking around your house and picking them all up. Remember, the funnier the story the more likely you are to remember.

You walk in the front door and there is the toothpaste on the doormat, you then go into the hall and there is your toothbrush bouncing on the settee..........

4 Chunking

This method is where you break the information up into smaller chunks or pieces. The largest group of numbers that most people can remember is 4, so that is why credit card numbers or phone numbers are grouped in 3 or 4 numbered chunks. How do you remember your phone number?

5 Acrostics (say across-tiks)

Perhaps your teacher helped you to remember the order of the colours of a rainbow by teaching you a strange sentence like:

Richard Of York Gave Battle In Vain

Red, Orange, Yellow, Green, Blue, Indigo, Violet

Use **mnemonics**

Small ants in danger – Said

Baby elephants can always understand small elephants – Because

Laugh and you get happy – Laugh

Focus and concentration

1 2 3

SESSION OBJECTIVES

To enable the children to understand that with practice they can train their mind to become more focused and notice more things.

SESSION OUTCOMES

✓ To be able to develop strategies that increase focus and concentration.

LESSON PLAN

➢ Ask the children to describe a time when they watched their class baby become really engrossed and focused on something. Ask them to describe what they observed, how did they know?

For those classrooms not able to undertake the Circles for Learning Project, video clips or photographs can be used to support the discussion around the topic and stimulate thoughts and ideas from the children and young people.

Task

KS1: To focus on blowing and observing bubbles.

KS2: To create two pictures to show focus and distraction and then to design a thought catcher.

KS3: To create a 'Puppy Brain Training Manual' to show how to bring the mind back to what you want it to focus on.

KS1

1 Ask the children what the word CONCENTRATION means. Explore what it feels like when they are fully engrossed in something and really concentrating.

2 When do they get this feeling? How does their body feel? How quickly or slowly does time pass? Are they aware of what is going on around them? Do they enjoy what they are doing? Can they get this focused on something they really don't like? What about something they are not able to do?

3 Ask the children to draw a picture of themselves doing something where they are fully engrossed, concentrating and focused and then write around the picture what this feels like. Can they come up with a simile to describe this?:

Concentrating is like swimming under the sea, it is peaceful, quiet and calm.

4 Explain to the children that the brain is always learning – show the video clip of neurons firing and making new connections as it learns to do new things.

5 Explain to the children that the neuron pathways are like paths in the jungle – the more they are used, the clearer they become and the easier they are to travel down. Neurons are like this – the more the neuron pathways are used, the easier it becomes – so that is why we practise things.

6 Explain to the children that you are all going to practise concentrating and focusing on something.

7 Share the bubbles with the children: explain that you are going to go outside and sit calmly somewhere with space around them so they feel as if they are on their own and then you are going to ask them to blow bubbles and watch and really observe and focus on the bubbles. You would like them to try and not think about anything else but the bubbles. If their mind wanders off you would like them to gently bring it back and remind it that you would like it to watch and think about the bubbles.

8 Ge the children to practise this for 1 minute and then talk about how it feels – link this to the forest path and the fact that the path has only just been made and needs to be used to keep it clear and for the neurons to know what they are doing.

9 Ask the children to do the exercise again for another minute. Discuss what they noticed, how they felt and how long they were able to just think about the bubbles.

10 Keep practising this skill. Next time use a candle in the classroom and ask the children to watch and focus on the flame dancing.

KS2

1 Ask the children what the word CONCENTRATION means. Explore what it feels like when they are fully engrossed in something and really concentrating.

2 When do they get this feeling? How does their body feel? How quickly or slowly does time pass? Are they aware of what is going on around them? Do they enjoy

what they are doing? Can they get this focused on something they really don't like? What about something they are not able to do?

3 Ask the children to draw a picture of themselves doing something where they are fully engrossed, concentrating and focused and then write around the picture what this feels like. Can they come up with a simile to describe this?:

Concentrating is like swimming under the sea, it is peaceful, quiet and calm.

4 Ask the children to fold a piece of paper in half. On one side draw a picture of themselves focusing and concentrating on something and then on the opposite side of the paper draw them being very distracted and not concentrating.

5 Explore with the children what it is like to not be able to concentrate, how does it feel? What is happening in their mind? What is their mind doing? Is it thinking about lots of other things?

6 Explain to the children that you would like them to design a 'Thought Catcher', a gadget that can help people concentrate and not be distracted by thoughts or other things. Ask them to two work in pairs and

- Design a 'Thought Catcher', labelling what it does
- Write a description of how it works
- Create an advert to get people to buy it.

7 When they have finished, get the children to present their idea to the class as if they were asking for money –*Dragons' Den*-style. Ask for 6 volunteers to be the Dragons and give them £100,000.00 each. Ask the children to decide if they would back the idea and if so how much money would they give. The team with the most money at the end is the winner.

KS3

1 Introduce the word CONCENTRATION to the children. In pairs, ask them to define what it means and give an example of a time they are able to become focused and to concentrate really easily and a time/activity when they really struggle.

2 Ask the children to either write or draw to show what it feels like in the two different states – to be focused and engrossed in something and to be distracted and not be able to focus. This could be on one sheet of paper folded into 2 with 'Focused' on one side and 'Distracted' on the other. It could be a written description detailing how it feels or it could be an acrostic poem using the words CONCENTRATION or DISTRACTION.

3 Support the children to understand that the brain is always learning new things and that this is when groups of neurons learn to fire together to make a pattern. Once they have learnt they need to practise to ensure that the pattern is established. Therefore we need to practise things.

4 Share the video clip of neurons firing and discuss.

5 Ask the children to describe how they learnt to ride a bicycle – they practised over and over again. Help them understand that focusing is a little like this. It is about practising – bringing the brain back to what they want it to do.

6 Share strategies the children use to keep themselves on task or being able to concentrate.

7 Explain to the children they are going to see if they can keep their brain focused on something for 5 minutes.

8 Give each child 10 counters and explain that each time their brain becomes distracted they put a counter on the floor/table. The aim of the game is to keep their mind focused on the candle for as long as possible. Each time it wanders, bring it back and try again. Remind them of the pathways that need to be constantly walked along to keep them clear.

9 Light a candle and ask the children to watch the flame. They put a counter down each time their mind wanders. Undertake this exercise for a couple of weeks and see if the number of counters they put down changes with practice. Is it easier on some days? Explore why this might be?

10 Discuss when this is easy to do and more difficult. Link to motivation and reward – What's In It for Me – WII4Me.

11 Share with the children the video showing how a puppy keeps getting distracted and keeps changing what it is focusing on. The brain can feel a bit similar.

12 Ask them to work in pairs and create a 'Train Your Brain' leaflet describing how to practise getting their brain to focus and concentrate using the strategies that you have all discussed.

RESOURCES

1 Bubbles for the children

2 A candle

3 Toy money for the Dragons

4 YouTube: 'Imaging reveals patterns in neuron firing',

www.youtube.com/watch?v=t3TaMU_qXMc

5 YouTube: 'Neuron time lapse video',

https://www.youtube.com/watch?v=A9zLKmt2nHo&pbjreload=10

6 YouTube: 'Distracted puppy party',

www.youtube.com/watch?v=sZdOisWgsJw

IMPORTANT POINTS

Focus and concentration can be hard to develop. We are often able to focus on things we like, so we know the brain can do this but we are often not aware. If we practise, we can help ourselves to concentrate when we want to.

LEARNING LINKS

Curiosity, creativity, learning skills, knowledge and understanding, self-awareness, collaboration, emotional literacy.

REFLECTION

Questions:

Positive comment from child:

Positive comment from adult:

LEARNING DIMENSIONS		SOCIAL & EMOTIONAL SKILLS	
Strategic awareness		Emotional literacy	
Learning relationships		Neuroscience	
Curiosity		Self-regulation	
Creativity		Self-development	
Meaning making			
Changing & learning			
Resilience			

Motivation

1 2 3

SESSION OBJECTIVES

To explore a range of ways that we can use to motivate ourselves to do something.

SESSION OUTCOMES

✓ To be able to describe a range of ways that they use to motivate themselves and explore the use of methods that they haven't used before.

LESSON PLAN

➢ Ask the children to describe a time when they watched their class baby try to do something again and again. Why did they keep trying? What do they think the baby was thinking at the time? Collect and write their ideas.

For those classrooms not able to undertake the Circles for Learning Project, video clips or photographs can be used to support the discussion around the topic and stimulate thoughts and ideas from the children and young people.

Task

KS1/KS2: To create a 'Motivator' cartoon character to help keep you motivated.

KS3: 'What's In It for Me' poster – WII4ME.

KS1/KS2

1 Introduce the word MOTIVATION. Ask the children what it means. Collect definitions and write them on the board.

2 Ask the children to give examples of how they motivate themselves to do things they like – play a video game or cuddle the dog? What is the self-talk that is going on inside their heads? What do they get out of the action? Play the video game – they get enjoyment.

3 Now ask them how they motivate themselves when they don't want to do something. What is the self-talk that goes on?

4 Introduce the 'What's In It For Me' phrase – WII4Me and explain that if they can help themselves see and understand that they will get something out of the action, it is sometimes easier to do, for example, if you go to bed early, you don't feel tired and then getting up is easier and you don't row with Mum in the morning. If they then focus on the row with Mum – not pleasant – then this can be the WII4Me reason to go to bed at a reasonable time.

5 Introduce the concept of 'delayed gratification' – a benefit in the future. If you save your pocket money each week you can then have the toy you want in a month's time – you delay getting the toy and thus delay the enjoyment or gratification .

6 Watch the video of the marshmallow test. Discuss what the children did to stop themselves eating the marshmallow. How were they feeling and why?

7 Watch the YouTube clip of Mr Motivator – he was one of the first TV presenters who became famous for keep-fit workouts. He is a real character – what makes him so good? List all the characteristics that make him a really good motivator.

8 Ask the children to work in pairs and come up with an acrostic poem for MOTIVATION.

9 Share the poems and talk about what they say about motivation.

10 Discuss the different strategies and self-talk the children use.

11 Vote for the one that is used the most, that is the strongest, that is the most useful, etc.

12 Ask the children to draw a Motivator cartoon character and label what characteristics they have that make them so powerful.

13 Share the work they have completed by putting it on the desk and then the children all walking around and reading what people have written.

14 Ask the children to write 3 strategies that they would like to try over the next couple of weeks and when they think they would be useful, for example,

I am going to use positive self-talk as a way of getting myself focused on my maths work as it is something that is hard to settle to.

KS3

1 Introduce the word MOTIVATION. Ask the children what it means. Collect definitions and write them on the board.

2 Ask the children to give examples of how they motivate themselves to do things they like – play a video game or cuddle the dog? What is the self-talk that is

going on inside their heads? What do they get out of the action? Play the video game – they get enjoyment.

3 Now ask them how they motivate themselves when they don't want to do something. What is the self-talk that goes on?

4 Introduce the 'What's In It For Me' phrase – WII4Me and explain that if they can help themselves see and understand that they will get something out of the action it is sometimes easier to do, for example, if you go to bed early you don't feel tired and then getting up is easier and you don't row with Mum in the morning. If they then focus on the row with Mum – not pleasant – then this can be the WII4Me (I won't row with Mum so won't go to school feeling horrible) reason to go to bed at a reasonable time.

5 Introduce the concept of 'delayed gratification' – a benefit in the future. If you save your pocket money each week you can then have the toy you want in a month's time – you delay getting the toy thus delay the enjoyment or gratification .. Watch the YouTube clip of Mr Motivator – he was one of the first TV presenters who became famous for keep-fit workouts. He is a real character – what makes him so good? List all the characteristics that make him a really good motivator.

6 Ask the children to work in pairs and come up with an acrostic poem for MOTIVATION.

7 Share the poems and talk about what they say about motivation.

8 Discuss the different strategies and self-talk the children use.

9 Vote for the one that is used the most, that is the strongest, that is the most useful, etc.

10 Ask the children to work in pairs and design a poster that explains what motivation is and the concept WII4Me. Clarify the success criteria for a good poster together as a class

- Clear to see and read
- Gets the concept across
- Is fun
- Eye-catching

- Doesn't offend anyone
- Easy to understand

11 When the children have finished, you can have an exhibition with a range of puzzles to celebrate and to explore how the children keep themselves motivated when the puzzles get tricky – which strategies are they using?

RESOURCES

1. Motivation challenges slips/cards
2. YouTube: 'Mr Motivator Beautiful Morning No 1',

   www.youtube.com/watch?v=1M5-HzxswPw
3. Motivation acrostic poem sheet
4. YouTube: 'The marshmallow test',

   www.youtube.com/watch?v=QX_oy9614HQ

IMPORTANT POINTS

Motivation can be hard when we don't want to do something. However, we can motivate ourselves in a range of ways including self-talk, focus on the outcome, talk our way to success, coach ourselves and use other people to keep us going.

LEARNING LINKS

Collaboration, self-development, emotional literacy, self-awareness, knowledge and understanding, skills for learning.

REFLECTION

Questions:

Positive comment from child:

Positive comment from adult:

LEARNING DIMENSIONS		SOCIAL & EMOTIONAL SKILLS	
Strategic awareness		Emotional literacy	
Learning relationships		Neuroscience	
Curiosity		Self-regulation	
Creativity		Self-development	
Meaning making			
Changing & learning			
Resilience			

M

O

T

I

V

A

T

I

O

N

My Motivation Challenges

I am going to use …………………………………… As my Motivation Strategy so that I can ……………………………………	I am going to use …………………………………… As my Motivation Strategy so that I can ……………………………………
I am going to use …………………………………… As my Motivation Strategy so that I can ……………………………………	I am going to use …………………………………… As my Motivation Strategy so that I can ……………………………………
I am going to use …………………………………… As my Motivation Strategy so that I can ……………………………………	I am going to use …………………………………… As my Motivation Strategy so that I can ……………………………………
I am going to use …………………………………… As my Motivation Strategy so that I can ……………………………………	I am going to use …………………………………… As my Motivation Strategy so that I can ……………………………………

Self-regulation 1 2 3

SESSION OBJECTIVES

To understand how your mind believes whatever you think.

To understand that by changing what you think, you can change how you feel.

SESSION OUTCOMES

✓ To be able to describe strategies you can use to help yourself feel better.

✓ To be able to problem-solve a worry.

✓ To be able to create a plan to manage a worry.

LESSON PLAN

➢ Ask the children to think of all the emotions their class baby has shown when they have visited them.

➢ Ask them to remember a time when they were feeling sad or fed up. What did their parent do to support them?

For those classrooms not able to undertake the Circles for Learning Project, video clips or photographs can be used to support the discussion around the topic and stimulate thoughts and ideas from the children and young people.

Task

KS1: To explore the 'Zones of Regulation' posters and create a card that helps them move from one zone to another.

KS2: To create a 'Wow Moments' box.

KS3: To problem-solve an anxiety.

To create a ladder to show the stages needed to challenge an anxiety.

KS1

1 Share the zones of regulation with the children

Green Zone – ready to go

Blue Zone – sad, flat, tired or unwell

Yellow Zone – wiggly, silly, frustrated

Red Zone – angry, cross, not managing

2 Explain to the children that we all feel these things but we learn how to manage them and change zones.

3 Ask how the children change from silly/wiggly to Green and ready to go. Write their ideas on the board.

4 Ask the children how they go from flat or tired to Green and ready to go. Record their ideas and strategies.

5 Ask the children how they go from the Red Zone to the Green Zone. Record their ideas.

6 Ask the children to work in pairs and talk to their partner about their strategies to Green from each of the zones. Share their top 3 ideas.

7 Once they have shared and talked about them to their partner, ask the children to make their cards. Use the card template below.

8 Practise using their strategies to change state and regulate themselves.

KS2

1 Ask the children to share all their ideas for unhelpful thoughts. Record them on the board with how they make you feel:

I can't do this ------- makes me feel useless or stupid

I always get spellings wrong ----------- makes me feel fed up and stupid

Bad things always happen to me ------------- makes me feel unlucky, horrid

2 Now think of a magic thought – a magic thought is a thought that doesn't have a negative effect:

I can't do this. Magic thought: OK this is hard but I can give it my best; that is what is important.

I always get spellings wrong. Magic thought: Last time I got 2 right; I am going to try and beat my record.

3 Ask the children to work in pairs and write a negative thought in black on a strip of paper and then a magic thought in a rainbow colour to show the difference.

4 Put the thoughts up around the room to help children start to use them.

5 Ask the children to make a 'Wow Moments' box. Decorate it to make it special and then, using small strips of paper, get the children to write notes of successes that they have and post into the box.

6 Suggest to the children that when they are fed up or down in the dumps, they can look into their box and remind themselves how well they can do things and in so doing change their state.

7 Celebrate all the small moments and get children to write notes for their box.

KS3

1 Discuss what the children think anxiety is, how it makes them feel, what strategies they have for managing this feeling.

2 Explain that anxiety isn't something we choose; it is affected by our genes, temperament and our experiences. Some people are more anxious than others but there are strategies that can be used that can help.

3 If we are anxious about something, we tend to keep thinking about it and trying to work it out. The thoughts go round and round inside our minds. This is called RUMINATING. It is what a cow does with its cud, chewing it eight times before it finally lets it go into its stomach – children like this silly bit of information as it helps them tackle this very unhelpful action.

4 Explain that one way of tackling an anxiety is to problem-solve it.

5 Ask the children to work in pairs and give out the 'Anxious Problems'.

6 Explain how the Problem Solving Game works: The problem is placed in the middle of the paper and then as many solutions as possible are put around the outside. These can be silly, ridiculous, imaginative as well as sensible and practical. Do one as an example with the children:

Some of the young people who I play football with keep teasing me about my goalkeeping; this is making me really anxious each week as I don't know what they are going to say and it is spoiling the game and I hate it.

Put this in the middle of the board and get them to give you solutions – these can be sensible or silly, e.g. change teams, don't go (sensible) or run away, blast them with a snow machine, get aliens to transport the players into outer space (silly). It is important to have the silly, non-sensible ones as they will make you laugh, which reduces tension and allows for better thinking. It also frees up the creative mind to help solve the problem.

Once you have come up with a variety of 'possible solutions', the next stage is to cross off all those that could cause harm – physically, emotionally or psychologically. Once you have done this, stage 3 is to write the pros and cons for each of the remaining solutions. Once this has been done, it will be easy to work out which solution is the best one. The last phase is to work out what you need to carry out that solution – this could mean a friend to help you or an adult to practise what you want to say or an adult to talk to someone.

7 Ask the children to work in pairs and work out the solution to a problem.

8 Share the problems and the solutions the pairs have come up with. Discuss the process they went through.

9 Sometimes anxiety can be caused by something that you have to do – having injections, for example. If this is the case, then one way of dealing with this is to create a ladder to success. This is where you break down what you need to do into small steps and then work on each step one at a time.

10 Share the 'Steps to Success for Injections' with the children as an example.

11 Ask them to work in small groups to create a 'Steps to Success' for one of the following: spiders, interviews, exams, going to a shopping centre, going on a school trip for a week, rock climbing, dogs, standing up and presenting a talk to a new class, playing an instrument in front of an audience, singing in front of an audience, etc.

12 Share the ladders when they have completed them by placing them on tables and then allowing children to walk around and read what people have come up with. Give them sticky notes to write positive comments on about each of the ladders, sharing what they liked, which steps they felt were the most positive and the design and layout of the work.

RESOURCES

1 'Zones of Regulation' posters

2 'Changing Zones' cards

3 'Wow Moments' box template

4 'Wow Moment' scrolls

5 'Steps to Success' ladders

6 'Problem-Solving Solutions Pros and Cons' sheet

IMPORTANT POINTS

We can regulate how we feel by doing a range of things and using a variety of strategies.

LEARNING LINKS

Collaboration, emotional literacy, self-awareness, knowledge and understanding, speaking and listening, creativity, skills for learning.

REFLECTION

Questions:

Positive comment from child:

Positive comment from adult:

LEARNING DIMENSIONS		SOCIAL & EMOTIONAL SKILLS	
Strategic awareness		Emotional literacy	
Learning relationships		Neuroscience	
Curiosity		Self-regulation	
Creativity		Self-development	
Meaning making			
Changing & learning			
Resilience			

Box template: WOW Moments Box

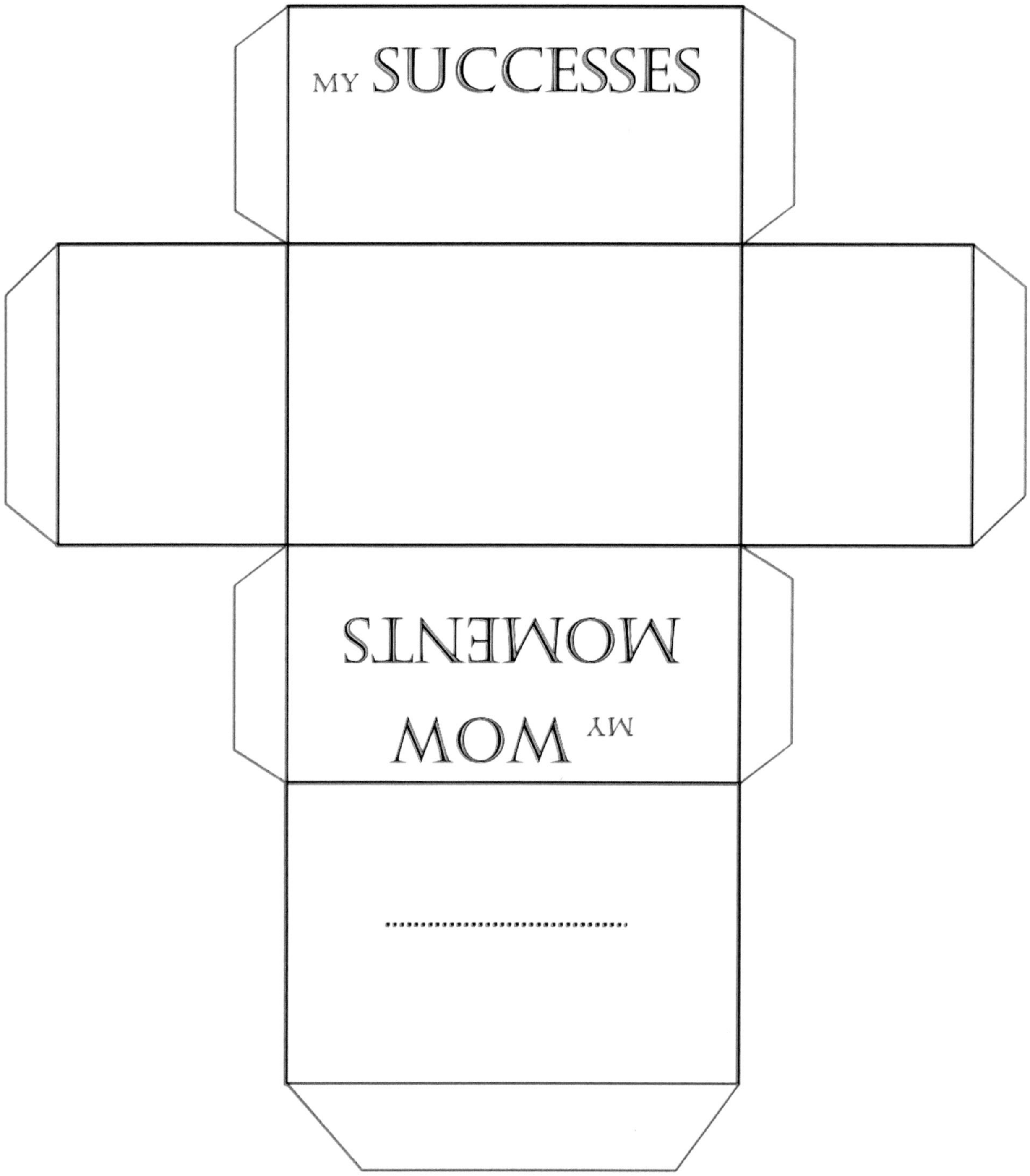

Anxious Problems	
You don't want to go to the Saturday Theatre Workshop anymore. You know your Mum and Dad are not going to like this but you hate it and dread Saturdays.	You are going on the school residential to France for a week but two friends want you to share a room with them and you don't want to upset one by choosing the other.
You have a birthday party coming up. It is a laser quest party and you have friends coming from school and also from your family. You know that two of the young people coming don't like each other and are likely to argue and spoil the party.	Your Mum and Dad are no longer together. They both want you to go on holiday with them in the summer and they want to go in the same week. You want to spend time with both of them but don't know how to manage this and it is causing you to feel ill every time you think about it.
You have to choose what project to do for your History Teacher. Your Mum thinks a good project would be about medicine over time but your Dad has lots of books on food. You want to research weapons as you would like to make something for your project. They both keep trying to persuade you to do their idea and you are dreading having to choose and don't think you can do the project on what you would like.	You went over to a friend's house to work on your school science project. But when you got there they were fed up as they had had a row with their step-dad and wanted to get out of the house and go to the cinema. You went as you felt sorry for them but didn't tell your parents. Your parents had been invited to your friend's house for a BBQ on Saturday and you are worried that they will find out that you skipped the project work and went out.
Your friends keep daring each other to steal sweets from the shop on the corner. They keep picking on you as you haven't done it yet. You know it is wrong but you don't want them to make fun of you. You have persuaded your Mum that you are sick and have avoided it today but this cannot go on.	You have been a scout for a couple of years and really like the activities and have a lot of friends there that you meet each week. A group of girls at school keep picking on another girl as they know she is a scout. You are frightened that they will find out about you and start to pick on you.

Problem Solving Solutions Pros and Cons

Solution	Pros or Positives	Cons or Negatives	Overall thoughts

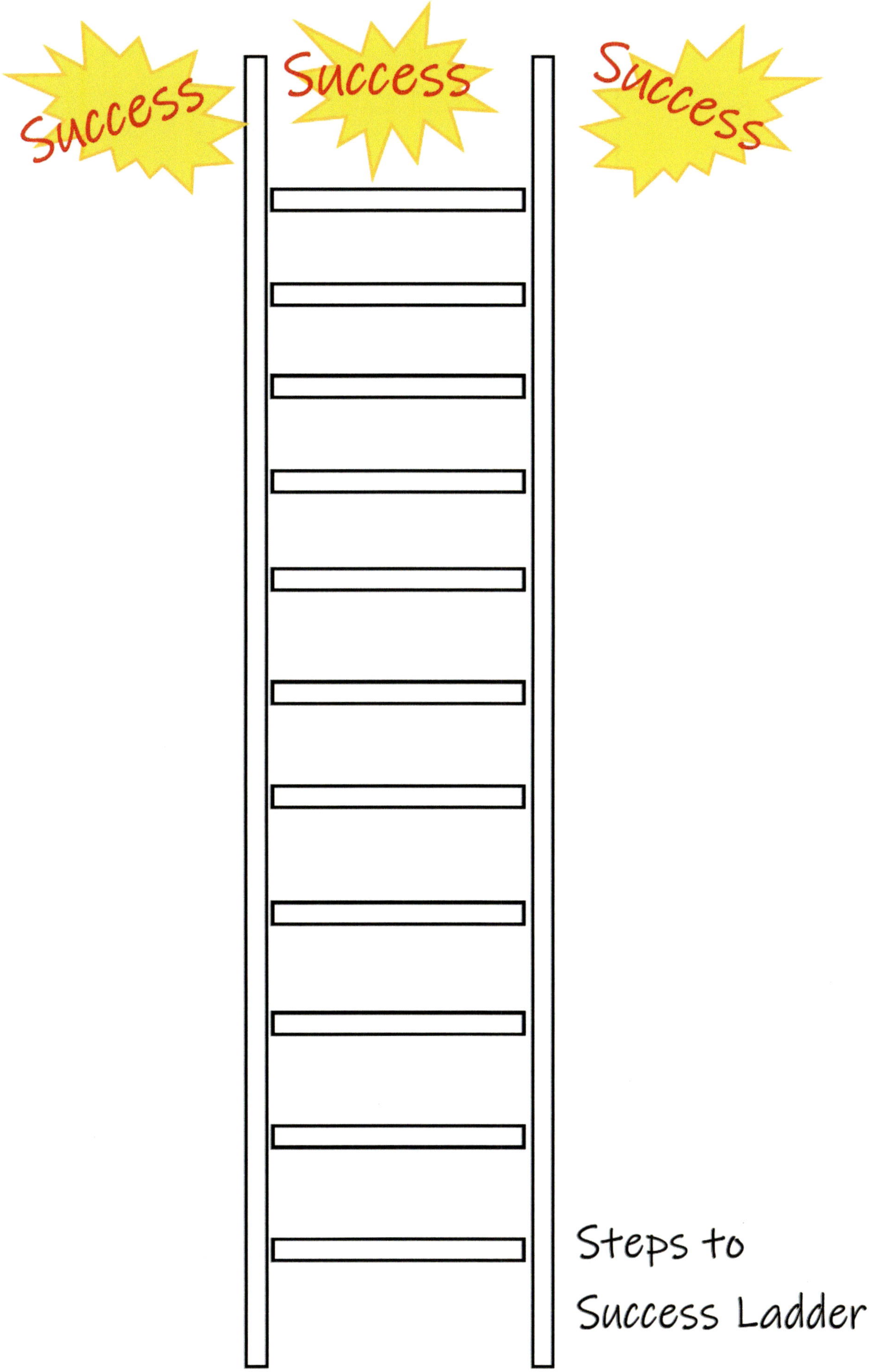
Success
Success
Success
Steps to
Success Ladder

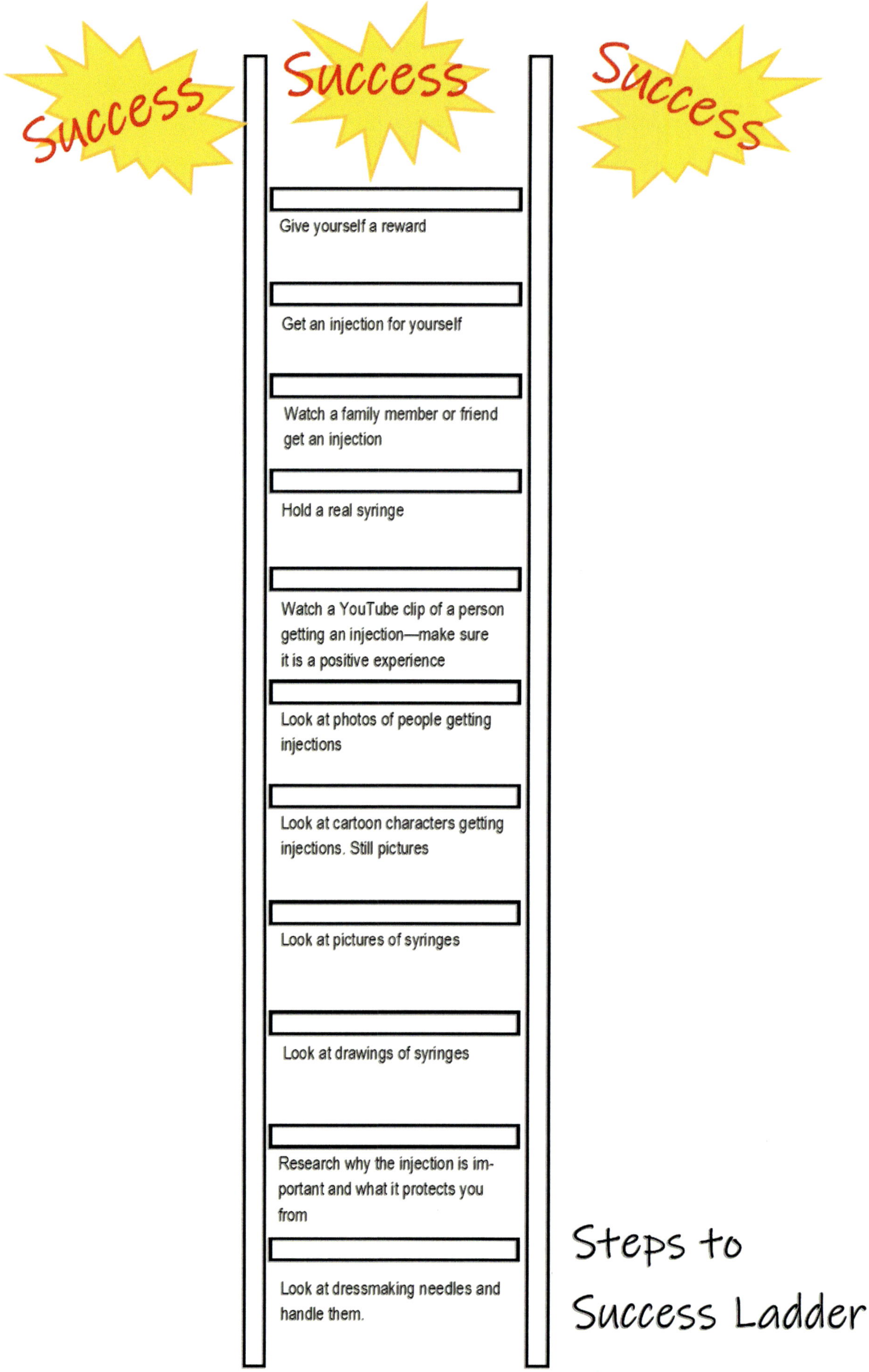
Success
Success
Success
Give yourself a reward
Get an injection for yourself
Watch a family member or friend get an injection
Hold a real syringe
Watch a YouTube clip of a person getting an injection—make sure it is a positive experience
Look at photos of people getting injections
Look at cartoon characters getting injections. Still pictures
Look at pictures of syringes
Look at drawings of syringes
Research why the injection is important and what it protects you from
Look at dressmaking needles and handle them.
Steps to Success Ladder

WOW Moment Scrolls

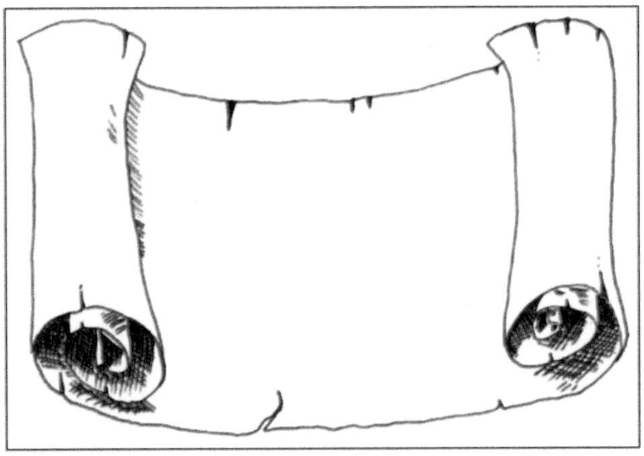
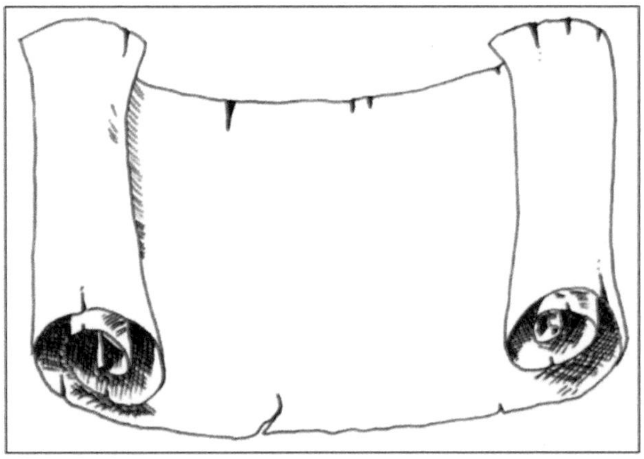
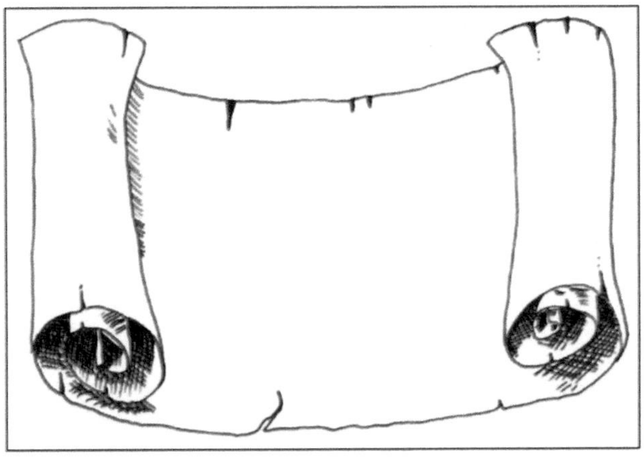
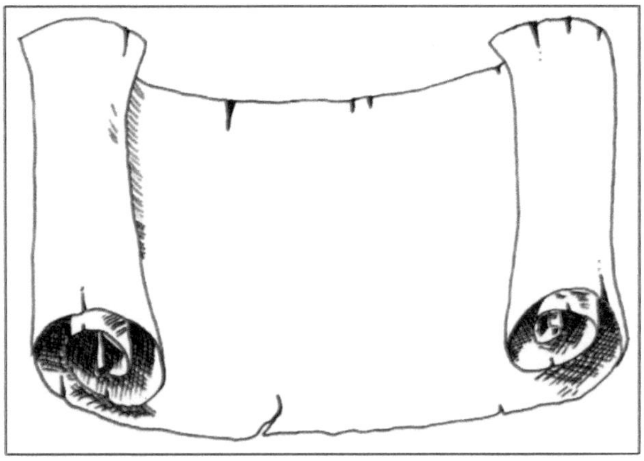
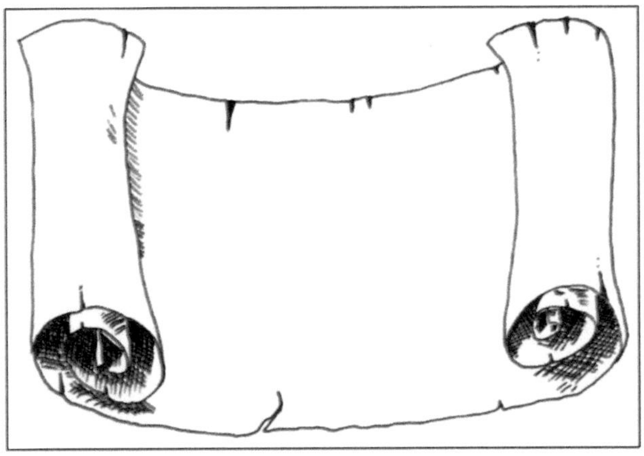
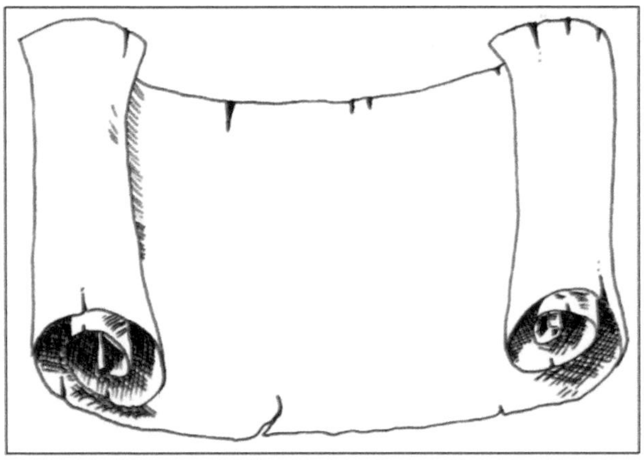
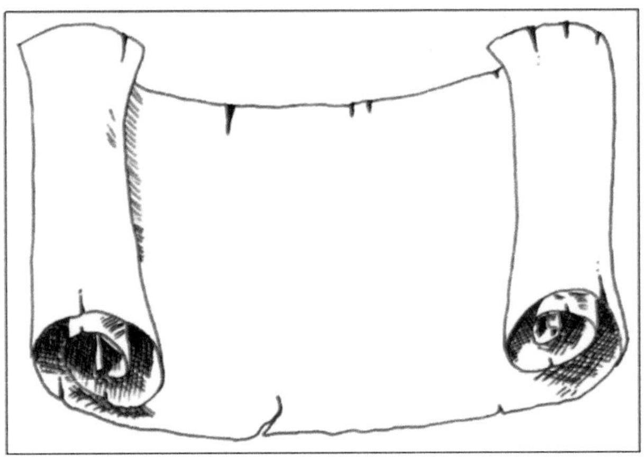
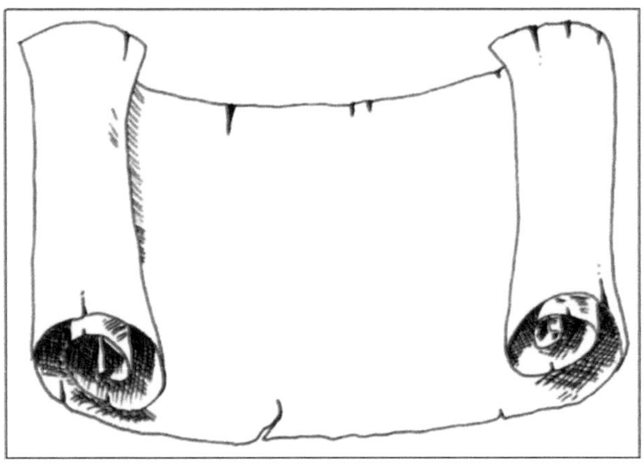

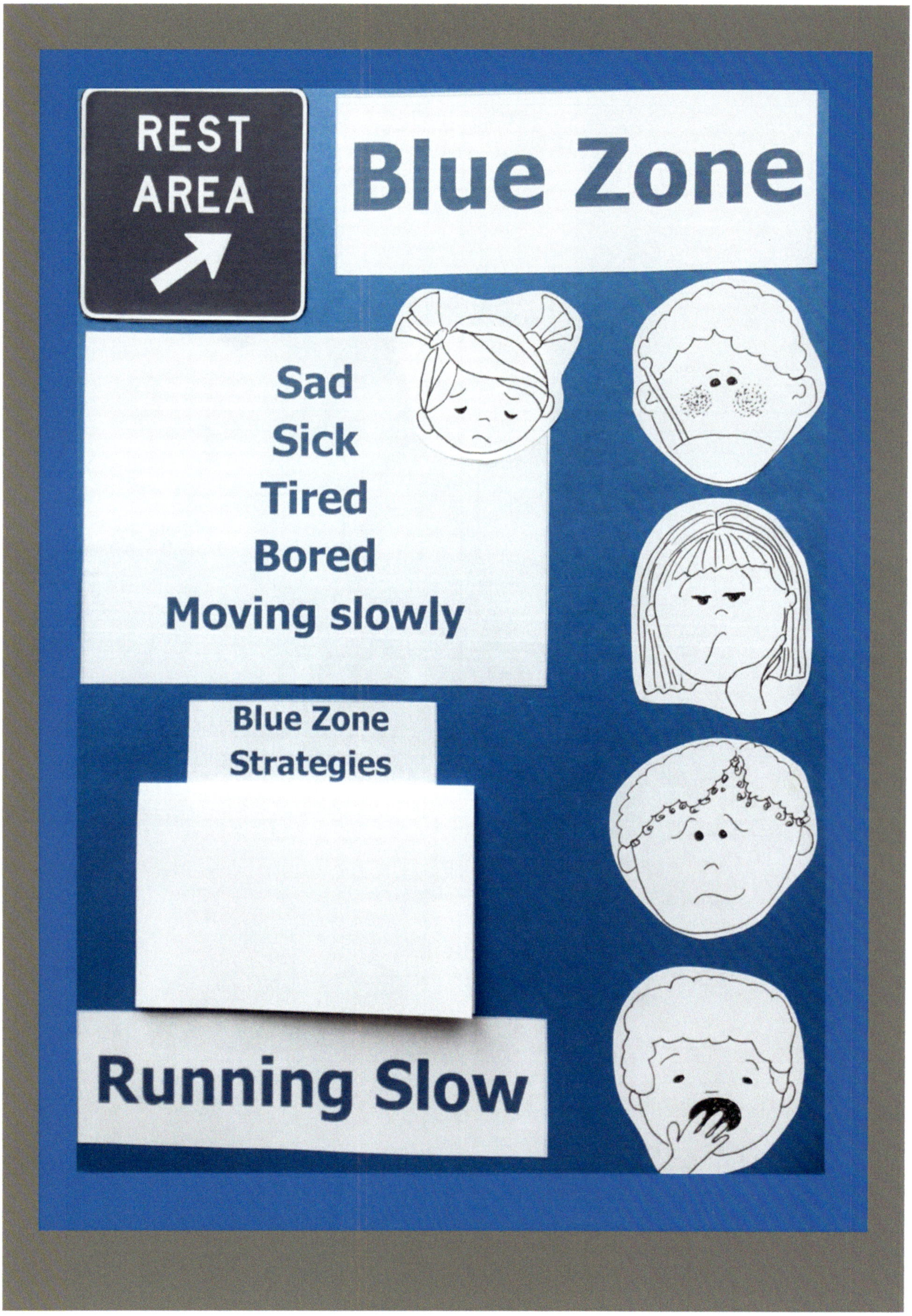
REST
AREA
Blue Zone
Sad
Sick
Tired
Bored
Moving slowly
Blue Zone
Strategies
Running Slow

GO
Green Zone
Happy
Calm
Feeling OK
Focused
Ready to Learn
Green Zone
Strategies
Good to Go

SLOW
PROCEED
WITH
CAUTION
Yellow Zone
Frustrated
Worried
Silly/Wiggly
Unfocused
Loss of some control
Yellow Zone
Strategies
Caution!

STOP
Red Zone
Mad/angry
Hands on
Yelling
Refusing to work
Out of control
Red Zone
Strategies
STOP
No!! I wont do it.

Changing Zone Cards

My Change Card

I am feeling

Red	☐	Red	☐
Green	☐	Green	☐
Blue	☐	Blue	☐
Yellow	☐	Yellow	☐

I need to get to the .... Zone

What I need to do

My Change Card

I am feeling

Red	☐	Red	☐
Green	☐	Green	☐
Blue	☐	Blue	☐
Yellow	☐	Yellow	☐

I need to get to the .... Zone

What I need to do

My Change Card

I am feeling

Red	☐	Red	☐
Green	☐	Green	☐
Blue	☐	Blue	☐
Yellow	☐	Yellow	☐

I need to get to the .... Zone

What I need to do

My Change Card

I am feeling

Red	☐	Red	☐
Green	☐	Green	☐
Blue	☐	Blue	☐
Yellow	☐	Yellow	☐

I need to get to the .... Zone

What I need to do

Mindfulness

SESSION OBJECTIVES

To understand that the brain and body are partners and affect each other.

SESSION OUTCOMES

- ✓ To be able to be able to describe how the mind affects the body and the body affects the mind.

LESSON PLAN

- ➢ Ask the children to describe a time when they observed their class baby laugh. What had caused the laughter? How did they feel when they heard it?
- ➢ Help them understand the steps the body went through to laugh: saw or felt something that made them happy, message went to the brain, messengers sent from the brain to the face to smile and to the voice box to laugh.
- ➢ How long did it take? The messages sent via the nervous system are very fast.

For those classrooms not able to undertake the Circles for Learning Project, video clips or photographs can be used to support the discussion around the topic and stimulate thoughts and ideas from the children and young people.

Task

KS1: To draw a thought feeling different things.

KS2: To create the brain body system and show how you can change things.

KS3: To create a play script to show the 'Power of a Thought'.

KS1

1 Draw the body brain circuit on the board and ask the children what they think is happening.

2 The mind has a thought and the body responds.

3 Ask them to have a sad thought – give them some examples: the day you had an argument with your friend, the day you were poorly and couldn't do something you had been looking forward to, the day you lost your special toy, the day you moved house, etc. Help the children understand that there are BIG sad memories or small ones and that you would like them to choose a small one.

4 Look around the class and help the children see that body language and faces are all showing you their sad thoughts.

5 Ask the children to think of a happy thought again and give examples of what this could be.

6 Then ask the children to think of an excited thought, one with lots of energy.

7 Ask the children to imagine what a 'Thought' might be like, what shape might it be? Would its shape change depending on the thought? Would a sad one be one shape and a happy one another? Would they be different colours?

8 Ask the children to draw a thought – one that is bored and has nothing to do. Then ask them to draw a range of different thoughts all feeling different things.

9 Ask them to draw the thought having a thought, showing what they are thinking about. If it is a happy thought, then have them show the happy thought the thought was thinking!

10 Create a display of thoughts.

11 Ask the children why this piece of information about thoughts affecting the body might be useful. It might help them change how they feel.

12 Try using this at the beginning of a lesson. Ask the children to think of a time when they were able to understand something and work at their best. Ask them to picture this in their mind and remember how good it felt to be able to do something well. It could have been riding their bike, doing maths or writing a story.

13 Before they go to play, ask them to think of a calm thought – one that helps them be still and relaxed.

KS2

1 Draw the body brain circuit on the board and ask the children what they think is happening.

2 The mind has a thought and the body responds. Or the body is poorly (chemicals not working properly) and then these affect the mind.

3 Ask them to have a sad thought – give them some examples: the day you had an argument with your friend, the day you were poorly and couldn't do something you had been looking forward to, the day you lost your special toy, the day you moved house, etc.

Help the children understand that there are BIG sad memories or small ones and that you would like them to choose a small one.

4 Look around the class and help the children see that body language and faces are all showing you their sad thoughts.

5 Ask the children to think of a happy thought and again give examples of what this could be.

6 Then ask the children to think of an excited thought, one with lots of energy.

7 Ask the children to think of ways that they can change the system, if their senses have sent information to the brain and the brain has decided that there is danger and has triggered the stress system. What could they do? If the senses have sent information to the brain (two people arguing) and this has triggered a memory of them arguing with their best friend and now they feel sad as they remember that time. What could they do? They can calm one part of the system – the mind or the body.

8 Ask the children to think of ways to calm their body – their self-soothe boxes or relaxation, breathing exercises or physical exercise.

9 Ask the children about ways to calm their minds. These could be visualisation, distraction, relaxation, watching a film or listening to music.

10 Introduce the concept of mindfulness – mindfulness means to be aware of the mind and how it is feeling, what it is thinking, how hard it is working and that thoughts are just that – thoughts. They are not facts.

11 Ask the children to draw a cartoon strip showing:

- How to change a thought
- How a thought can impact on the body
- How a negative thought can come into existence
- How a positive thought can make you feel good.

12 When the children have finished, ask them to write a short description about their piece and then create a display in the school. See what reactions you get by putting a 'Write Your Comment' sheet by the display.

KS3

1 Draw the body brain circuit on the board and ask the children what they think is happening.

2 The mind has a thought and the body responds. Or the body is poorly (chemicals not working properly) and these affect the mind.

3 Ask the children to think of ways that they can change the system, if their senses have sent information to the brain and the brain has decided that there is danger and has triggered the stress system. What could they do? If the senses have sent information to the brain (two people arguing) and this has triggered a memory of them arguing with their best friend and now they feel sad as they remember that time. What could they do? They can calm one part of the system – the mind or the body.

4 Ask the children to think of ways to calm their body – their self-soothe boxes or relaxation, breathing exercises or physical exercise.

5 Ask the children about ways to calm their minds. These could be visualisation, distraction, relaxation, watching a film or listening to music.

6 Introduce the concept of mindfulness – mindfulness means to be aware of the mind and how it is feeling, what it is thinking, how hard it is working and that thoughts are just that – thoughts. They are not facts.

7 Ask the children to work in pairs and create a play script entitled 'The Power of a Thought', showing that your mind believes whatever you think.

8 When they have finished, ask the children to set them out on their table and then have a silent exhibition.

9 Ask the children to vote for the one that best shows how the mind believes what you think and shows how you can change this. Give the children 6 counters each. Ask them to put 3 counters on their favourite script, 2 on their second favourite and 1 on their third favourite. Then add up the counters and choose the winning script.

10 Ask the pair who write it to produce this – they can choose the people to play the characters and oversee how it is done.

11 Record the script or show it in an assembly.

RESOURCES

1 'The brain and the body are partners' resource sheet

2 Paper, pens, rubbers, colours or paints

3 Tablet computer or other way of recording a play script.

IMPORTANT POINTS

Your mind believes whatever you think. However, a thought is not always true – it is just a thought. We have the power to change how we feel by changing our thinking.

Mindfulness is the ability to be aware of our mind, how it is thinking and how hard it is working. By doing mindfulness exercises we learn to control our minds and understand that our thoughts can be managed.

LEARNING LINKS

Working collaboratively, creativity, learning skills, knowledge and understanding,

REFLECTION

Questions:

Positive comment from child:

Positive comment from adult:

LEARNING DIMENSIONS		SOCIAL & EMOTIONAL SKILLS	
Strategic awareness		Emotional literacy	
Learning relationships		Neuroscience	
Curiosity		Self-regulation	
Creativity		Self-development	
Meaning making			
Changing & learning			
Resilience			

The Brain and the Body are Partners.

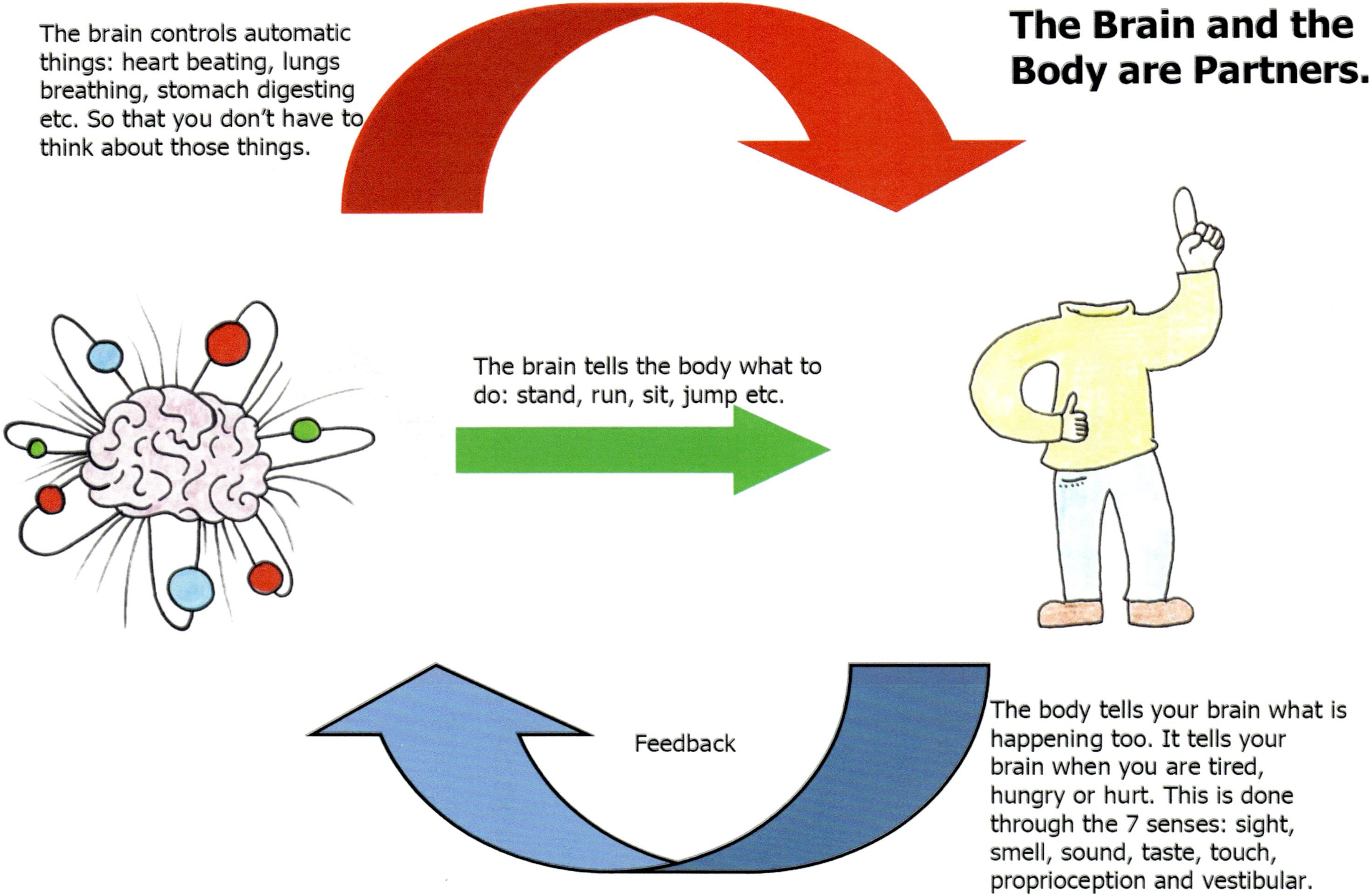

Chapter 4

The brain and emotions

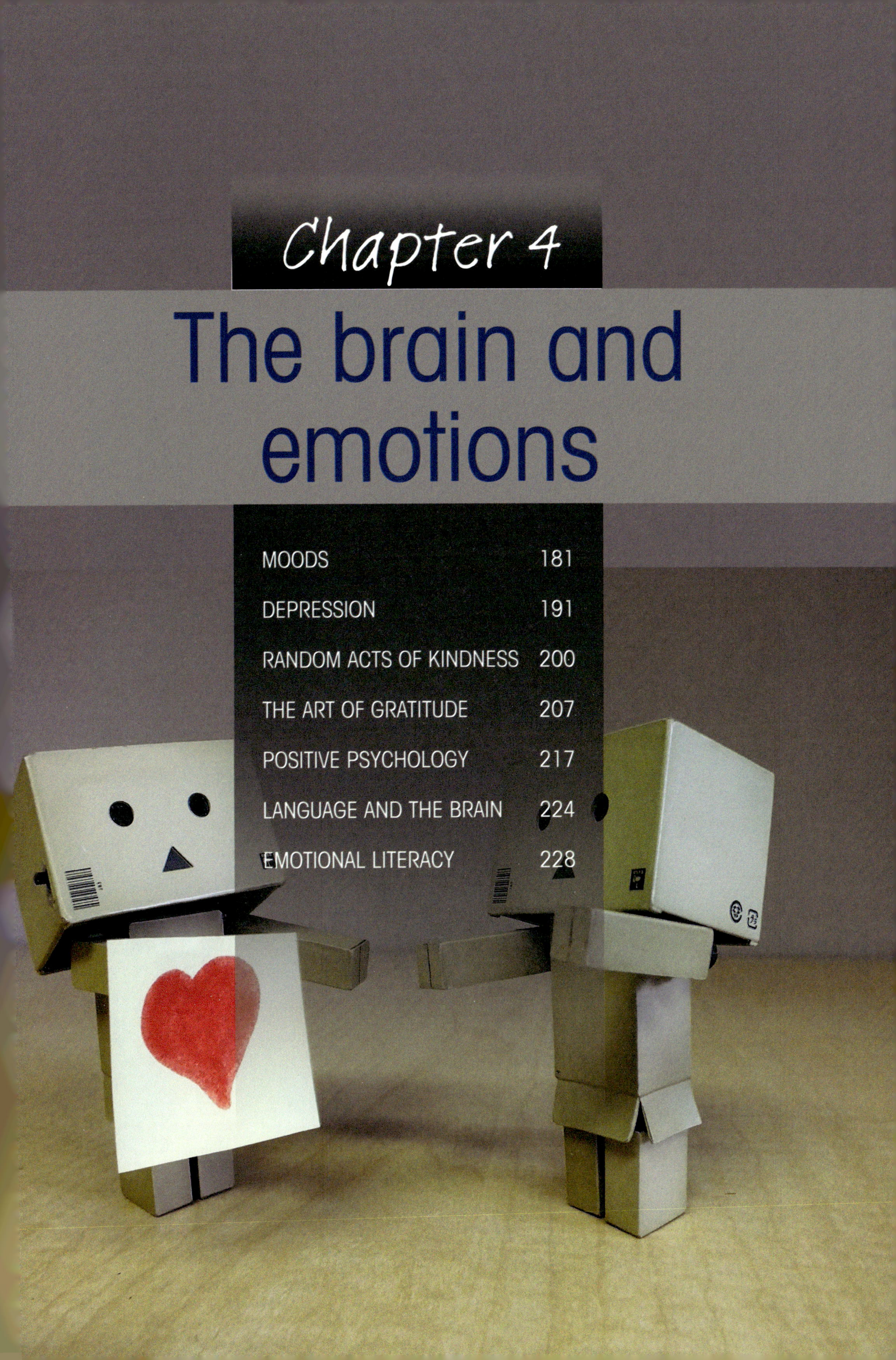

Moods

1 2 3

SESSION OBJECTIVES

To understand that moods change the way you see and interpret the things that go on around you.

To understand that you have the power to change your mood.

SESSION OUTCOMES

✓ To be able to describe strategies that help change your mood.

✓ To identify triggers and mood busters.

LESSON PLAN

➢ Ask the children to think of the times that they have observed their class baby in a particular 'mood'. What sort of moods have they observed – this could be a bad mood, a silly mood, a cranky mood or a happy mood.

➢ Discuss what they think may have caused this mood and the sort of behaviour that went with it.

For those classrooms not able to undertake the Circles for Learning Project, video clips or photographs can be used to support the discussion around the topic and stimulate thoughts and ideas from the children and young people.

Task

KS1: To create good mood and bad mood glasses.

KS2: To create a mood buster song or poem and a moody robot.

KS3: To create a triggers and mood buster table.

KS1

1 Ask the children to think and name as many moods that they have experienced or watched others experience. Write them all up on the board. As each one is shared, ask the children for the 'trigger' that may have caused it.

Bad mood – trigger: getting told off

Good mood – trigger: having a friend over for a playdate after school

2 Explore with the children how the world seems depending on your mood. List the moods on the board and find a picture to go with each. Under each one, write how the world might be experienced

Bad mood – things go wrong, people argue a lot, you can't do the things as well as you normally can, people keep telling you off for no reason, etc.

Good mood – things go well, people are kind and friendly, you can get things right a lot of the time, etc.

3 Share the book *In My Heart* by Jo Witek.

4 Ask the children to work in pairs. One person's job is to make some good mood/happy/excited/fearless glasses and the others job is to make the opposite glasses, bad mood/sad/fed up/fearful glasses. If you wear the glasses you experience the world in one of these ways.

5 Explain to the children that they can be as creative as they like but the glasses must show how they will make the wearer feel if they choose to put them on.

6 Once the children have made their glasses, ask them to try them on and for each pair write something that they experience.

'As I put the glasses on all of a sudden the world changed. The sky cleared and the sun came out. People were laughing and playing. My friends came running up and asked if I'd like to play it – my most favourite game ever.'

KS2

1 Ask the children to think and name as many moods that they have experienced or watched others experience. Write them all up on the board. As each one is shared, ask the children for the 'trigger' that may have caused it.

Bad mood – trigger: getting told off

Good mood – trigger: having a friend over for a playdate after school

2 Explore with the children how the world seems depending on your mood. List the moods on the board and find a picture to go with each. Under each one, write how the world might be experienced.

Bad mood – things go wrong, people argue a lot, you can't do the things as well as you normally can, people keep telling you off for no reason, etc.

Good mood – things go well, people are kind and friendly, you can get things right a lot of the time, etc.

3 Remind the children of the different chemicals the body produces as a trigger to manage what is happening – dopamine, cortisol, serotonin.

Low serotonin levels are often attributed to anxiety, depression, panic attacks, insomnia, negative thoughts, low self-esteem, obsessive thoughts and behaviours.

Cortisol is a hormone, which is mainly released at times of stress and has many important functions in your body. Having the right cortisol balance is essential for human health and you can have problems if your adrenal gland releases too much or too little cortisol.

Dopamine, serotonin, oxytocin and endorphins are the quartet responsible for your happiness. Many situations can trigger these neurotransmitters, but instead of being in the passenger seat, there are ways you can intentionally cause them to flow.

4 Remind the children of the 90-second rule – the chemicals that are released into the body have a 90-second effect; however, if our brain gets involved, its thoughts can continue to make the chemicals active and so the effects can last for longer than 90 seconds.

5 Ask the children to work in pairs. Explain that they have a challenge: to make a mood-bustin robot and a poem that the robot says as a way to help them bust the mood.

6 Read some of the poems by Brian Moses.

7 Have a selection of books about feelings for the children to read and be inspired by.

8 Challenge the class to work on as many moods as possible – write up the ones the children want to do and see if each pair can work on a different one.

9 When the work is completed, set up an exhibition and invite another class to come and look around. Which Mood Busting Robot would be the most sought after?

KS3

1 Ask the children to think and name as many moods that they have experienced or watched others experience. Write them all up on the board. As each one is shared, ask the children for the 'trigger' that may have caused it.

Bad mood – trigger: getting told off

Good mood – trigger: having a friend over for a playdate after school

2 Explore with the children how the world seems depending on your mood. List the moods on the board and find a picture to go with each. Under each one, write how the world might be experienced.

Bad mood – things go wrong, people argue a lot, you can't do the things as well as you normally can, people keep telling you off for no reason, etc.

Good mood – things go well, people are kind and friendly, you can get things right a lot of the time, etc.

3 Remind the children of the different chemicals the body produces as a trigger to manage what is happening – dopamine, cortisol, serotonin.

Low serotonin levels are often attributed to anxiety, depression, panic attacks, insomnia, negative thoughts, low self-esteem, obsessive thoughts and behaviours.

Cortisol is a hormone, which is mainly released at times of stress and has many important functions in your body. Having the right cortisol balance is essential for human health and you can have problems if your adrenal gland releases too much or too little cortisol.

Dopamine, serotonin, oxytocin and endorphins are the quartet responsible for your happiness. Many situations can trigger these neurotransmitters, but instead of being in the passenger seat, there are ways you can intentionally cause them to flow.

4 Remind the children of the 90-second rule – the chemicals that are released into the body have a 90-second effect; however, if our brain gets involved, its thoughts can continue to make the chemicals active and so the effects can last for longer than 90 seconds.

5 Ask the children to work in pairs or small groups to think of as many moods as possible, both good and bad. *The Book of Human Emotions* is a great resource as it lists all the emotions – even ones you have never heard of – e.g., 'Dolce far niente' (The pleasure of doing nothing!).

6 Share the exciting ones and then ask the children to choose 15 of the negative emotions and fill in the triggers for them.

7 Share and discuss. Is everyone's trigger the same? Do some triggers set us off on some days but not on others? Can we control the triggers? Can we trigger ourselves?

8 Ask the children to complete the table – what mood-busting strategies can they use?

RESOURCES

1 Coloured cellophane
2 Glasses templates
3 Card, paper and collage materials
4 Old magazines with pictures
5 Items for the robot creations – plastic post, tubes, boxes, etc.
6 *Badger's Bad Mood* by Hiawyn Oram
7 *The Cross with Us Rhinoceros* by John Bush and Paul Geraghty
8 *In My Heart: A Book of Feelings (Growing Hearts)* by Jo Witek
9 *Feelings: Inside My Heart and in My Head* by Libby Walden
10 *Poems About Emotions* by Brian Moses
11 *The Book of Human Emotions* by Tiffany Watt Smith
12 'Triggers and mood busters' sheet

IMPORTANT POINTS

Moods can be good or bad and are triggered by a thought or action. They are changeable.

LEARNING LINKS

Creativity, collaboration, knowledge and understanding, emotional literacy, self-awareness.

REFLECTION

Questions:

Positive comment from child:

Positive comment from adult:

Learning Dimensions		**Social & Emotional Skills**	
Strategic awareness		Emotional literacy	
Learning relationships		Neuroscience	
Curiosity		Self-regulation	
Creativity		Self-development	
Meaning making			
Changing & learning			
Resilience			

Triggers and Mood Busters

Mood	Triggers	Busters

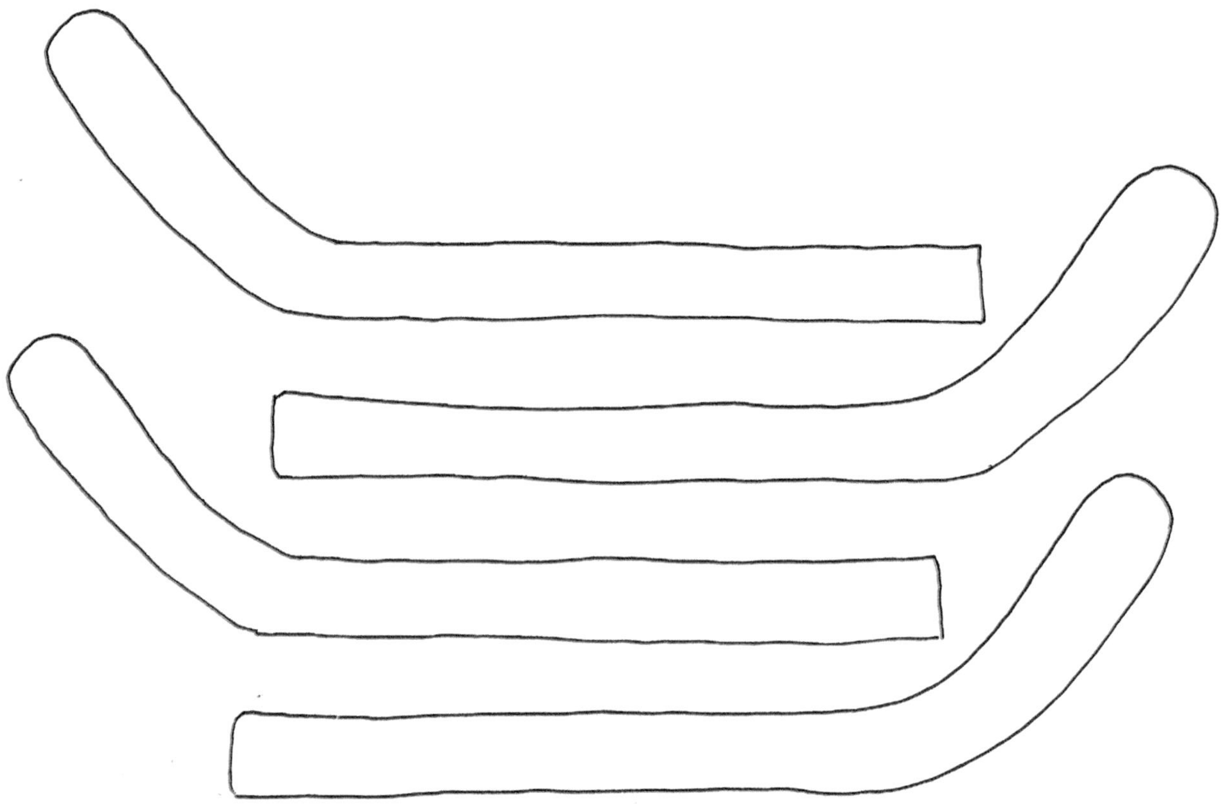

Depression

1 2 3

SESSION OBJECTIVES

To be able to explore a range of words that link to being sad and helpless.

To be able to discuss a range of books that explore depression.

SESSION OUTCOMES

✓ To be able to group words that link to sadness, helplessness, anger and happiness.

✓ To be able to engage in a book-tasting session.

LESSON PLAN

- Ask the children to remember a time when their class baby was happy – what sort of behaviours did they show?
- Now ask them to describe a time when they were sad – what sort of behaviours communicated they were sad?
- Explore a time when their class baby was cross or angry. What did they see? How did their class parent manage this?

For those classrooms not able to undertake the Circles for Learning Project, video clips or photographs can be used to support the discussion around the topic and stimulate thoughts and ideas from the children and young people.

Task

KS1: To create a sad thermometer using a range of words.

KS2/KS3: To take part in a book-tasting session exploring books about depression.

KS1

1 Explore with the children what the word 'sad' means. How does it make you feel inside? What can we see when someone's sad on the outside?

2 Ask the children to work in groups and sort the words and pictures into groups:

Sad, Happy, Helpless and Angry.

3 Share the words they have come up with and ask the children to put them into sentences to explore the different meanings.

4 Ask the children to use the thermometer and put the words in order, with saddest at the top and least sad at the bottom of the thermometer.

5 Share what they have come up with.

6 Now do the same for the other words. You might rather ask different groups to work on different words.

7 Share the story *What Makes Me Sad?* with the children or *The Color Monster*.

KS2/KS3

1 Set up your classroom as a restaurant and put a big menu board up to tell the children about book tasting.

2 Each table needs to be set out with a tablecloth (checked ones are good and have a brilliant effect), a candle (you can get battery-operated ones), napkins and plates.

3 On each plate put the book menu,

4 On each table put a variety of books (choose depending on the age group and the children you have in the class). Ensure that you are mindful about the children and their backgrounds and also their ability to read – ensure you have a selection of books with different reading ages – some books with no words – *Meh* and some graphic novels.

5 Ask the children to sit at a table and to choose a starter book to 'taste'. They have 3 minutes to look at the book, read the first few pages and read the blurb and look at the cover.

6 After 3 minutes, you will ring the bell and then they need to write up the menu for the book they tasted.

7 After the short write-up, explain that they can now choose their main course – they can have 5 minutes looking and tasting this book. Then you will ring the bell and they can write up their menu.

8 Their penultimate choice is their pudding or dessert course. They will be given 3 minutes to explore and taste their dessert book. Then you will ring the bell and they will be able to write up their menu for that book.

9 Their final choice is their coffee and mints course. For this they will have 2 minutes to choose and taste their book.

10 Remind the children that they need to give each book a star rating and to say which is their first, second and third choice of books that they would like to continue reading.

11 When the tasting is over, discuss the books and then move children into groups so that they can continue reading their first- or second-favourite book.

12 Ask the children to write a review for the library and then set up a book menu display in the library with the different books and reviews.

RESOURCES

1 Words

2 Pictures showing emotions – sad, happy, angry and helpless

3 *What Makes Me Sad?* by Heidi Howarth and Daniel Howarth

4 *The Color Monster: A Story about Emotions* by Anna Llenas

5 *Meh: A Story About Depression* by Deborah Malcolm

6 *The Colour Thief: A Family's Story of Depression* by Andrew Fusek Peters

7 *The Princess and the Fog: A Story for Children with Depression* by Martyn Lloyd-Jones

8 *Not Today, Celeste!: A Dog's Tale about Her Human's Depression* by Liza Stevens

9 *Michael Rosen's Sad Book* by Michael Rosen

10 *The Heart and the Bottle* by Oliver Jeffers

11 YouTube: 'I had a black dog, his name was depression',

www.youtube.com/watch?v=XiCrniLQGYc

12 *I Had a Black Dog* by Matthew Johnstone

13 Book-tasting menu

14 Tablecloths

15 Candles

16 Plates

Books for teenagers

1 *All the Bright Places* by Jennifer Niven

2 *Meh: A Story About Depression* by Deborah Malcolm

3 *Don't Stop Thinking About Tomorrow* by Siobhan Curham

4 *Forgive Me, Leonard Peacock* by Matthew Quick

5 *Playlist for the Dead* by Michelle Falkoff

6 *Hey, Kiddo* by Jarrett J. Krosoczka

7 *I Would, but My DAMN MIND Won't Let Me!: A Teen's Guide to Controlling Their Thoughts and Feelings* by Jacqui Letran

8 *Marbles: Mania, Depression, Michelangelo, and Me: A Graphic Memoir* by Ellen Forney

IMPORTANT POINTS

Depression can be a debilitating illness that is hard to manage. Thinking about things differently, socialising and exercise can all have an impact on depression. For some people the only way to manage is with medication.

LEARNING LINKS

Co-operation, self-awareness, emotional literacy, curiosity, knowledge and understanding.

REFLECTION

Questions:

Positive comment from child:

Positive comment from adult:

LEARNING DIMENSIONS		SOCIAL & EMOTIONAL SKILLS	
Strategic awareness		Emotional literacy	
Learning Relationships		Neuroscience	
Curiosity		Self-regulation	
Creativity		Self-development	
Meaning making			
Changing & learning			
Resilience			

Happy	Angry
Great	Furious
Merry	Cross
Delighted	Annoyed
Cheerful	Mad
Glad	Irritated
Ecstatic	Upset
Overjoyed	Aggressive
Joyful	Fuming
OK	Unhappy
Fine	Enraged
Pleased	Fed Up

Helpless	Sad
Vulnerable	Tearful
Despair	Unhappy
Woeful	Pessimistic
Useless	Sorrowful
Stupid	Dismayed
Hesitant	Lousy
Frustrated	Upset
Distressed	Miserable
Pathetic	Terrible
Uncertain	Disappointed
Powerless	Hurt

Menu

On your table you have Tasting Etiquette

1. Choose one book to 'taste'. You don't need to eat/read the entire thing to know if you like it. Try a little bite!

2. Critique your selection by filling in answers on your menu.

3. Repeat steps 1–2 for another dish/book.

4. Enjoy!

My Book Review

Name of the Book...

Author..

Illustrator..

Rating: ☆☆☆☆☆

Three words to describe the cover

....

Summary of the Book

....
....
....
....
....

Your Favourite Character

....
....
....

Your Favourite Aspect of the Book

....
....
....

My Book Review

Name of the Book...

Author..

Illustrator..

Rating: ☆☆☆☆☆

Three words to describe the cover

....

Summary of the Book

....
....
....
....
....

Your Favourite Character and Why

....
....
....

Your Favourite Aspect of the Book

....
....
....

Random acts of kindness

1 2 3

SESSION OBJECTIVES

To understand how acts of kindness can make the giver and receiver feel good.

SESSION OUTCOMES

✓ To create and then undertake a Random Acts of Kindness challenge.

LESSON PLAN

➢ Ask the children how the baby feels when they smile or do something positive for the baby. Explain that when a parent smiles and holds a baby in a loving way, the chemical dopamine is released into the blood.

➢ Ask the children how they think all these acts of kindness influence the baby as they grow? What sort of map of the world does the baby create? What will be their expectations of the way people will react or behave?

For those classrooms not able to undertake the Circles for Learning Project, video clips or photographs can be used to support the discussion around the topic and stimulate thoughts and ideas from the children and young people.

Task

KS1/KS2: To create a Random Acts of Kindness calendar for the class.

KS3: To create a story or drawing showing the impact of an act of kindness.

KS1/KS2

1 Ask the children to work in pairs and define what kindness is. Then ask them to think of 3 examples of kindness.

2 In their pairs ask one person to draw a heart showing how it feels when they undertake a kind gesture and the other to draw a heart to show how it feels to receive the kindness.

3 Read the story *Have You Filled a Bucket Today?* by Carol McCloud.

4 Watch the YouTube clip 'The science of kindness' and discuss with the children.

5 Explain to the children that you are going to set a class challenge and that is to make a Random Acts of Kindness calendar.

6 Each child is going to create a kindness challenge and then these will all be put together to create enough kindness acts for a whole month.

7 Give each child the Kindness Square and ask them to write what their act of kindness is and draw a picture to illustrate it or show how it might make someone feel.

Examples: Say 'Good Morning' to the first 5 people you meet as you come into school.

Ask someone new to play

Let someone else go first

Give someone a compliment

8 Create a huge calendar of all the different acts of kindness and choose one each day for someone to do. Alternatively, get the whole class to do each act for 30 days. The calendar could be a large display, with each act of kindness covered by a piece of paper with a number on so that it is like a huge advent calendar. Each day, one child uncovers the challenge for the class. Watch out for the 'let someone go first' if you do this as a class or you won't get a sensible line and be able to get anywhere!

9 Watch the short film 'A short story on kindness'.

KS3

1 Ask the children to work in pairs and come up with a definition of kindness and then 3 examples.

2 Ask the children to divide into small groups. The challenge is for them to find and present a video that they believe shows and promotes kindness and argue why their video is the one that has the biggest impact.

3 Examples are:

'How you treat people is who you are! (kindness motivational video)'

'Life vest inside – kindness boomerang'

'Color your world with kindness'

RESOURCES

1 You Tube: 'A short story on – kindness must see',

www.youtube.com/watch?v=8WiOUWLeT9I

2 Read the story *Have You Filled a Bucket Today?* by Carol McCloud

3 YouTube: 'How you treat people is who you are! (kindness motivational video)',

www.youtube.com/watch?v=mTsvSAltPqA

4 YouTube: 'Life vest inside - kindness boomerang - "One Day"',

www.youtube.com/watch?v=nwAYpLVyeFU

5 YouTube: 'Color your world with kindness',

www.youtube.com/watch?v=rweIE8yyYOU

6 YouTube: 'The science of kindness',

www.youtube.com/watch?v=O9UByLyOjBM

IMPORTANT POINTS

Kindness affects the giver and the receiver. Kindness starts with one person and grows.

LEARNING LINKS

Collaboration, knowledge and understanding, emotional literacy, self-development, self-awareness.

REFLECTION

Questions:

Positive comment from child:

Positive comment from adult:

LEARNING DIMENSIONS		SOCIAL & EMOTIONAL SKILLS	
Strategic awareness		Emotional literacy	
Learning relationships		Neuroscience	
Curiosity		Self-regulation	
Creativity		Self-development	
Meaning making			
Changing & learning			
Resilience			

My Heart Feels.................................

When someone is kind to me

My Heart Feels ……………………
When I do something kind for someone else

Kindness is FREE

Sprinkle it wherever you can

and watch happiness

spread.

My Act of Kindness is

....

....

Kindness is FREE

Sprinkle it wherever you can

and watch happiness

spread.

My Act of Kindness is

....

....

The art of gratitude

1 2 3

SESSION OBJECTIVES

To understand that if we focus our thoughts and mind on the positive, this can develop happiness.

SESSION OUTCOMES

✓ To be able to create a gratitude tree.

✓ To create a gratitude calendar.

LESSON PLAN

➢ Ask the children to think of their class baby and all the things that they class parent does for their baby. Why do they do them? What makes them want to? How will these things affect their baby? What messages do the actions convey to the baby?

➢ Ask the parent what makes it all worth it.

For those classrooms not able to undertake the Circles for Learning Project, video clips or photographs can be used to support the discussion around the topic and stimulate thoughts and ideas from the children and young people.

Task

KS1: To create a gratitude tree.

KS2: To create gratitude stones and have a gratitude scavenger hunt.

KS3: Create a special gratitude calendar.

KS1

1 Ask the children to define gratitude.

2 Share the research: practising being grateful on a daily basis enables people to feel happier. Why do they think this is? Might it be a skill that develops which is about looking and seeing the positive? Or might it be the increase of neurotransmitters that are released when they practise being positive which the body likes and is rewarded by?

3 Share with the children that you are going to set up a gratitude tree in the classroom.

4 Ask the children what they think you should hang on the tree. This could be hearts or leaves or stars or something else.

5 Use the templates below and ask the children to write something at the end of the day that they were grateful for. Ensure that all the adults join in with this activity.

6 Hang the 'gratitudes' on the tree as they go home each day. Make it a special celebration.

7 Ensure that you have a pile of gratitude shapes available for children to use each day.

KS2

1 Ask the children to define gratitude.

2 Share the research: practising being grateful on a daily basis enables people to feel happier. Why do they think this is? Might it be a skill that develops which is about looking and seeing the positive? Or might it be the increase of neurotransmitters that are released when they practise being positive which the body likes and is rewarded by?

3 Explain to the children that you have a gratitude scavenger hunt for them to do (this will need to be done at home as homework as they will need access to a range of things).

4 Give the children the sheet and ask them to find an object or a picture of that object for each item on the list.

5 Explain to the children that they are going to make gratitude stones for their family. They will each have 6 stones/pebbles. On each pebble they can draw and colour a symbol – heart, star or something else. They then take the stones and hide them in different places around their house so that they can easily be seen. Each time someone finds a pebble they have to take a minute to think about something in their life that means a lot to them – this could be a person, an object, a pet, the weather or an experience they have had.

6 Get the children to make the stones and then write a short set of instructions about how to use them and then create a little bag or box to put them in.

7 Share and let the children tell you about how their family respond.

8 You can make some for the school and hide them around the classrooms, staffroom, etc.

KS3

1 Ask the children to define gratitude.

2 Share the research: practising being grateful on a daily basis enables people to feel happier. Why do they think this is? Might it be a skill that develops which is about looking

and seeing the positive? Or might it be the increase of neurotransmitters that are released when they practise being positive which the body likes and is rewarded by?

3 Share with the children that you are going to give them a gratitude calendar for them to create and then try out.

4 The calendar is a bit like an advent calendar – each day you open a door and try and achieve the challenge that it has set you.

5 Pair the children up and ask them to create a calendar for their partner. They need to think about the person and make sure that the challenges are achievable for that person. If they have a quiet partner, they need to ensure that the challenges don't involve them having to be to extravert; they need to be mindful of their partner.

6 Give the children the two templates. Template 1 is the outside and the squares have to be cut carefully so that they can open – like doors. Template 2 is the hidden message/ challenge that the door will reveal.

7 Ask the children to share ideas that they could put in their door. Collect these on the board to help as examples and idea generators.

Send a note to a friend who has done something special
Say thank you to the canteen staff at school
Send an email to a grandparent
Give Mum or Dad a sticky note saying thank you for something they have done.
Find a charity you would like to support and either make a money donation or give them some old toys, clothes or books that you no longer need.
Do a job for a teacher as a way of saying thank you for helping you in the past.
Notice 3 kind things that people have done that day
Make a thank you bookmark for someone

Which job in school do you think is least recognised? Do something for that person to ensure they know they are appreciated

Hold a door open for someone
A memory you are grateful for
An experience you are grateful for
A skill you have that you are proud of
A present you have received that you loved
Etc.

8 When the calendars are completed, ask the children to give them to their partner.

9 Check on how people are doing and what sort of response they are getting.

10 How does it make them feel?

RESOURCES

1 Pictures showing people being grateful

2 Twigs and branches to make the tree in the classroom

3 String

4 Shapes to hang on the tree

5 Gratitude calendar templates 1 and 2

6 Gratitude scavenger hunt

7 A collection of pebbles from the beach (these need to big enough to put small gold stars or hearts on

8 Sharpies or pens that can write on pebbles

IMPORTANT POINTS

Practising gratitude can make people feel happier. There are many ways to do this; however, it has to be practised and kept going.

LEARNING LINKS

Collaboration, knowledge and understanding, self-awareness, emotional literacy, creativity.

REFLECTION

Questions:

Positive comment from child:

Positive comment from adult:

LEARNING DIMENSIONS		SOCIAL & EMOTIONAL SKILLS	
Strategic awareness		Emotional literacy	
Learning relationships		Neuroscience	
Curiosity		Self-regulation	
Creativity		Self-development	
Meaning making			
Changing & learning			
Resilience			

GRATITUDE SCAVENGER HUNT

A gratitude scavenger hunt is a way to celebrate and focus on the small things that we enjoy and make us happy. It helps us to focus on the things we can be grateful for.

1 Something that makes you happy
2 Something to give to someone else to make them smile
3 Find one thing that you love to smell
4 Find one thing that you enjoy looking at
5 Find something that is your favourite colour
6 Find something that you enjoy in nature
7 Find something that is useful to you that you wouldn't be without
8 Find something that tastes good
9 Find a holiday photo you love
10 Find something that you know will make someone happy
11 Find something that makes you laugh
12 Find something that is unique to you
13 Your favourite place
14 Favourite toy
15 Something that you enjoy doing with friends
16 A game you love to play with your family or friends
17 Find a book that you enjoyed reading
18 Something that you are proud of doing
19 Something that you enjoyed learning
20 Something that you would give you joy when you share with others.

SHAPES FOR GRATITUDE TREE

8 17 5 4

11 25 20

3 15 21 12

23 22 18

6 16 13 14

9 24 19

1 2 10 7

Positive psychology

1 2 3

SESSION OBJECTIVES

To understand what makes me happy, what qualities make a good person and what makes someone a positive member of a community.

SESSION OUTCOMES

- ✓ To be able to describe the things that make them happy.
- ✓ To be able to describe positive character strengths.
- ✓ To be able to describe what social responsibility is and how it can be supported to develop.

LESSON PLAN

- ➢ Ask the children what the role of the parent is. How does society help parents? What does society or the community do to teach adults how to be parents?
- ➢ Ask them to come up with a list of questions for their class parent about what it is like to be a parent and how do they know what to do, etc.

For those classrooms not able to undertake the Circles for Learning Project, video clips or photographs can be used to support the discussion around the topic and stimulate thoughts and ideas from the children and young people.

Task

KS1: To create a 'things that make me happy' lolly.

KS2: To create a list of positive and negative personal characteristics and explore how these are developed and taught and why.

KS3: To explore what social responsibility is, how it is developed and taught and why it makes a difference.

KS1

1 Ask the children to share with a partner 3 things that make them happy.

2 Share these together.

3 Working with their partner, again share 3 things that they can do that make other people happy.

4 Share the different ideas they have come up with.

5 Give the children the 'things that make me happy' lolly and ask them to fill them in.

6 Share what they have created and discuss.

7 Explore questions like:

What happens if something makes me happy but makes someone else unhappy?

Whose responsibility is it to be happy?

Can we train our brains to be happy?

Are some people born happy?

Is it parents' responsibility to make children happy?

Is it good to be happy all the time?

Should all children be happy?

KS2

1 Ask the children what qualities make a good person.

2 Ask the children to work in pairs and then on a large piece of paper A3 draw a good person who has lots of good qualities one end and a person with very negative qualities the other.

3 Ask them to surround each person with the qualities that they think they would have.

4 Share what they have decided and discuss. Ask questions to expand their understanding.

Are we born with good or negative qualities or do we learn them?

Is it parents' responsibility to ensure that children develop positive or negative qualities?

How does school support the development of these qualities?

Who is a person they hold in their minds as being a person with very positive qualities?

What qualities do they think are the most important?

How do you support children who have developed very negative qualities?

How do you support adults who have developed very negative qualities?

If they were Prime Minister for the day, what would they do to support people who needed their help the most?

KS3

1 Ask the children to work with a partner and define social responsibility.

2 Share the definitions.

3 Is this something that they think is important?

At its core, being socially responsible means acknowledging accountability for the impact of one's choices on the larger world. This might be as simple as dropping your litter in the street or how you treat others. Businesses, in particular, are expected to make the welfare of society a priority when they make decisions, rather than focus exclusively on profit margins. This pertains not only to how companies spend money, but also to the ways in which they earn it. Do they look after the environment, do they pay people fair wages, do men and women earn the same?, etc.

4 Ask the children to research how big companies, such as banks, supermarkets, industries and large food and drinks manufacturers, are becoming more socially responsible.

5 Share what they have found – list the different ways businesses are working to look after the environment, people and their employees.

6 Discuss with the children how school should teach social responsibility. How should it promote it? Are rewards a good idea? If rewards are used, is it acceptable to use sanctions if people are not socially responsible?

7 In small groups or pairs ask the children to design a poster that shares what social responsibility is and the ways people can demonstrate this.

8 When the posters are complete, let the CYP undertake an assembly to share this with others.

RESOURCES

1 'Learned Optimism by Martin Seligman – animated book review',

www.youtube.com/watch?v=2hHNq45rEnU

2 YouTube: 'Individual social responsibility',

https://www.youtube.com/watch?v=gWff2Ne4v78

3 'Things that make me happy' lolly templates

4 Large sheets of paper

5 Pens, pencils, etc.

IMPORTANT POINTS

Positive psychology is the study of what makes people happy and able to thrive or flourish.

LEARNING LINKS

Collaboration, self-awareness, knowledge and understanding, emotional literacy.

REFLECTION

Questions:

Positive comment from child:

Positive comment from adult:

LEARNING DIMENSIONS		SOCIAL & EMOTIONAL SKILLS	
Strategic awareness		Emotional literacy	
Learning relationships		Neuroscience	(shaded green)
Curiosity		Self-regulation	
Creativity		Self-development	
Meaning making			
Changing & learning			
Resilience			

Things that make me Happy

Things I enjoy doing

Books and toys I enjoy reading and playing with

Things I do which I am proud of

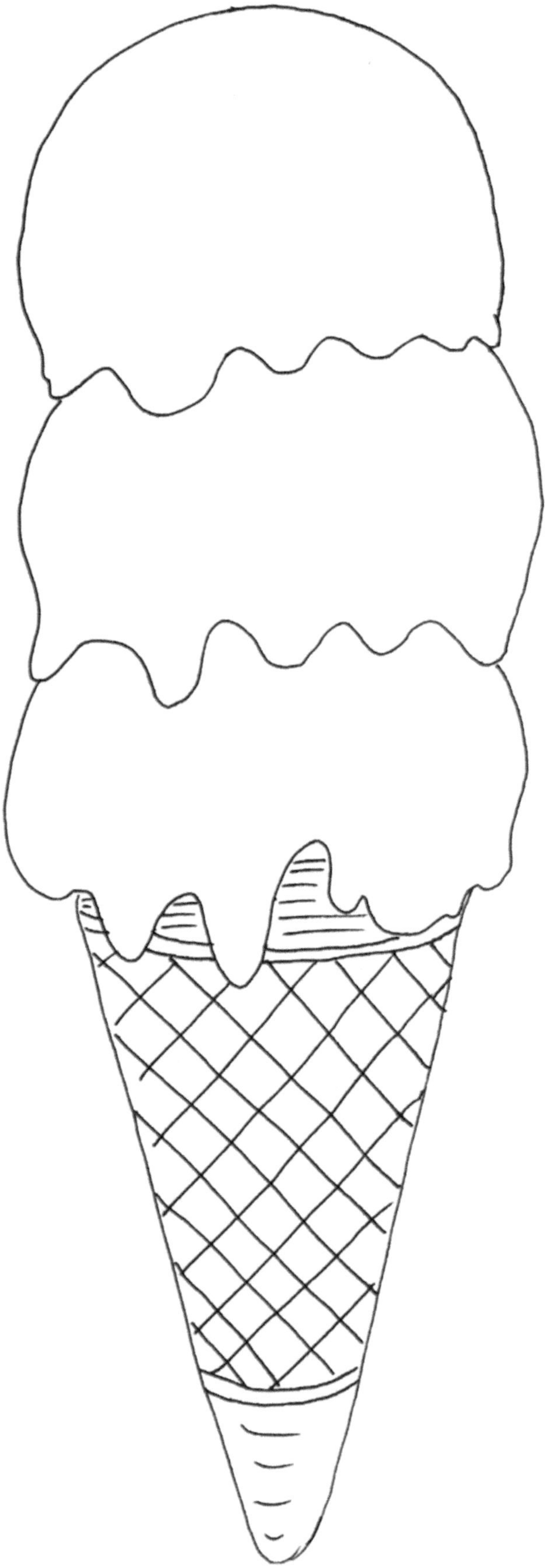

Things that make me Happy

Things I enjoy doing

Books and toys I enjoy reading and playing with

Things I do which I am proud of

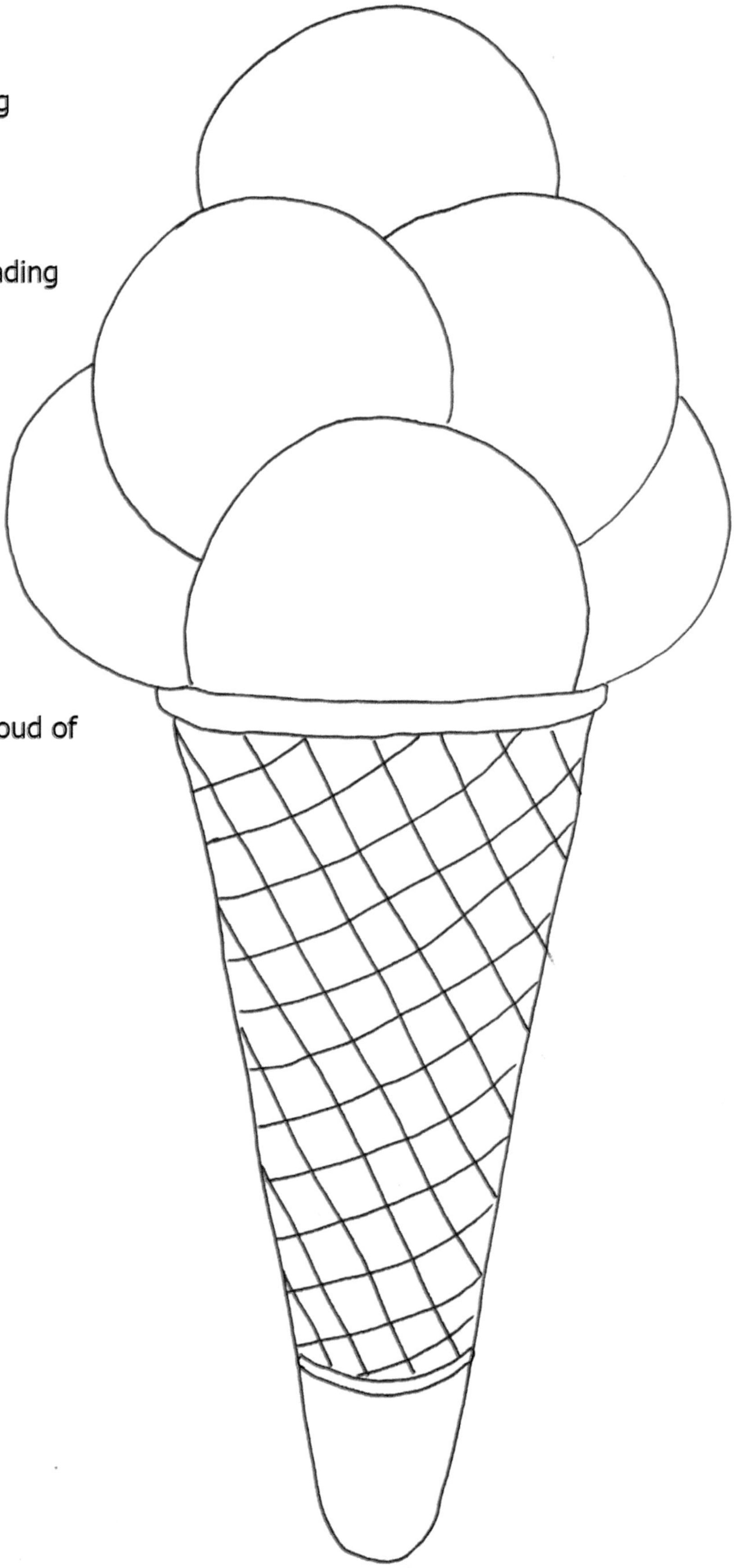

Things that make me Happy

Things I enjoy doing

Books and toys I enjoy reading and playing with

Things I do which I am proud of

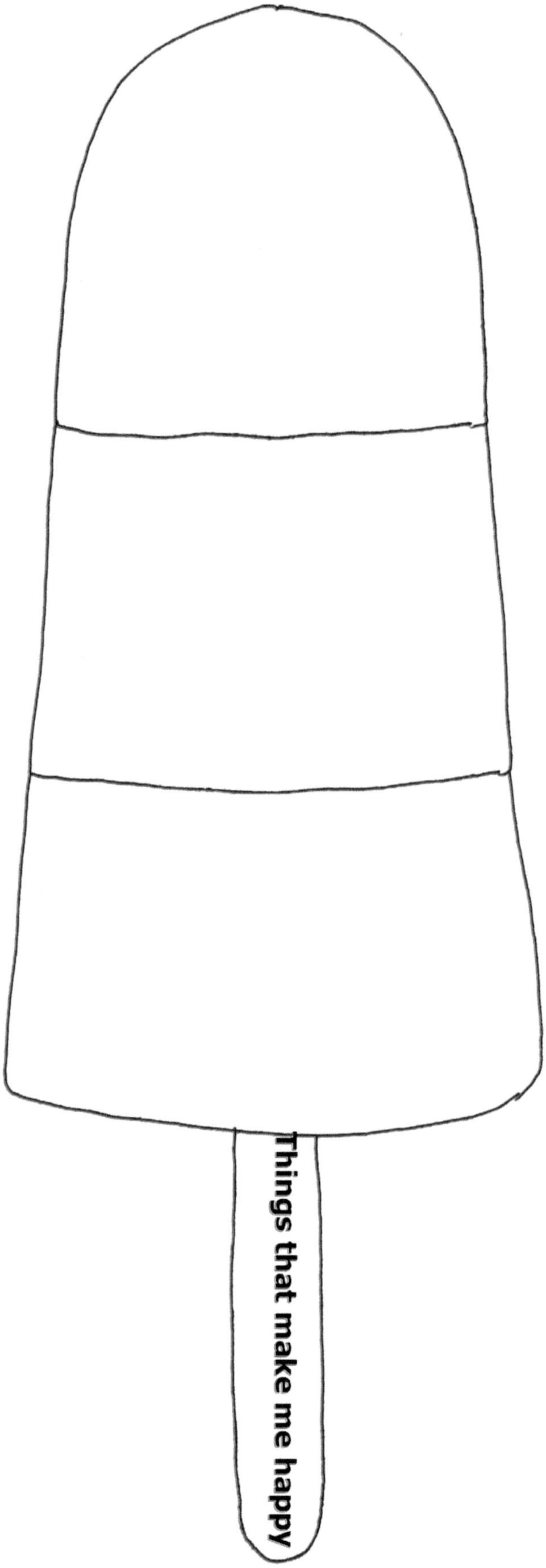

Language and the brain

1 2 3

SESSION OBJECTIVES

To understand how words or what people say can influence our thoughts and therefore how we feel and respond.

SESSION OUTCOMES

✓ To be able to create a cartoon comic strip that shows how words can make us feel good or bad.

LESSON PLAN

- Ask the children to remember the time before their class baby could talk. How did they understand what their parent was feeling – tone of voice, facial expressions, etc.?
- How did their parent use this to guide the baby or let them know if what they were doing was OK or not?

For those classrooms not able to undertake the Circles for Learning Project, video clips or photographs can be used to support the discussion around the topic and stimulate thoughts and ideas from the children and young people.

Task

KS1: To act out a chain of events to show how words can make people feel good or bad.

KS2/KS3: To create a comic strip to show how positive and negative words influence the nervous system and therefore feelings.

KS1

1 Tell the children about something they have done really well and how very pleased you are with them. How does that make them feel?

2 Now act out a short sketch with you TA or another adult letting them know how disappointed you are with them.

3 Ask the children how this person now feels.

4 Support the children discussing the differences between the two situations – why did the two people feel different?

5 Link this to the words or the message you were giving. Explore with the children who is responsible for the message? This is a tricky one as we are responsible for our words and actions but sometimes people don't want to hear what we are saying as it makes them mad or sad.

6 Get the children to work in groups of 4 (in each group, two children play the part of the person and the other two children play the part of their thoughts). Ask them to act out a short scene between two children and two thoughts, one for each of them. Ask the children to show how their words can make thoughts, good or bad, and then these thoughts make the child feel happy, sad, angry or something else.

7 Share the different sketches and discuss each one.

KS2/KS3

1 Explain to the children that you have a challenge – to communicate with other children that what we say has an impact on how someone can feel. You would like them to create a comic, story, poem or poster to show this.

2 Ask the children to work in pairs. They will each act as coach and mentor for the other person.

3 Ask the children to sketch out a rough idea and then share this with their coach or mentor – answer questions that arise. The work will all be making an exhibition for another class to attend to help think about the impact we have on each other and about responsibility.

4 Check in with the children at different times and discuss how they are feeling about the task, where they are, how the planning and organisation is going – do they need to check in with another person who is good at a particular way of working and talk something through with them?

5 Share the work when it is at the draft stage and get the children to give feedback about how they think the work is going and what they like. They can ask questions about whether the person has thought about a particular area and also what areas they feel could be explored further.

6 Set up a coaching station for children who need your support and help them think about what they are doing and the problems that they are encountering. Focus on the end product, a resource to support others in thinking about the impact their words have on someone else.

7 Set up the exhibition, with children explaining about their piece of work and why they chose to create what they have done.

RESOURCES

1 Comic strip blank

2 Large paper

3 Pens, pencils, rubbers

4 Cameras

5 Computers

IMPORTANT POINTS

What we say has an impact on the person we are talking to; our words cause them to feel an emotion. We are responsible for what we say and how we make people feel.

LEARNING LINKS

Collaboration, self-awareness, emotional literacy, knowledge and understanding, self-development.

REFLECTION

Questions:

Positive comment from child:

Positive comment from adult:

Learning Dimensions		Social & Emotional Skills	
Strategic awareness	(orange)	Emotional literacy	(orange)
Learning relationships		Neuroscience	(green)
Curiosity	(orange)	Self-regulation	
Creativity		Self-development	(orange)
Meaning making	(orange)		
Changing & learning	(orange)		
Resilience			

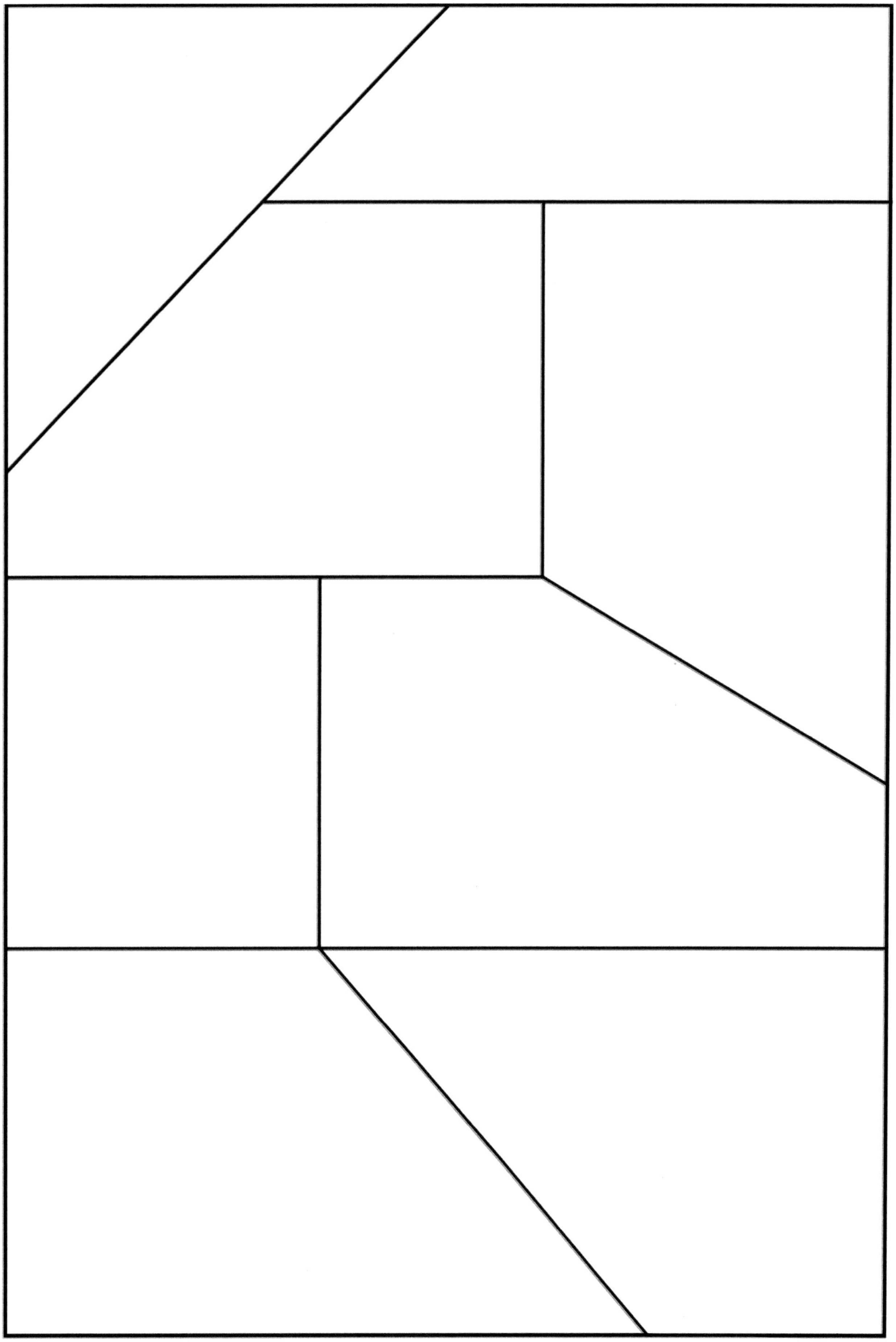

Emotional literacy

1 2 3

SESSION OBJECTIVES

To understand that what we do or say can have an effect on someone else.

SESSION OUTCOMES

- ✓ To be able to identify and talk about a range of different emotions.
- ✓ To be able to share what it means to be a good friend.
- ✓ To be able to create an A to Z of kindness.

LESSON PLAN

- ➢ Ask the children to think of a time when they observed their class baby do something which had an emotional impact on their parent.
- ➢ Can they think of a time when they did something which had an emotional impact on someone else.

For those classrooms not able to undertake the Circles for Learning Project, video clips or photographs can be used to support the discussion around the topic and stimulate thoughts and ideas from the children and young people.

Task

KS1: To make a feelings fishing game.

KS2: To create a 'Friends or not' poster.

KS3: To show how the mind deletes, distorts or generalises information sometimes, depending on our beliefs.

KS1

1 Ask the children to write/draw a positive emotion on a whiteboard and hold it up.

2 Then ask them what might have happened to cause a person to feel that emotion.

3 Finally ask them how that person might now behave as a result of that emotion.

Emotion – Happy. Cause of the happiness – It's their birthday. Actions/behaviour due to happiness – lots of laughter and enjoyment.

Emotion – Angry. Cause of anger – brother broke their Lego toy. Actions/behaviour due to the anger – hits out at brother.

Emotion – Frustration. Cause of frustration – not being able to do their maths. Actions/behaviour due to frustration – yells at the teacher.

4 Ask the children to work in pairs and list as many emotions as possible on the linking sheet.

5 Then ask them to put a cause on the sheet next and then finally an action/behaviour.

6 Explain to the children that they are going to make a game that links the feeling, cause and action together.

7 Ask the children to choose 10 emotions and write each one on a fish. Then cut out the fishes and put a paperclip on their noses.

8 Next ask them to put a cause on the shells and cut those out and once more put a paperclip on the shell.

9 Finally ask them to put an action or behaviour on the bubbles. When they have done this, cut the bubbles out and put a paperclip on them.

10 Tie a piece of string on a pencil and then on the other end add a magnet.

11 The idea of the game is to catch a fish, shell and bubble that go together to make a chain.

KS2

1 Ask the children what sort of thing can happen that can trigger an emotion.

2 Work together to list emotions and their triggers.

3 Ask the children to work in pairs to fill in the 'Power of Thought' sheet showing how a trigger sets off a thought that makes a feeling.

4 Share and discuss what they have found.

5 Pose the question, who is responsible for how somebody feels? Demonstrate how we are all responsible for each other but also how we are responsible for ourselves.

6 Get the children to write 10 sentences demonstrating actions that you would expect from a friend and 10 that are not good friendship actions. Write these on strips of paper, with one on each strip.

Listens and is interested in what I have to say.
Leaves me out of games.

7 Read through them and then fold them up and put them in a bowl. Make sure they are evenly done for and against friendship.

8 Take turns for children to choose a sentence. Once they have it they have to read it out and then decide if it is a friend or not a friend. If it is a friend, they go and stand by the Friendship sign, if not they stand under the Not Friends sign.

9 Discuss how their actions make other people feel. They are responsible for their actions, just as dog owners are responsible for their dogs.

KS3

1 Ask the children to work in pairs.

2 Give each pair the 'Our Filters' picture and ask them to discuss what they think it represents.

3 Share and feed back to the group.

4 Remind the children about the ways we create our beliefs – the way we interpret situations.

I can't do maths, I am useless at drawing, etc.

5 Share the fleas jumping video to reinforce this.

YouTube: 'Flea in a glass jar experiment'.

6 Read the book *We Are What We Think* by Kristy Hammill.

7 Work with the children to come up with examples for each section:

Deletion occurs when we overlook, tune out or omit. When we delete parts of our experience, either they fail to register or we discount them as unimportant.

I am a failure – this doesn't expand what has been failed at.
She excluded me – this doesn't share what or when or how.

Distortion is a personal prejudice that twists our perceptions. We amplify or diminish our experience.

He never talks to me.
Friends should always be there for each other no matter what.

Generalisation occurs when we reach a global conclusion based on one or two experiences, taking them as representative of the whole and paying no attention to exceptions.

I always get things wrong.
I am useless at maths. I never understand.

8 Ask the children to work together in pairs to complete an A-Z of kindness and then see if they can work their way through it together over the week.

RESOURCES

1 'Chain reactions' sheet

2 Fish pictures

3 Shell pictures

4 Bubble pictures

5 Friendship sign

6 No friends sign

7 YouTube: 'Flea in a glass jar experiment',

www.youtube.com/watch?v=TK2Hd9a05HM

8 *We Are What We Think* by Kristy Hammill

9 'Deletion, distortion and generalisation' poster

IMPORTANT POINTS

We are responsible for the way we treat others. If we are unkind or do not think, we can cause people to feel bad.

LEARNING LINKS

Collaboration, self-awareness, emotional literacy, knowledge and understanding, creativity.

REFLECTION

Questions:

Positive comment from child:

Positive comment from adult:

LEARNING DIMENSIONS		SOCIAL & EMOTIONAL SKILLS	
Strategic awareness		Emotional literacy	
Learning relationships		Neuroscience	
Curiosity		Self-regulation	
Creativity		Self-development	
Meaning making			
Changing & learning			
Resilience			

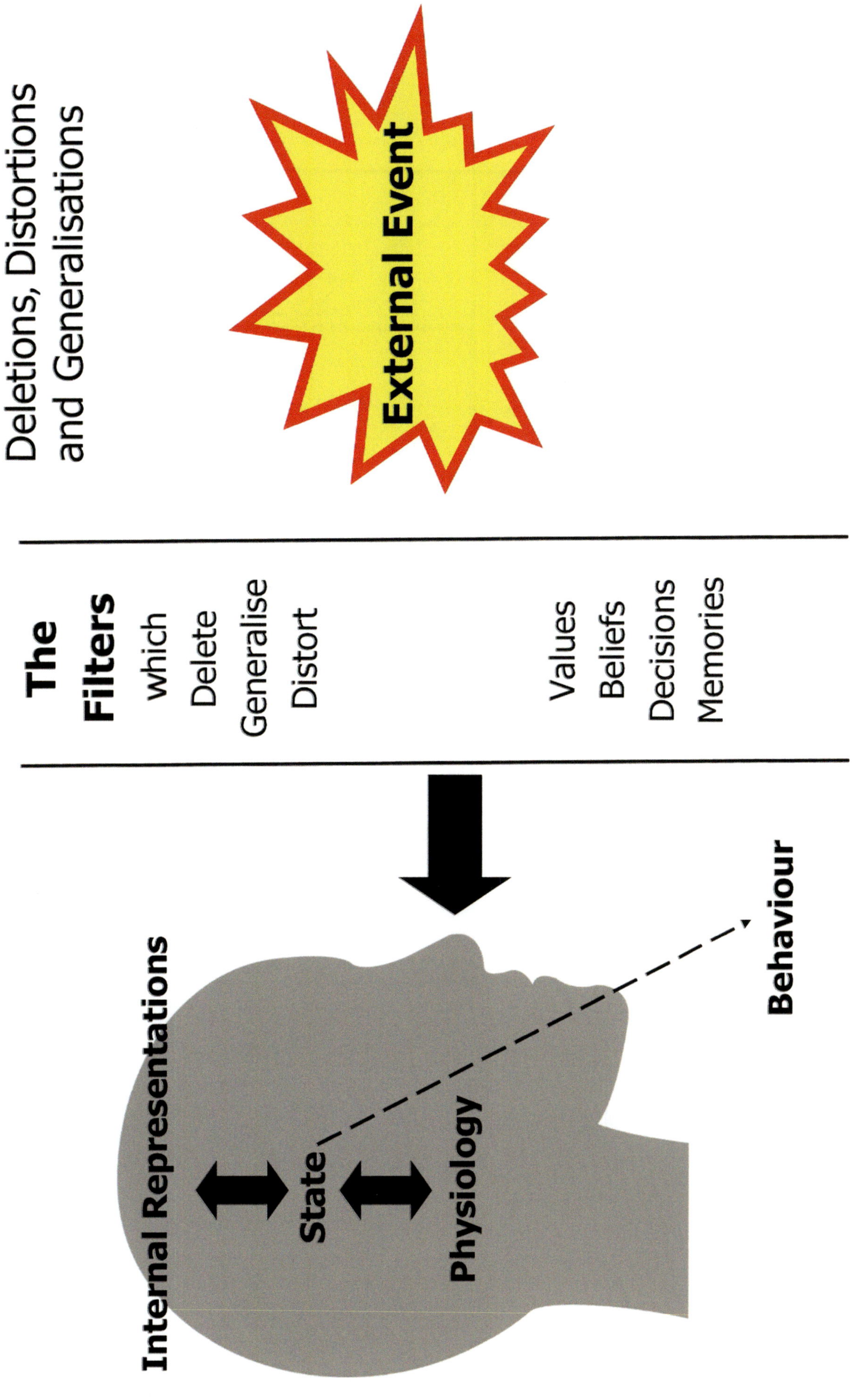
Deletions, Distortions
and Generalisations
External Event
The
Filters
which
Delete
Generalise
Distort
Values
Beliefs
Decisions
Memories
Internal Representations
State
Physiology
Behaviour

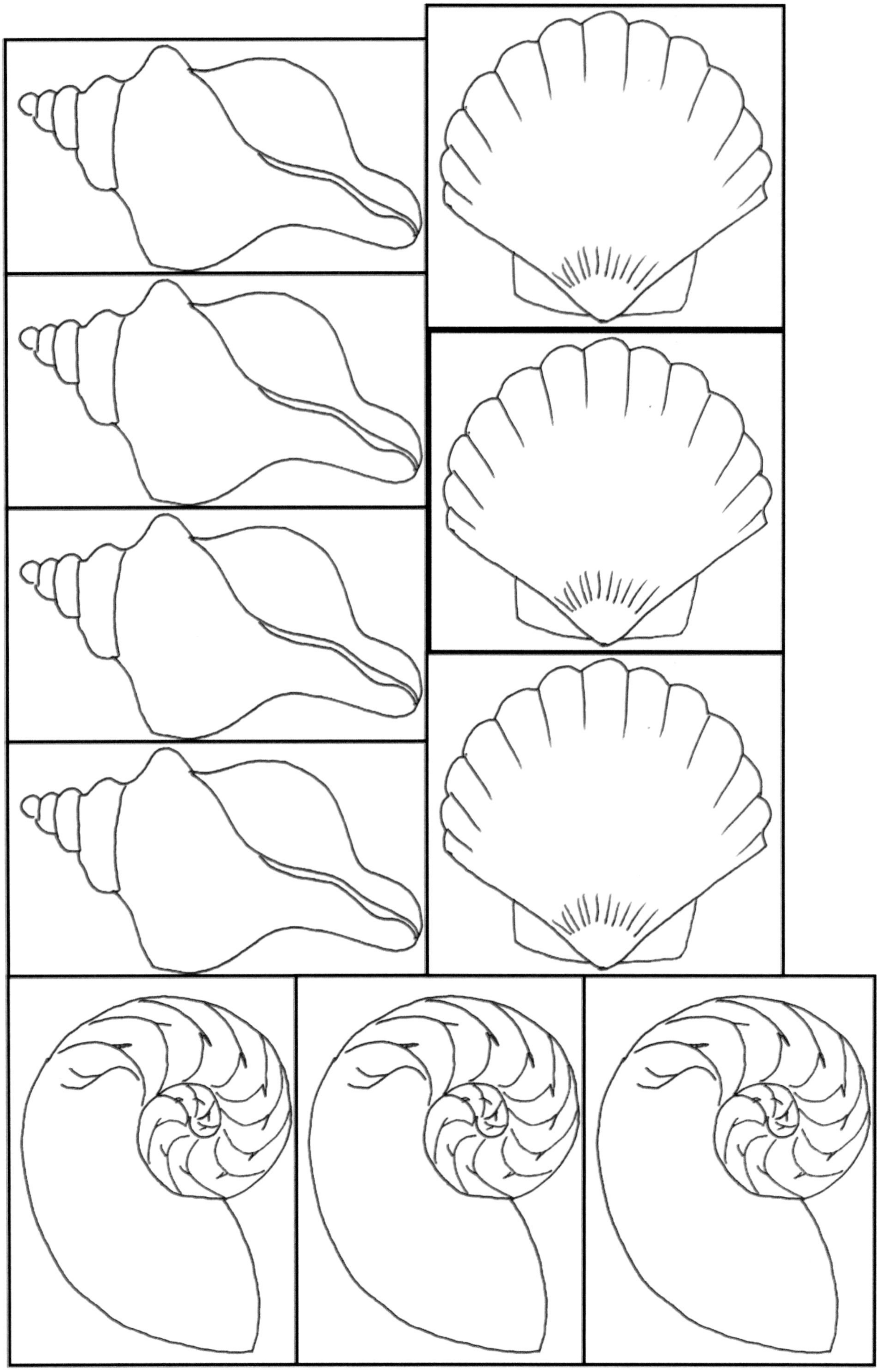

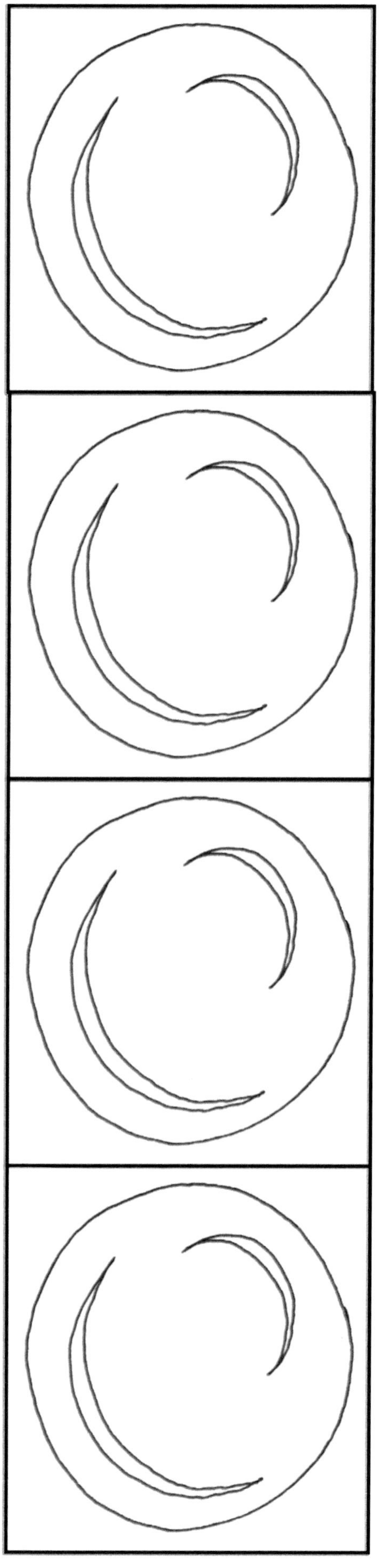

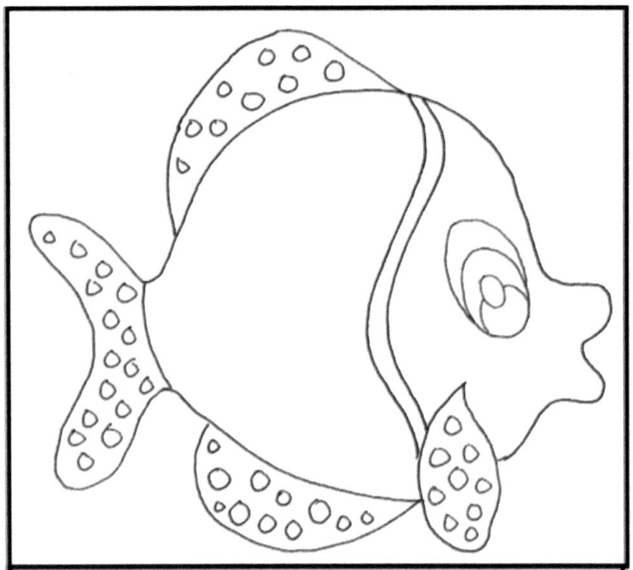

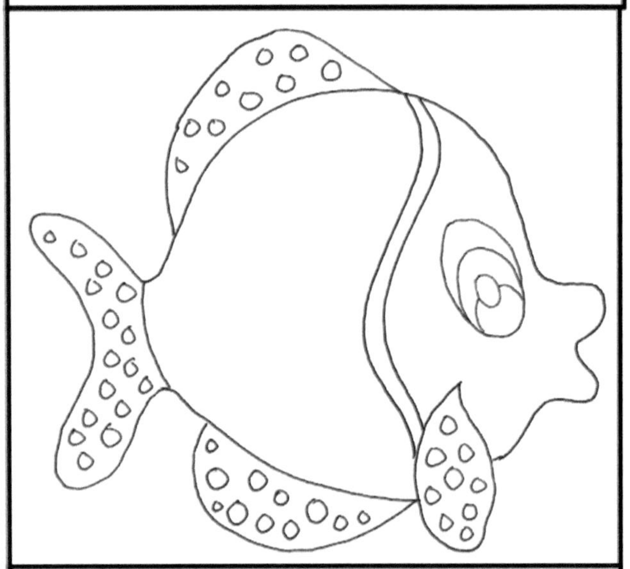

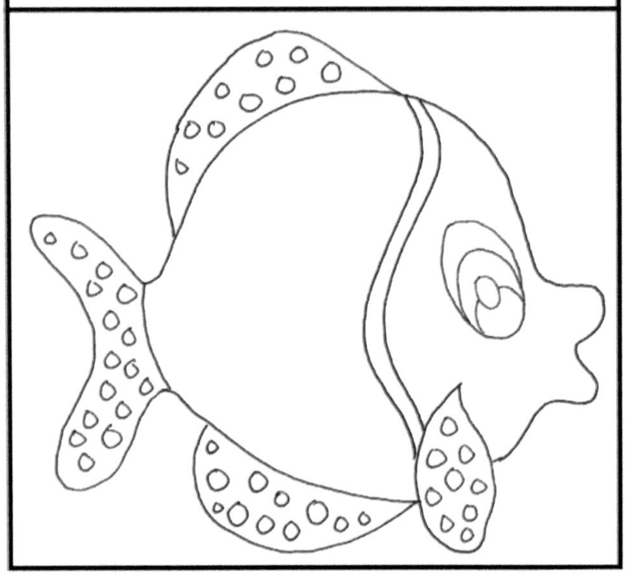

Chain Reactions

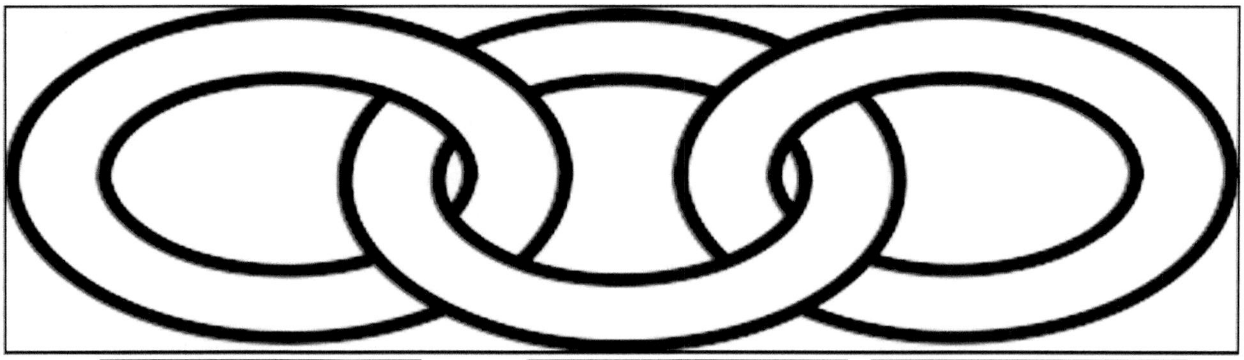

Emotion | Cause | Action

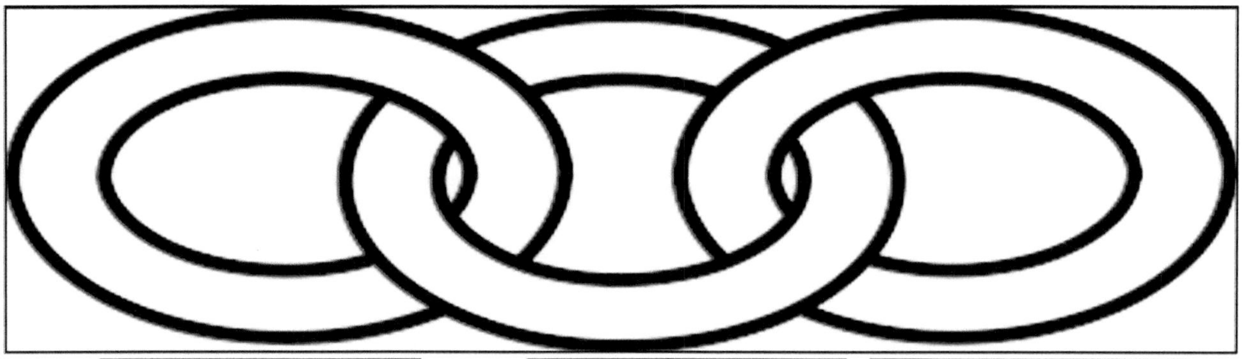

Emotion | Cause | Action

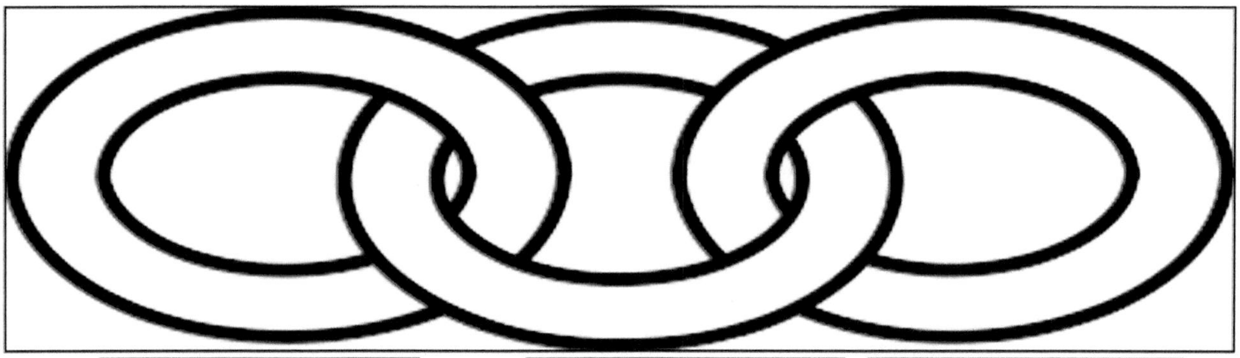

Emotion | Cause | Action

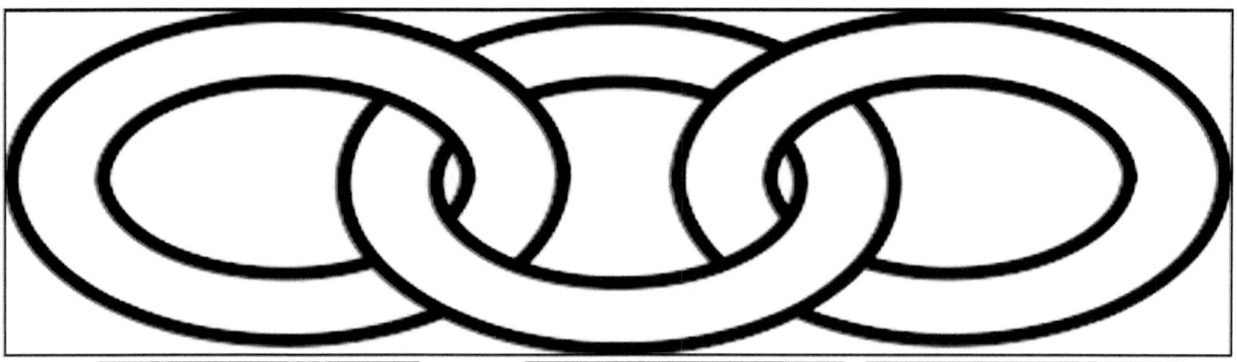

Emotion | Cause | Action

Chapter 5

How the brain can influence behaviour

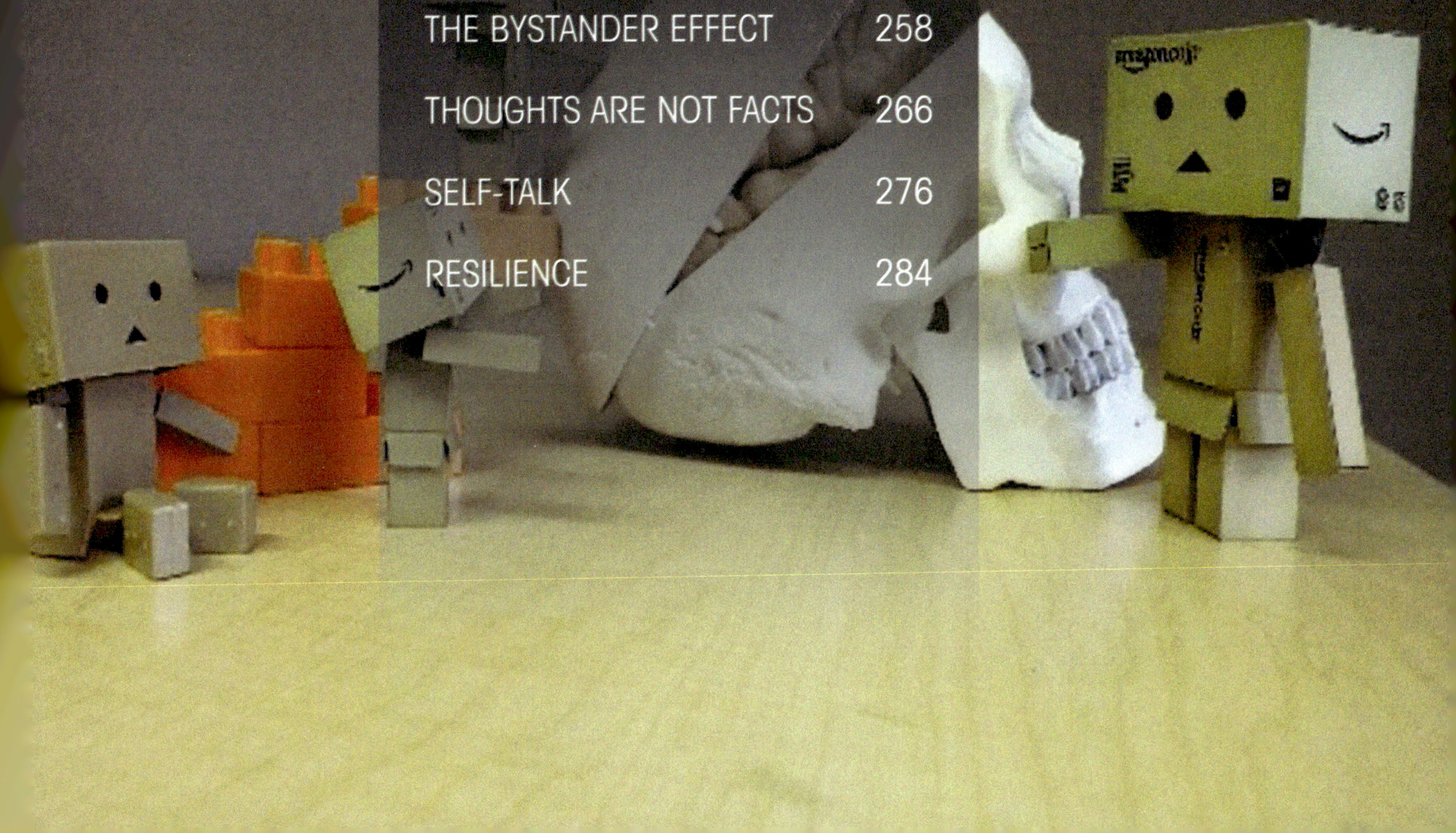

Initial Orientating Response

1 2 3

SESSION OBJECTIVES

To understand why the brain quickly sees a change in the environment and how this can aid memory.

SESSION OUTCOMES

✓ To be able to describe why the brain notices a change in the environment and how this can support memory.

LESSON PLAN

➢ Ask the children to describe a time when they were aware of their class baby remembering something.

➢ Explore what they observed and how they interpreted this.

For those classrooms not able to undertake the Circles for Learning Project, video clips or photographs can be used to support the discussion around the topic and stimulate thoughts and ideas from the children and young people.

The Initial Orientating Response (IOR), also called orienting reflex, is an organism's immediate response to a change in its environment, when that change is not sudden enough to elicit the startle reflex. The phenomenon was first described by Russian physiologist Ivan Sechenov.

Task

KS1/KS2: To be able to describe how they cope with a change or new things and create a 'Change Toolkit'.

KS3: To be able to describe what the Initial Orientating Response is and how it can affect our emotions and behaviour.

KS1/KS2

1 Come into the classroom with something different on – a pair of glasses if you don't normally wear them, a wig, or a hat and watch what the children do. Ask them why they think their brain was so quick to notice the difference? Remind them of the brain's function – to enable them to survive. Why is it important to notice new things if survival is important? Remember this was more important for the early humans than perhaps now. If they noticed where a new source of water could be found or they noticed where a new apple tree was growing – these things would then be remembered and so would support survival. Our brains remember new things or different things and sometimes this makes us feel good and sometimes it can trigger fear.

2 Ask the children to think of a time when they had to manage a change in their environment – this could be a change of classrooms, a change of teacher, a change of school, a change of bedroom or home.

3 Explore what this felt like and how it made them feel.

4 Ask the children to think about a change of classroom and teacher. How do they feel about this? Set out a line in the classroom with the statement 'I enjoy change and manage it well' and then the opposite, 'I find change scary and difficult to manage.' Ask the children to stand on the line where they are with managing change.

5 Focus on the fact that all people are different and enjoy different things and are good at different things.

6 Divide the children into small groups (ensure that you have some strong change managers in each group as well as children who struggle with change) and ask them to think of the things that they need or that support them in managing change in a positive way.

7 Give them the toolkit recording sheet to fill in together.

8 Share what they have come up with and create a class toolkit of things that support change, with each child drawing and writing about one strategy.

9 Ask the children to come up with their top 3 strategies and then add photo card change passports to the class information.

KS3

1 Come into the classroom with something different on – a pair of glasses if you don't normally wear them, a wig, or a hat and watch what the children do. Ask them why they think their brain was so quick to notice the difference? Remind them of the brain's function – to enable them to survive. Why is it important to notice new things if survival is

important? Remember this was more important for the early humans than perhaps now. If they noticed where a new source of water could be found or they noticed where a new apple tree was growing – these things would then be remembered and so would support survival. Our brains remember new things or different things and sometimes this makes us feel good and sometimes it can trigger fear.

2 Ask the children to work in pairs and come up with 5 reasons why this response has developed in early humans and supported survival.

3 Ask the groups now to list 3 reasons why this response may cause an individual a difficulty today and 3 reasons why it might be useful today.

4 Link the IOR to how the brain remembers things and discuss how this could support classroom practitioners and how they might use this natural response to support revision. Ask the pairs to come up with 3 things class practitioners could do to use this response to support classroom teaching and 3 ways that they could use this knowledge about how the brain remembers things to support revision – e.g., revise in different parts of the house, make sure that they use different methods of revision, if they use tapes or recordings, use different peoples voices, Mind Map pictures – unusual and funny, etc.

5 Introduce the word HABITUATION – once the brain has got used to the unusual stimuli, then it stops noticing it. This is called habituation.

6 Ask the children to draw and write a description of the IOR as a way of explaining this to others and how it can impact on the way they behave.

RESOURCES

1 Change survival passports

2 Change survival kit

IMPORTANT POINTS

The IOR is an organism's initial response to change which can affect the organism's emotions and behaviours.

LEARNING LINKS

Emotional literacy, self-development, self-awareness, knowledge and understanding, collaboration, creativity, problem solving.

REFLECTION

Questions:

Positive comment from child:

Positive comment from adult:

LEARNING DIMENSIONS		SOCIAL & EMOTIONAL SKILLS	
Strategic awareness		Emotional literacy	
Learning relationships		Neuroscience	
Curiosity		Self-regulation	
Creativity		Self-development	
Meaning making			
Changing & learning			
Resilience			

Change Survival Kit

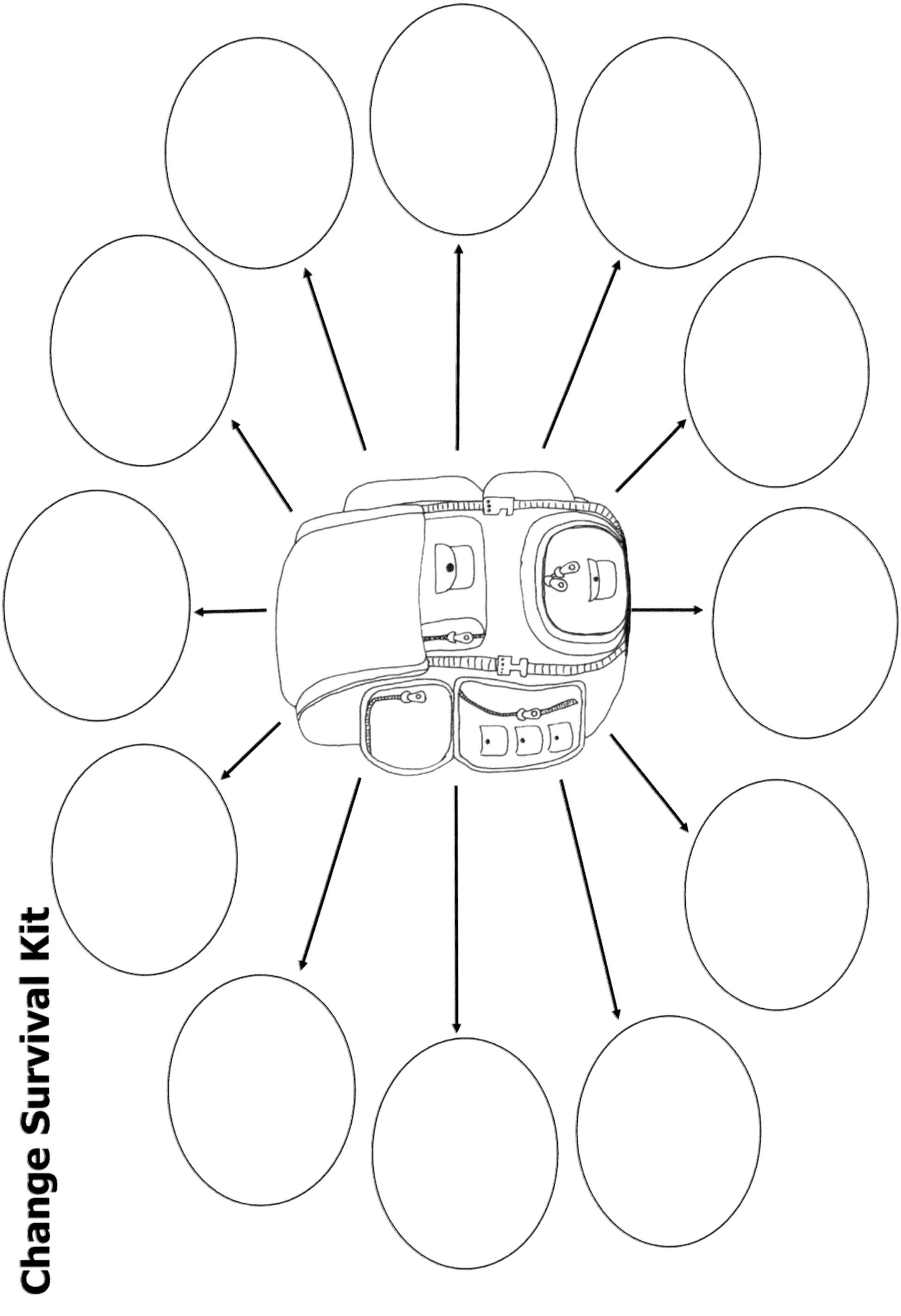

MY TOP STRATEGIES FOR CHANGE

Things I can do:

Things I can ask others to do:

INTERNATIONAL PASSPORT

PASSPORT **TYPE** **Code of issuing State** **Passport No** AA 012345678

SURNAME

GIVEN NAMES

NATIONALITY

DATE OF BIRTH **SEX** **PLACE OF BIRTH**

>>>>>>>>>>>>>>>>>12345678//>>>>>>>>>>>>>>>>>>>>>

Perspectives and points of view

SESSION OBJECTIVES

To be able to discuss and understand how different people can experience situations in a different way.

SESSION OUTCOMES

✓ To be able to share the different points of view of characters in a story.

LESSON PLAN

- Ask the children to think of a time when they have heard their class parent describe their child by giving them a label, such as 'She is such a good eater' or 'He really loves playing in water', etc.
- Ask the children to describe why the parent might say this, what they are noticing and what CONCLUSIONS they are making. This is a way of introducing the fact that everyone draws their own conclusion from a situation and not all people will see things the same way.

For those classrooms not able to undertake the Circles for Learning Project, video clips or photographs can be used to support the discussion around the topic and stimulate thoughts and ideas from the children and young people.

Task

KS1: To be able to interview different story characters and show their different points of view.
KS2: To be able to map the different points of view of the characters in a story.
KS3: To be able to interview different people, hear their points of view and support them in reaching an agreement.

KS1

1 Read a story to the children which has characters that experience the story in a different way, such as 'Jack and the Beanstalk' or 'Goldilocks'.

2 Ask the children to work in small groups one person for each character. Jack, Jack's Mum, Traveller and the Giant. Give each of the groups either a mask or an object to represent the character. This could be

Jack – a red scarf
Mum – an apron
Traveller – jar of beans
Giant – a knife and fork
Ask the children to think how the different characters might feel about what has happened in the story.

3 Ask each of the characters to join together – all the Jacks, Giants, Mums and Travellers. Together ask them to think about the questions.

How do you feel?
What were you thinking at the time?
Has anything like this happened before?
How has this all affected you?
What would you like to do?

4 Divide the children up so they sit in different places in the classroom – one in each quarter. Then act as the reported for the daily newspaper, asking each other questions about what had happened and how they felt.

5 Finish by asking how Jack's behaviour had affected everyone?

How had Jack's Mum felt about him coming home with beans and no money?
How had Jack's Mum felt about him bringing home gold? Did she know it was stolen?
How did the Giant feel about having his chicken that laid the golden egg stolen?
What does he think should happen to Jack?
How does the Traveller feel about buying a cow for a handful of beans?
What did he think Jack's Mum would say at the sale?

Help the children to see that how we behave affects lots of people. Sometimes it can be in a positive way, other times in a negative way.

KS2

1 Ask the children to work in pairs and come up with a way to describe and show what different points of view means.

2 Ask them to choose a story and show how the different characters experience things differently. Good stories to choose are: *Going Places, Necks out for Adventure* or 'Jack and the Beanstalk', 'Goldilocks' or 'The Three Billy Goats Gruff' or 'Hansel and Gretel'. You could have different stories on different tables.

3 To illustrate how to work with the children, *Going Places* has been used.

4 Ask the children to work in groups of four. One person in each group must take on the character of one of the people within the book. Rafael, Maya, Teacher and a child in the class.

5 Ask each child to write a short piece about the day, sharing how they felt and what happened. It can be written as a diary account or as a letter to a friend telling them about the day.

6 Then ask them to share what they have written. They can ask each other questions about how they felt and why (in their character).

7 Give the children the points of view sheet and ask them to fill this in as a group.

8 Share the points of view sheets by having each group display theirs on their table with their book. Ask the groups to go round and read what has been written.

9 Discuss any points that come up.

10 Finish by asking each group to answer:

How did your character affect the others in the story?
Was this effect on other characters positive or negative?
What did your character learn from the experience?
How will what your character learnt affect them in the future?

Help the children to see that how we behave affects lots of people. Sometimes it can be in a positive way, other times in a negative way.

KS3

1 Ask the children to work in pairs and come up with a way to describe and show what 'different points of view' means.

2 Ask them to choose a story and show how the different characters experience things differently. Good stories to choose are: *The Island, Rose Blanche, The Harmonica, Star of Fear, Star of Hope* or *Erika's Story*. You could use one book for each group.

3 Ask the children to work in groups of four. One person in each group must take on the character of one of the people within the book. Rafael, Maya, Teacher and a child in the class. These would be the characters from the book *Going Places*.

4 Ask each child to write a short piece about the story, sharing how they felt and what happened. It can be written as a diary account or as a letter to a friend telling them about the day.

5 Then ask them to share what they have written. They can ask each other questions about how they felt and why (for their character). This will help expand the understanding of each character.

6 Give the children the points of view sheet and ask them to fill this in as a group.

7 Share the points of view sheets by having each group display theirs on their table with their book. Ask the groups to go round and read what has been written.

8 Discuss any points that come up.

9 Finish by asking each group to answer:

How did your character affect the others in the story?
Was this effect on other characters positive or negative?
What did your character learn from the experience?
How will what your character learnt affect them in the future?

Help the children to see that how we behave affects lots of people sometimes it can be in a positive way, other times in a negative way.

RESOURCES

1 *The Harmonica* by Tony Johnston

2 *Rose Blanche* by Ian McEwan

3 *The Island* by Armin Greder

4 *Going Places* by Peter and Paul Reynolds

5 *Necks Out for Adventure* by Timothy Basil Ering

6 *When Mum Turned into a Monster* by Joanne Harrison

7 *Star of Fear, Star of Hope* by Jo Hoestlandt

8 *Erika's Story* by Ruth Vander Zee

IMPORTANT POINTS

Each person interprets what has happened in their own way. Their experiences and ways of thinking all have an effect on how they interpret a situation. Their behaviour is linked to how they feel and how they have experienced the situation.

LEARNING LINKS

Collaboration, creativity, curiosity, knowledge and understanding, skills for learning, emotional literacy.

REFLECTION

Questions:

Positive comment from child:

Positive comment from adult:

LEARNING DIMENSIONS		SOCIAL & EMOTIONAL SKILLS	
Strategic awareness		Emotional literacy	
Learning relationships		Neuroscience	
Curiosity		Self-regulation	
Creativity		Self-development	
Meaning making			
Changing & learning			
Resilience			

Points of View and Different Perspectives

Character	Character ....
How did they feel?	How did they feel?
Why did their feel this way?	Why did their feel this way?
How did they behave?	How did they behave?
Why do you think they behaved this way?	Why do you think they behaved this way?
Who affected them most?	Who affected them most?
Why do you think this was?	Why do you think this was?

Story

Character	Character ....
How did they feel?	How did they feel?
Why did their feel this way?	Why did their feel this way?
How did they behave?	How did they behave?
Why do you think they behaved this way?	Why do you think they behaved this way?
Who affected them most?	Who affected them most?
Why do you think this was?	Why do you think this was?

Negativity bias 1 2 3

SESSION OBJECTIVES

To understand why our brain notices and remembers negative things more quickly and powerfully than positive things and why challenging this has a positive impact on our wellbeing.

SESSION OUTCOMES

- ✓ To be able to describe what negativity bias is and why in evolutionary times this was important.
- ✓ To be able to identify strategies that challenge this.

LESSON PLAN

- ➢ Ask the children to describe a time when they watched their class baby become nervous or frightened of something new.
- ➢ How did they deal with this? Why was this experience important for them? How did their parent support them overcome their anxiety/fear.

For those classrooms not able to undertake the Circles for Learning Project, video clips or photographs can be used to support the discussion around the topic and stimulate thoughts and ideas from the children and young people.

Task

KS1: To be able to create an optimistic cartoon character and a pessimistic character.

KS2/KS3: To be able to describe what negativity bias is and ways to challenge this.

KS1

1. Introduce the words 'optimistic' and 'pessimistic' to the children and explore their understanding of these.
2. Make a class acrostic poem out of the words to help the children remember them and their meaning.
3. Share a range of cartoon characters with the children and discuss what they do and how.

4 Ask the children to draw a cartoon character for 'pessimism' and 'optimism' and to give the character a name – Oliver/Olive/Owen/Oriana the Optimist, Peter/Paula/Percy Pessimist, etc.

5 Ask them to create a story to show how they thought about something that happened using thought bubbles around their character.

6 Share the different stories – you can add music to them – e.g. 'Always look on the bright side of life'. (Be careful which part you use as there is a swear word incorporated in this song however it has a good tune and a lovely bit to whistle to!)

KS2/KS3

1 Watch the video with the children that explains about negativity bias and then discuss what they have learnt and what they think.

YouTube: 'The negativity bias and how to beat it', www.youtube.com/watch?v=0LfteZ9k8YU&t=51s

Stop the video clip before it starts to discuss how to beat the negativity bias and discuss the brain's need to notice and think about all the negative things. Is this something that the children recognise? Can they share an example of a time they couldn't get a negative event or incident out of their mind?

2 Share the next part of the video on how to beat the negativity bias.

3 Discuss the 4 strategies:

- Awareness that the brain works in this way and why,
- Look for the positive or Velcro the positive times,
- Gratitude supports us in focusing on the good things and stops the brain going searching for the negative things,
- Kudos folder – a box that contains the good things we have done or achieved to remind us of the positive things in our life.

4 Share the 'Beat the negativity bias' sheet with the children and ask them to work in small groups to fill this in and create a poster to remind them about letting the negative things slide off and sticking the good things in their mind.

5 Share the different posters or worksheet the children have come up with.

6 Ask the children to bring in a small box – a shoe box is ideal. Let them decorate this and make a box to collect WOW moments in. This might be certificates, photos, reports, badges from guides or scouts, great pieces of work, etc.

The amygdala uses 2/3 of its neurons to look for bad news or dangers. Once it detects them, it fires the alarm and then those negative events and experiences get quickly stored in our memory as a reference for future events. Positive memories are not stored as quickly.

RESOURCES

1 'Always Look on the Bright Side of Life' song

2 Pens, paper and colours

3 Cartoon characters to discuss and share

4 YouTube: 'The negativity bias and how to beat it',

www.youtube.com/watch?v=0LfteZ9k8YU&t=51s

5 'Beat the negativity bias' sheet

6 Pens, paper and coloured pens

7 Magazines

8 Coloured paper and collage materials

9 Paints

IMPORTANT POINTS

Negativity bias is the brain's way of keeping us safe. However it was more useful in times past when human kind was dealing with a much more dangerous environment. It is important to understand why the brain looks for and focuses on negative things so that we can challenge this and ensure we both see and hold onto the positive things we experience.

LEARNING LINKS

Collaboration, self-awareness, self-development, creativity, emotional literacy, knowledge and understanding.

REFLECTION

Questions:

Positive comment from child:

Positive comment from adult:

LEARNING DIMENSIONS		SOCIAL & EMOTIONAL SKILLS	
Strategic awareness		Emotional literacy	
Learning relationships		Neuroscience	
Curiosity		Self-regulation	
Creativity		Self-development	
Meaning making			
Changing & learning			
Resilience			

The Negativity Bias

The Negativity Bias ....
....
....
....
....

Ways to beat the Negativity Bias

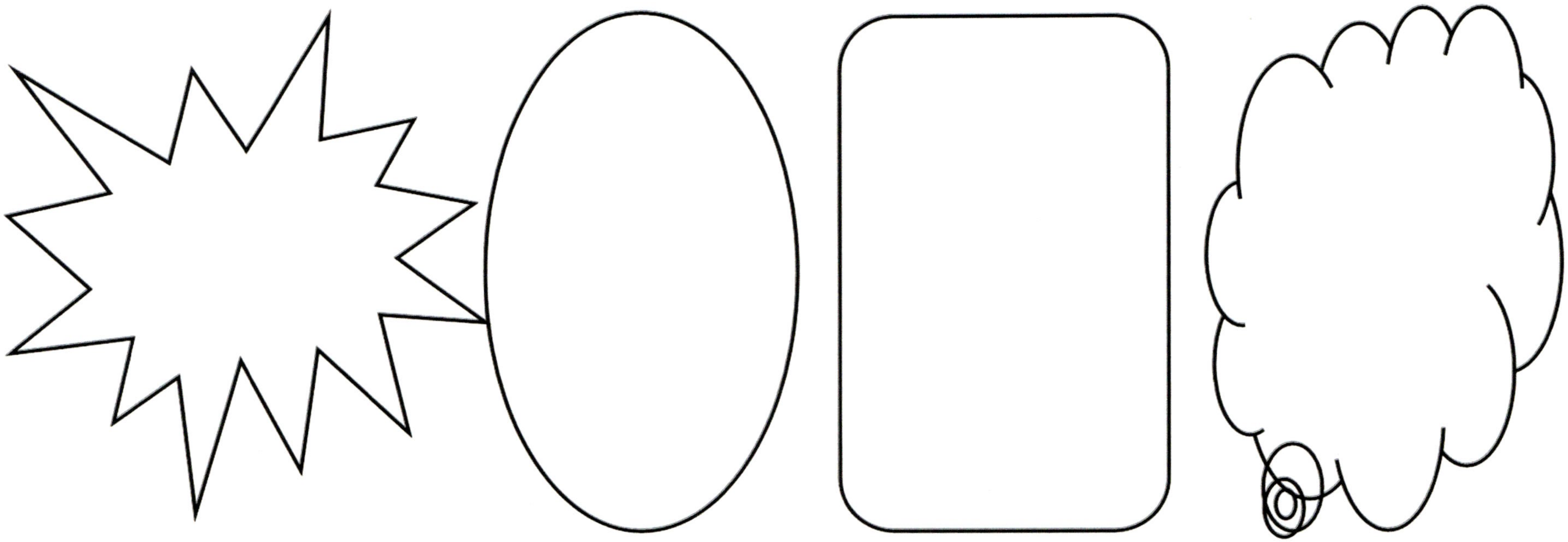

The bystander effect

1 2 3

SESSION OBJECTIVES

To understand the bystander effect and ways to challenge this.

SESSION OUTCOMES

✓ To be able to describe what the bystander effect is and be able to suggest ways of challenging this.

LESSON PLAN

➤ Ask the children to think about their class baby and their parents. If they could give the baby 3 things, what would they be?

➤ What three things do they think the parent would want for their child and how are they supporting the child in developing those skills as they look after them.

For those classrooms not able to undertake the Circles for Learning Project, video clips or photographs can be used to support the discussion around the topic and stimulate thoughts and ideas from the children and young people.

Task

KS2/KS3: To be able to describe what the bystander effect is and how this can be challenged.

KS2/KS3

1 Watch the YouTube videos: 'The bystander effect' and 'The bystander effect – the science of empathy'.

2 Ask the children to work in pairs and discuss what they have seen. What did they think? Have they ever been in a position where they wanted to help but didn't feel able to? Have they ever been in a position where they needed help?

3 Working in pairs, ask them to come up with as many ways that people can harm others as possible – bullying, harassment, violence, intimidation, unkindness, persecution, making fun of them, etc.

4 Share the different situations they have come up with and record them on the board.

5 Now ask the pairs to think of the potential consequences for the targets of harmdoing. This could be fear, unhappiness, depression, suicide, lack of belief in themselves, etc.

6 Share the definition sheet with the children so that all can be clear about the terminology that will be used in the session.

7 Divide the group into 4: Targets, Harmdoers, Bystanders, School Culture.

8 Ask them to work in their groups to answer the following questions

How is this person feeling while harm is going on?
What happens as a result of the incident now or later?
What lesson is being learnt from the incident of harmdoing?

9 Share the different points of view and impact the harmdoing can have on the different people involved.

10 Ask the children to work individually to record a time when they did something that harmed another person and the impact this had on the other person and themselves. The 'Impact of Harmdoing' record sheet can be used.

11 Pose the question – What stops us from taking action? Discuss thoughts ideas and information from the two video clips. Ask the children to work in pairs and then ask them to join with another pair and share their ideas.

12 Feed back to the class – if you can identify the 5 different categories do so as you go.

13 Share the 'What Stops Us' information sheet.

14 Ask the children to work in their pairs again and come up with an example for each of the areas:

Masks – You watch a young person push another young person into a fence, you walk away pretending not to notice or see what they have done. You may even look away or in the opposite direction.

Who me? – A group of young people have gathered around two people fighting. You don't do or say anything to stop them as you are waiting for someone else to step in and stop it.

Confusion – This is when you might see a young person teasing another young person. You are not sure how difficult this is or whether the young person is managing what is happening. Is it hurtful or are they OK and think it is funny?

Danger – You see two people shouting and yelling at each other. Tempers are running high and they are about to have a fight. You don't want to step in in case one of them attacks you.

Fear of disapproval – Two young people are jumping on desks and chasing another young person around the class throwing paper at them. You don't want to get involved in case a teacher walks in and accuses you of being involved. The rest of the class are laughing and you don't want them to turn on you and accuse you of spoiling their fun.

15 Share the different examples and discuss how they each feel from the different people's perspectives.

16 Ask the class to divide into 5 groups and give each one, one of the inhibitors: Masks, Who me?, Confusion, Danger and Fear of disapproval. Ask each group to come up with solutions to the harm-doing. This could be linked to what the bystander could do to reduce the power of this inhibiting effect or what they could say.

Masks – You walk up and ask the person who has been pushed if they are OK
You go and tell a teacher
You find your friends and all walk over to where the incident happened and check out the person pushed into the fence

17 Share what each group has come up with and discuss the different solutions.

RESOURCES

1 'The bystander effect – the science of empathy',

www.youtube.com/watch?v=Wy6eUTLzcU4

2 'The bystander effect',

www.youtube.com/watch?v=OSsPfbupOac

3 The 'Impact of Harmdoing' record sheet

4 Definition sheet

5 'What Stops Us' information sheet

IMPORTANT POINTS

The bystander effect is a social psychological phenomenon in which individuals are less likely to offer help to a victim when other people are present. The greater the number of bystanders, the less likely it is that one of them will help. There are several things that the bystander can do to reduce the power of the harmdoer and support the target.

LEARNING LINKS

Collaboration, self-development, knowledge and understanding, emotional literacy, self-awareness, problem solving.

REFLECTION

Questions:

Positive comment from child:

Positive comment from adult:

LEARNING DIMENSIONS		SOCIAL & EMOTIONAL SKILLS	
Strategic awareness		Emotional literacy	
Learning relationships		Neuroscience	
Curiosity		Self-regulation	
Creativity		Self-development	
Meaning making			
Changing & learning			
Resilience			

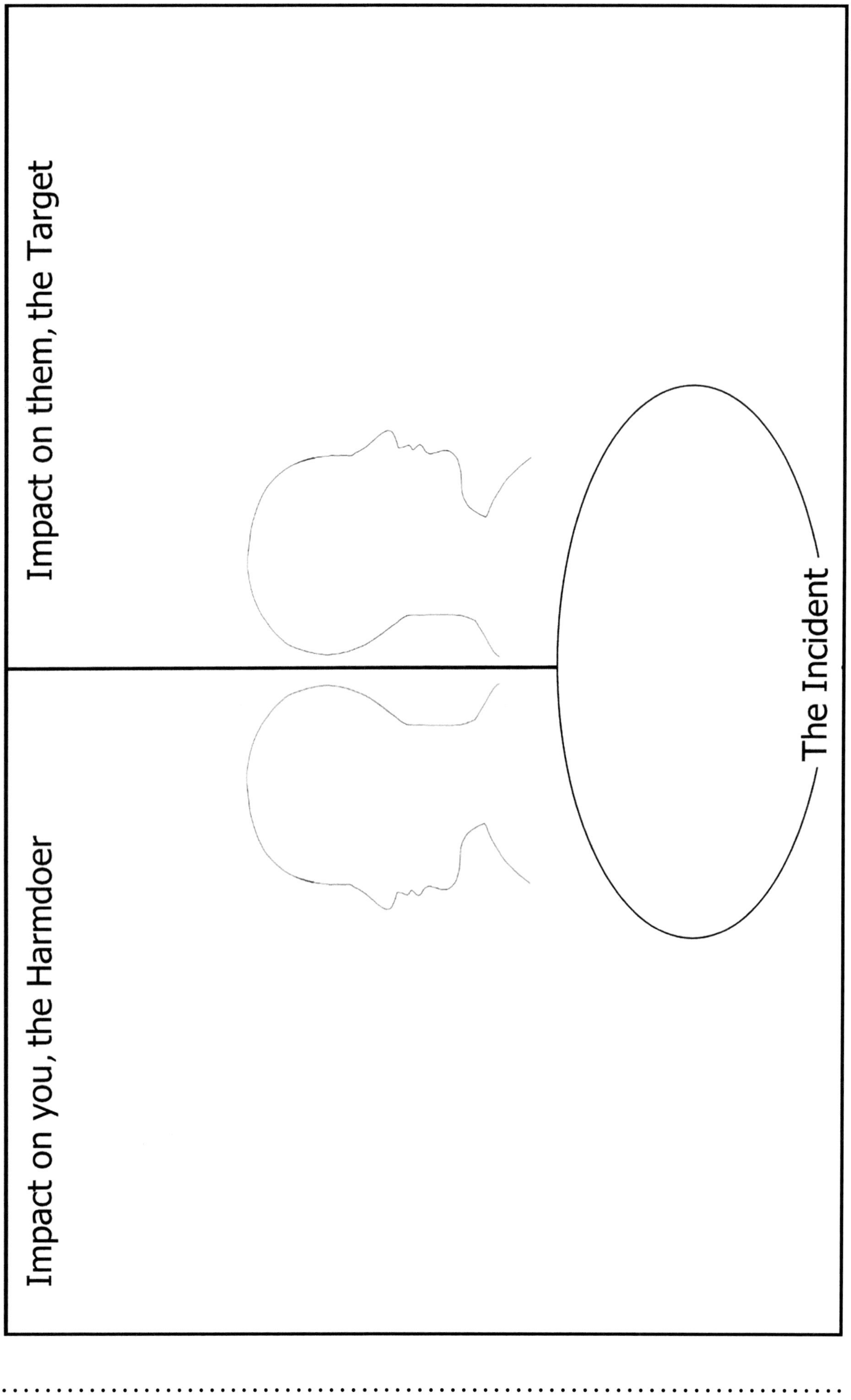
The Impact of Harmdoing on the Harmdoer and the Target
Impact on you, the Harmdoer
Impact on them, the Target
The Incident

THE BYSTANDER EFFECT TERMINOLOGY

What is a bystander?

A bystander is a witness, someone who is in a position to know what is happening and is in a position to take action.

What is a passive bystander?

For some people, the word bystander means passive, however 'bystander' is a neutral term. Therefore a bystander can be passive or they can become active.

Passivity in a bystander might show itself as:

1. Acceptance and/or approval of what the harmdoer is doing.
2. The bystander might not be feeling they accept or approve, but by being passive, others might think the bystander accepts or approves of the harmdoer's actions.
3. The harmdoer might think that his/her actions are accepted and/or approved.
4. This is likely to lead to further harmful actions.
5. Passivity can create a negative change in what the larger community sees as normal or acceptable behaviour.
6. Less trust: the target and the bystanders may begin to feel less trusting of others in general.
7. The passive bystander may feel guilt for not doing the right thing.
8. A very few witnesses might enjoy the suffering of another.

Complicity

Sometimes, bystanders are not only passive, but also complicit. Complicity means any words, actions, or non-verbal reactions by which a bystander supports a harmdoer. This would include facial expressions, gestures such as clapping or cheering, laughing, joining in with comments or actions, or saying things to support the harmdoer. Sometimes bystanders may laugh because they are nervous and do not know what to do. This laughter can be interpreted by the harmdoer as supporting what they are doing and might even egg them on.

Moral courage

This is the ability and willingness to act according to our values (to do the right thing) even though others might disapprove of our actions, or do harm to us. Moral courage means doing what you believe is the right thing even when these actions are different from the values, beliefs or expectations of other people.

Harmdoing

There is a lot of harmdoing (bullying, harassment, violence and intimidation) in schools, the community and the world both among young people and the adult population. Sadly most young people experience being a target at some point, and at some point nearly everyone hurts another person through something they say or do, sometimes without even meaning to. Unfortunately some young people become targets or regular harmdoers for long periods of time. This means that every young person is likely to experience being a bystander at some point.

Targets

Targets are the focus of the harmdoing – the target of the attack either physically, verbally or emotionally. They can experience distress, unhappiness, depression and have negative moods, all of which are the result of the actions of the harmdoers. The presence of passive bystanders makes people feel worse as they are aware that no one has stepped forward to help them and this raises the question why? Are they not worth it? Is something wrong with them? Studies show that people who were targets when bystanders were passive felt worse than if there was no one to see.

Harmdoers

Harmdoers are the people who inflict harm on another person. Often the only way that they can make what they have done acceptable is to devalue those they harm. This may mean focusing on their targets as different, bad, strange, stupid, outsiders, as 'them' not 'us'. For some people who are aggressive harmdoers, their violent behaviour can become habits. When harmdoers get what they want through their harmdoing behaviour, it reinforces the way of behaving.

INHIBITING BEHAVIOURS

MASKS: Pluralistic ignorance

This is when people do mask or cover their feelings so that when they look at each other they do not show that anything is needed. In public, many people do not show they are upset; they wear a mask to cover their feelings. If you ask people they will say they are 'fine'. Their faces don't show feelings of fear, concern, anxiety distress, anger, sadness, etc. The bystanders look around them and all they see are other bystanders with no expressions on their faces – no clue as to what is needed – and so no one does anything. They just walk by.

People tend to look to other people to see what they are doing or thinking before they act. If all the people around are wearing their masks, then all the bystanders decide there cannot be a problem and therefore they do not need to do anything.

WHO ME?: Diffusion of responsibility

When there are other people present, each person or bystander feels they have less responsibility because there are others present who could also respond. The people look to each other to do something which therefore means no one acts. Studies show that the more people there are at an emergency, the less likely it is that any one person helps.

CONFUSION: Unclear as to whether help is needed.

When the people who are around and watching – bystanders – are unclear if help is needed, they are less likely to help. People receive more help more if they call for help. The targets don't always want to be seen to need help as being a target can feel shameful. This means that the targets choose to act as if there is nothing wrong and everything is OK; sometimes they can even laugh or joke. When they do this, it is really hard for the bystanders to understand if help is really needed.

DANGER: Danger or cost of helping

Sometimes the bystanders understand that by helping they could put themselves in danger either at the time or later. Sometimes the emotional cost of helping the target can be seen as being too high or the effort that they might need to go to might be perceived as being too much. If the target is unpopular, then by helping them, the active bystander could be picked on, teased or even excluded from a group. If the target is someone the active bystander does not like, the target might then turn to the bystander for continued support and friendship after the event and this may be something that they do not want. Individuals often don't like people because, for whatever reason, their group dislikes them. When this is the case, the underlying belief is that there is something wrong with the individual because they are not liked.

FEAR: Fear of disapproval

This is a fear of looking foolish or getting something wrong whilst others are watching. The bystander may be unsure as to whether they have the skills to help or if they can solve the problem or make a difference. This may be linked to the judgement of others. When a person chooses to act or do something in front of a group, they are likely to feel a little self-conscious and anxious. Added to this, if they are also acting against the opinion or attitudes of an individual or a group, then they are likely to feel very uncomfortable.

Thoughts are not facts

1 2 3

SESSION OBJECTIVES

To explore the idea that thoughts are just that – thoughts – and not real.

SESSION OUTCOMES

✓ To be able to create a poster that demonstrates why thoughts should not always be believed.

LESSON PLAN

For those classrooms not able to undertake the Circles for Learning Project, video clips or photographs can be used to support the discussion around the topic and stimulate thoughts and ideas from the children and young people.

Task

KS1: To draw a picture of a thought that grows when someone is kind to us and another to show what happens to our thoughts when we experience someone being unkind.

KS2: To create a poster to demonstrate how thinking impacts on our wellbeing.

KS3: To create a poster to demonstrate how thinking impacts on our wellbeing.
To explore a range of scenarios and how they make the CYP think, feel and then behave.

KS1

1 Share the book *The Magic Is Inside You* and explore with the children how positive and negative thoughts can make them feel.

2 Share the poster showing you saving your good thoughts and throwing away the bad ones and ask the children whether thoughts are real. Help them understand that thoughts are just that – thoughts – and are not real.

3 Ask the children to draw a picture of a thought that develops in their mind when they experience someone being kind and nice to them and then another picture to show the thought that grows when someone is unkind to them.

4 Share the work they have created.

5 Pose the question 'If you walk your dog, who is responsible for the way it behaves?' The owner is. We are the owners of our thoughts, words and actions and so we have to learn to take responsibility for this and learn how to manage them, just like the dog has to learn how to walk on a lead or behave. Help them to understand that what we say or do is our responsibility and that our words or behaviours can cause other people harm if we are not thoughtful and considerate.

KS2

1 Lay out the different sayings about thoughts on the tables around the room.

2 Ask the children to walk around the room and read the different sayings.

3 Ask them to choose the one that they like the best or that they believe is most powerful and write this on a sticky note.

4 Come back together and share the saying that they have chosen and why.

5 Discuss why they think the sayings are important and why they think they can have an impact on wellbeing.

6 Set the challenge – to create a poster using the phrases that they have chosen to help others realise that thoughts can have a powerful impact on our wellbeing and yet they are just thoughts and not real.

7 Discuss the success criteria for a good poster:

Easily understood
Clearly seen from a distance
Eye-catching
Interesting
Gets the message across well
Creates interest
Creates discussion
Is memorable
Etc.

8 Allow the children to work on a draft design and then share with their learning coach. Their learning coach supports them in thinking about whether the poster meets the success criteria and supports them to share why they have chosen the idea they have and how it might be improved.

9 Once the children have shared their idea with their learning coach, let them work on the final poster.

10 Once the posters are complete, ask the children to display them in a silent exhibition. The posters are all laid out around the room on tables and the class walk around silently. Each person has 3 sticky notes. On the notes, they write something they really like about 3 of the posters and stick them on the posters for the artist to read.

11 No one can write the same comment on a poster.

KS3

1 The poster competition can be undertaken as for KS2.

2 After the competition, ask the children to work in small groups.

3 Give them the different scenarios and ask them to discuss what the characters might think and how this would make them feel and behave.

4 For each of the scenarios, ask the children what self-talk the characters could use and also what their best friend might say to them as a way of supporting them in thinking about what to do.

RESOURCES

1 *The Tale of Two Fishes* by Juliette Ttofa

2 'Good thoughts, bad thoughts' poster

3 *The Magic Is Inside You* by Cathy Domoney

4 *We Are What We Think* by Kristy Hammill

IMPORTANT POINTS

Don't believe all that you think; thoughts are just that – thoughts.

LEARNING LINKS

Collaboration, knowledge and understanding, emotional literacy, self-development, self-awareness.

REFLECTION

Questions:

Positive comment from child:

Positive comment from adult:

LEARNING DIMENSIONS		SOCIAL & EMOTIONAL SKILLS	
Strategic awareness		Emotional literacy	
Learning relationships		Neuroscience	
Curiosity		Self-regulation	
Creativity		Self-development	
Meaning making			
Changing & learning			
Resilience			

The Power of Thoughts
Negative thought
Cause
Positive thought
Cause

A negative mind will never give a positive life.
You must master a new way to think if you are to master a new way to be.
Slowly replace negative thoughts with beautifully coloured thoughts and positive energy.

Don't believe everything you think, thoughts are just that, thoughts.
To worry about the past or future is to worry about things that don't exist.
The happiness in your life depends on the quality of your thoughts.
Thoughts are just visitors, let them come and go.

What a wonderful thought it is that the best days of our life haven't happened yet.
Don’t listen to the negative thoughts in your head throw them our and stop them polluting your mind.
Thoughts are just words and images passing through your mind.

Let the bright vibrant positive thoughts settle and grow in your mind so that the negative thoughts have no where to grow.
Thoughts have no power until you take them and somehow impregnate them with the power of belief.

Situations and Negative Thinking that Can Emerge

Situation	Negative Thoughts	Behaviour	Self-talk that could be used	Supportive Friend
A new girl joins the school; she used to go to school with your best friend. At the end of school you see them talking and when you approach they stop. Later your friend reads your WhatsApp message but doesn't answer.				
You play football in the school team. Several of the team keep having a go about your goalkeeping. The next time you meet for practice you realise that they all met up and went bowling and you didn't get invited.				
Your boyfriend puts a photo on social media of him having fun playing crazy golf with his friend. This was the night he said he couldn't come over as he had to revise for a Science exam.				
Your girlfriend keeps ignoring you in school and every time you see her she starts whispering to her friend.				
While you are on holiday your best friend puts several photos of her having fun out and about with some other people from the youth club you both go to.				
Your Mum and Dad forgot about the school trip to Alton Towers at the end of term and booked to go to a family event. You keep getting sent photos of your friends having fun.				

Situations and Negative Thinking that can Emerge

Situation	Negative Thoughts	Behaviour	Self-talk that could be used	Supportive Friend

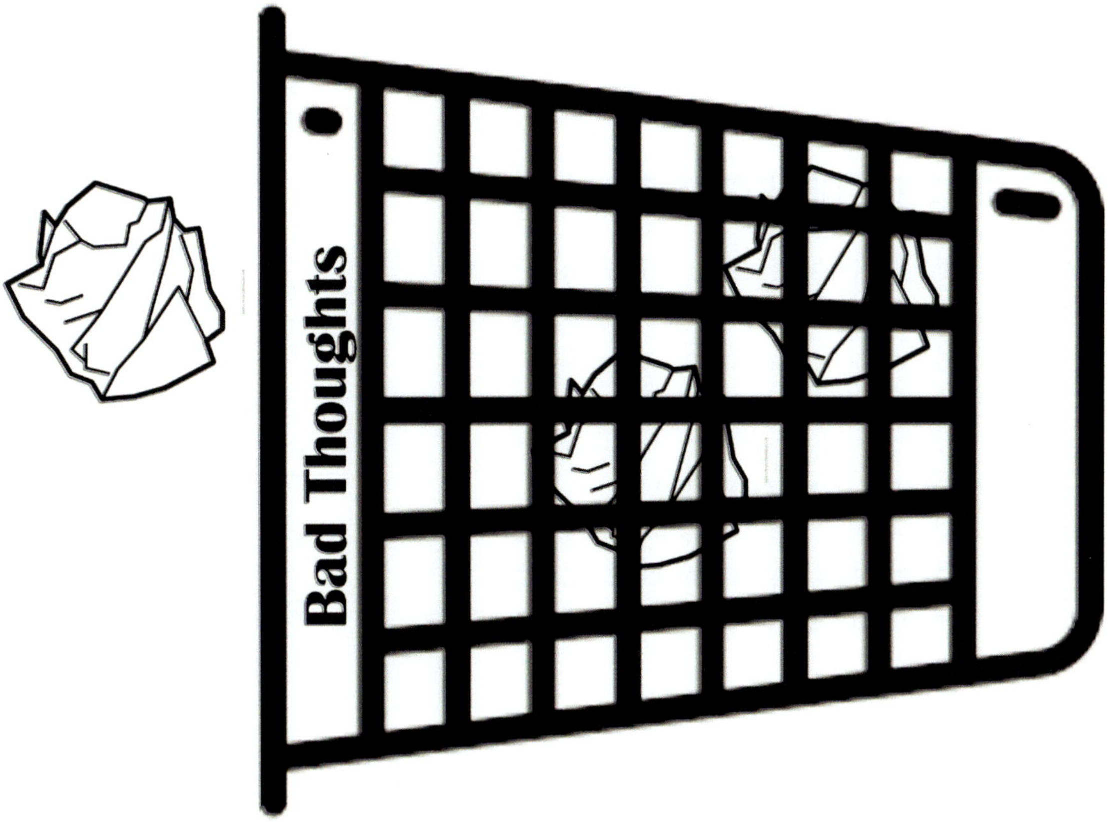
Bad Thoughts

Good Thoughts

Self-talk

1 2 3

SESSION OBJECTIVES

Negative self-talk keeps you down. If you train your mind to speak to yourself as you would your best friend then it has a big impact on how you think and feel.

SESSION OUTCOMES

✓ To be able to notice unwanted thoughts and do something about them.

LESSON PLAN

- Ask the children to remember a time when their heard their class parent share that being a parent was really hard. Remind them about what they said or ask the children to come up with questions they would like to ask their class parent about being a parent.
- What are the 'nagging doubts' that they face each day?

For those classrooms not able to undertake the Circles for Learning Project, video clips or photographs can be used to support the discussion around the topic and stimulate thoughts and ideas from the children and young people.

Task

KS1: To create a positive self-talk flower.

KS2: To create an assembly to show the impact positive self-talk can have on how you think, feel and behave.

KS3: Create a personal picture book full of positive self-talk.

KS1

1 Act out for the children a short sketch where you get something wrong and are mean to yourself – 'Oh for goodness sake, how stupid I am. I can't even get . . . right.'

2 Ask the children if they have ever felt like that. Ask them if what you said to yourself was a useful thing to say. What do they say to themselves?

3 Get another adult to ask you if you would speak to your best friend the way you just spoke to yourself. Ask the children what they think – if their best friend spoke to them the way you had just spoken to yourself, how would they feel?

4 Pose the question – If you wouldn't talk to your best friend that way, why is it OK to talk to yourself that way?

5 Work with the children to come up with times when they might use negative self-talk:

When they make a mistake
When they get something wrong
When they don't know what to do
When they get stuck or fed up
When someone does something that upsets them
When they upset someone
When they say something silly
When they do something that gets them into trouble.
When they do something and people laugh
Etc.

6 Get them to share what they might say:

You are so stupid
Oh how could you be so dumb
You are such a fool, no one likes you
Everyone's laughing at you because you are being so stupid
Etc.

7 Give the children one of the negative self-talk sentences on a strip of paper and ask them to come up with a positive thing to say to themselves.

'You are so stupid' could become 'OK, so you got that wrong. Don't worry, everyone gets things wrong; that is how you learn.'

8 Share the YouTube video: 'Positive self-talk'.

9 Ask the children to make a positive self-talk flower with different things they can say on the petals.

10 Share what they have come up with and display in the classroom.

11 Read the story *I Am Human* and help the children think about making mistakes and how valuable these can be to learning how to do something.

KS2

1 Share the video with the children YouTube: 'Positive self-talk' and discuss.

2 How do they talk to themselves? Do a class poll – negative or positive?

3 Pose the question – Would they talk to their best friend this way? If not why is it OK to talk to themselves this way?

4 Work with the children to come up with some times when they might use self-talk.

5 Ask the children to work in groups. Give them strips of paper and ask them to write two negative and two positive self-talk phrases for each of the situations; each must be different.

6 Share what they have come up with and create a negative and positive list.

7 Explore the reasons why negative self-talk may not be good for the mind or the body – increases stress, has a negative effect on how we feel, has a negative effect on how we think, can cause us to feel bad about ourselves and may have an impact on what we try to do or if we succeed at what we are doing.

8 Why should we teach ourselves to be more positive in our self-talk? It can reduce our stress levels, help us feel better about ourselves, have a positive impact on our learning and our relationships and ultimately help us achieve our goals.

9 Share the book *Why Am I Here?* with the children and talk about the impact self-talk can have on being the best version of yourself.

10 Explain to the children that you are going to share this very important piece of information with the whole school in an assembly – positive self-talk is good for you and negative self-talk is bad for you.

11 Ask the children to get into groups of 3. One person is going to be positive self-talk, one negative self-talk and one the human being. Ask them to come up with a short sketch showing a situation which produces self-talk and then share what the negative and positive self-talk might be.

12 Share what they have come up with together.

13 Ask the children to show what would happen if the person only had negative self-talk to listen to – they can show by body language how down and fed up the person would be after each negative comment, until they stop believing in themselves.

14 Now ask them to show what would happen if they just had positive self-talk. How would they show this in their body language?

15 Create an assembly out of the sketches to show the importance of positive self-talk. Give each person in assembly a blank self-talk flower to take away and fill in.

KS3

1 Share the YouTube clips with the children and discuss.

2 How do they use self-talk, when do they use it and have they ever been aware of the impact of it before?

3 Share the book *Ishi* with the children and explain that as a class you are going to make a book that shows mistakes, things going wrong, learning, difficulties, etc. Ask the children to work in pairs. Each pair has to take two photos (one for each person) of something going wrong or a mistake being made. (You can use a pebble as in *Ishi* or a pink bendy toy person or other such toy.)

4 Once they have taken the photo, they need to write in the thought bubble what the negative self-talk could be and then the positive self-talk that could be used instead.

5 Take all the photos and all the sayings and create a book for the class to use or a large display to remind the young people of the importance of self-talk.

6 Help the children identify positive self-talk questions that can be used to focus them on the positive aspect of the mistake or the difficulty.

What can you learn from this situation or this experience which will be helpful for you in the future?

What was the positive that this experience/situation gave you?

What did you do right?

How could this help you in the future?

What went well?

What are you pleased about?

All of these questions help focus the mind on the positive and not the negative and thus challenge the brain's normal response of negativity bias.

RESOURCES

1 YouTube video: 'Positive self-talk – Ginther Elementary School',

www.youtube.com/watch?v=8AQQqJEwkjw

2 YouTube clip: 'Unit 2 clip 2 of Helpful Thinking and Self Talk (SenseAbility)',

www.youtube.com/watch?v=AS7tUD97k7g

3 YouTube clip: 'Unit 1 clip 1 of Helpful Thinking and Self Talk (SenseAbility)',

www.youtube.com/watch?v=YQz11MmUoYO

4 *Why Am I Here?* by Matthew Kelly

5 *I Am Human* by Susan Verde

6 *Ishi* by Akiko Yabuki

7 Pink bendy person/pebbles/small toy

8 Positive and negative self-talk signs

9 Positive self-talk flowers

10 Speech bubbles

IMPORTANT POINTS

Positive self-talk is when we talk to ourselves in a kind and thoughtful, reassuring and optimistic way. It affects how we think and feel. It reduces stress and can inspire us to achieve great things.

LEARNING LINKS

Collaboration, creativity, knowledge and understanding, self-awareness, emotional literacy.

REFLECTION

Questions:

Positive comment from child:

Positive comment from adult:

LEARNING DIMENSIONS		SOCIAL & EMOTIONAL SKILLS	
Strategic awareness		Emotional literacy	
Learning relationships		Neuroscience	
Curiosity		Self-regulation	
Creativity		Self-development	
Meaning making			
Changing & learning			
Resilience			

POSITIVE SELF-TALK FLOWERS

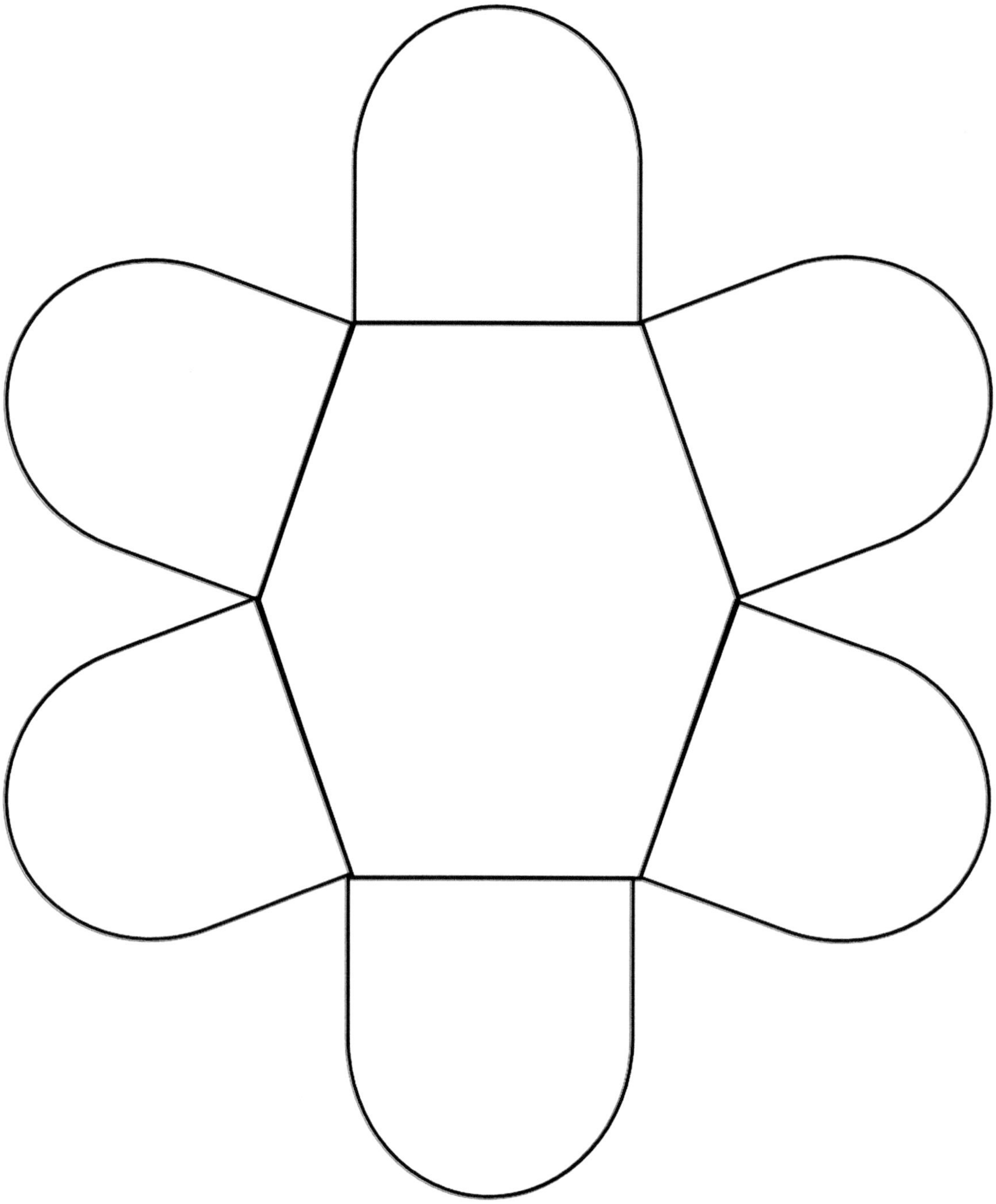

Resilience

1 2 3

SESSION OBJECTIVES

To discuss and identify what enables people to keep going when life gets difficult.

SESSION OUTCOMES

✓ To be able to identify a range of behaviours, thoughts and characteristics that enable people to keep going when life gets difficult.

LESSON PLAN

- Ask the children to think of a time when their class baby struggled. Ask them to describe the different behaviours that they have observed their class baby demonstrate.
- Ask the children to identify how their class parent supported their class baby carry on with what they were doing. Did they 'steal' the class baby's learning or coach them through the difficulty?
- Explain that by doing something for the baby, the parent 'steals' their learning, as the baby doesn't get the chance to learn how to do something for themselves.

For those classrooms not able to undertake the Circles for Learning Project, video clips or photographs can be used to support the discussion around the topic and stimulate thoughts and ideas from the children and young people.

Task

KS1: To create a puppet show that demonstrates resilience.

KS2/KS3: To read a variety of books and identify the different things that keep people going when life makes it difficult.

KS1

1 Explain to the children you are going to read them a story a day for a week and that you have a challenge for them. Each story tells of a journey or a challenge that is really difficult. Their job is to come up with all the things that they can find that tell them how and why the different things managed to keep going.

2 Share the stories, one a day for a week. After each story, ask the children to think of all the things that the people or objects did to keep going when life became difficult.

3 List all the things that they did or used to help them keep going on a large sheet of paper. These can be coloured or grouped to help the children think of new things and to help them identify the sorts of things that the different stories showed, e.g., in *Strictly No Elephants*, one thing that helps us when things go wrong or get difficult is our friends; another is the self-talk that we use – the little boy explains that the people don't know any better; creativity – the boy and girl start their own club, look after each other, help each other to be brave.

4 Once you have shared all the books and come up with a range of things that allow the characters in the books to keep going when things get tough, ask the children to think of a time when they found things tough – this could be when they argued with a friend, lost a special toy, missed Mum and Dad, moved schools, couldn't do something at school, etc. Ask them to draw a picture of a time when they found life tough and then what had helped them.

5 Introduce the word 'resilience' and help the children understand its meaning.

6 Ask the children to create a puppet show that shows what resilience is and the sort of things that can help keep their character going when life throws them a big challenge.

7 Collect different things that can help us be resilient or keep going when life gets tough.

KS2/KS3

1 Set up a book-tasting session with the children (see Chapter 4 for how to do this and for all the resources needed).

2 Set out a variety of books on each table so that the children are able to access different books.

3 Set the challenge for the children to identify as many things as possible that support the different characters in keeping going when life gets difficult.

4 Books to use are listed in the resources section.

5 Remind the children that this is a book-tasting – they do not need to read the whole thing. By tasting the different books, they can choose which one they wish to read in full later.

6 Once the children have read their books, they can fill in the 'resilience' sheet to show what strategies, ways of thinking or other things the characters use to keep going when their life is getting difficult.

7 Once the children have read several of the books and you have collected the information, create a session to share what they have found.

RESOURCES

1 *Pete the Cat and His Four Groovy Buttons* by Eric Litwin

2 *Jabari Jumps* by Gaia Cornwall

3 *The Tiny Seed* by Eric Carle

4 *A Perfectly Messed-Up Story* by Patrick McDonnell

5 *The Adventures of Beekle: The Unimaginary Friend* by Dan Santat

6 *Strictly No Elephants* by Lisa Mantchev

7 *A Mouse So Small* by Angela McAllister

8 A box of puppets or a range of finger puppets

9 *The Harmonica* by Tony Johnston

10 *Rose Blanche* by Ian McEwan

11 *Emmanuel's Dream: The True Story of Emmanuel Ofosu Yeboah* by Laurie Thompson

12 *The Hugging Tree* by Jill Neimark

13 *Salt in His Shoes: Michael Jordan in Pursuit of a Dream* by Deloris Jordan

14 *The Boy Who Harnessed the Wind* by William Kamkwamba, Bryan Mealer

15 *El Deafo* by Cece Bell

16 *The Thing Lou Couldn't Do* by Ashley Spires

17 *Out of My Mind* by Sharon M. Draper

18 *Ben's Trumpet* by Rachel Isadora

19 Hope in a Ballet Shoe by Michaela DePrince

20 *Hatchet* by Gary Paulsen

IMPORTANT POINTS

When we face a challenge, there are many things that can support us to keep going, these can be internal – self-talk, our beliefs, self-esteem, motivation, determination, etc. – or they can be external – friends and family, people who have inspired us, signs that we believe are showing us the way, etc.

LEARNING LINKS

Emotional literacy, knowledge and understanding, creativity, self-development, self-awareness.

REFLECTION

Questions:

Positive comment from child:

Positive comment from adult:

LEARNING DIMENSIONS		SOCIAL & EMOTIONAL SKILLS	
Strategic awareness		Emotional literacy	
Learning relationships		Neuroscience	
Curiosity		Self-regulation	
Creativity		Self-development	
Meaning making			
Changing & learning			
Resilience			

Things that help us keep going when life gets tough

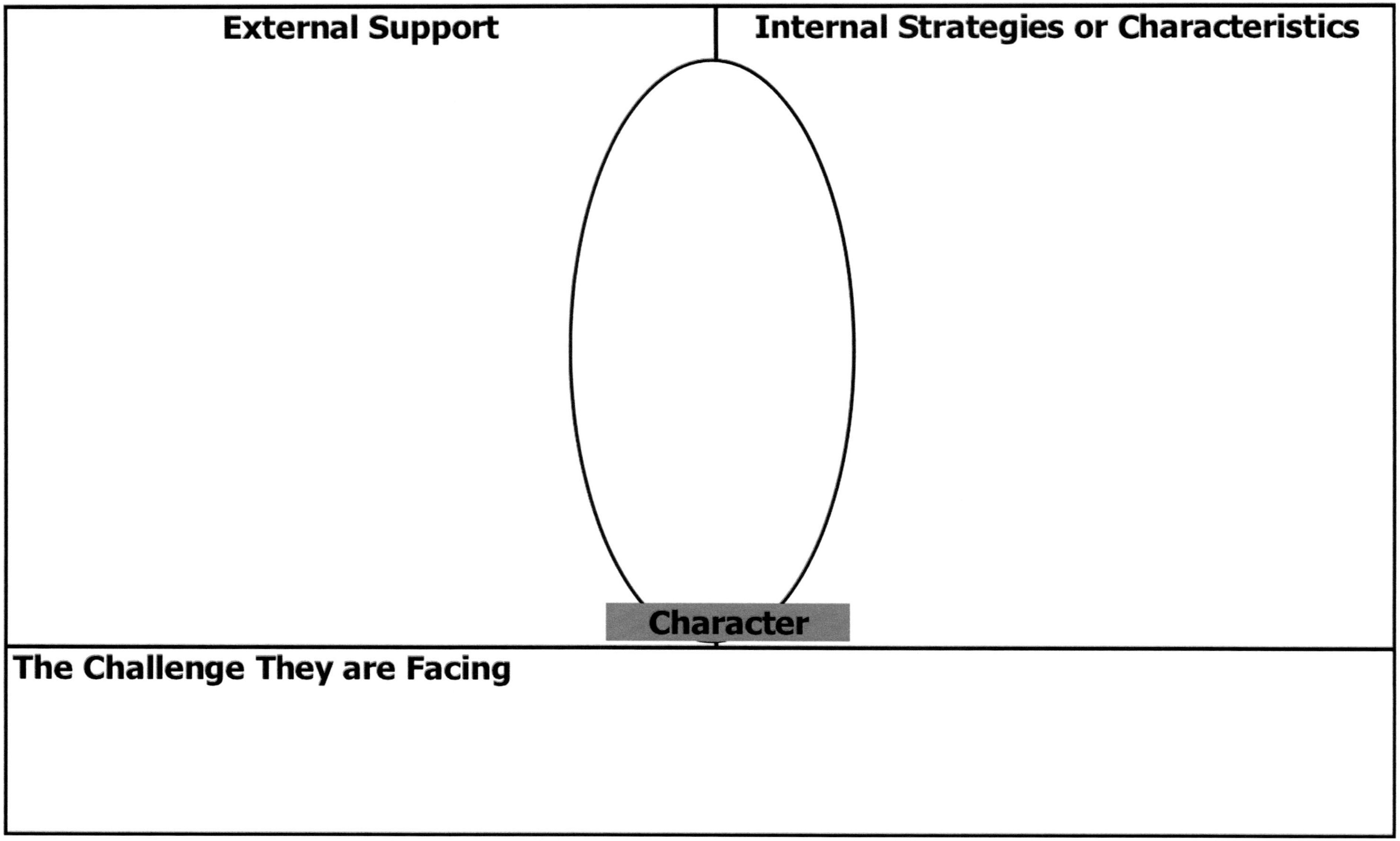

Bibliography

'Are brains like computers?', www.youtube.com/watch?v=rjnRiEaud0Y (accessed 10 September 2019).

'A short story on kindness', www.youtube.com/watch?v=8Wi0UWLeT9I (accessed 10 September 2019).

Bell, C. (2014). *El Deafo.* Amulet Books.

Binnion, J. (2017). *You're So Clumsy Charley,* 2nd edition. Explainer HQ, Your Stories Matter.

'Brain vs computer', www.youtube.com/watch?v=TIUK69Wsk6g (accessed 10 September 2019).

Brown, B. (2012). *Daring Greatly: How the Courage to Be Vulnerable Transforms the Way We Live, Love, Parent, and Lead.* Penguin Life.

Burgham, N. (2012). 'Fairy tales as play scripts', *TES,* www.tes.com/teaching-resource/fairy-tales-as-play-scripts-6233715 (accessed 10 September 2019).

Bush, J., & Geraghty, P. (1989). *The Cross-with-Us Rhinoceros.* Red Fox.

Carle, E. (1997). *The Tiny Seed.* Puffin.

'Color your world with kindness', www.youtube.com/watch?v=rwelE8yyYOU (accessed 10 September 2019).

Churches, R., Dommett, E., & Devonshire, I. (2017). *Neuroscience for Teachers: Applying Research Evidence from Brain Science.* Crown House Publishing.

Cornwall, G. (2018). *Jabari Jumps.* Walker Books.

Cozolino, L. (2013). *The Social Neuroscience of Education: Optimizing Attachment and Learning in the Classroom.* W.W. Norton & Company.

Curham, S. (2018). *Don't Stop Thinking About Tomorrow.* Walker Books.

Deacon, A. (2016). *I am Henry Finch.* Walker Books.

DePrince, M. (2015). *Hope in a Ballet Shoe.* Faber & Faber.

Desautels, L., & McKnight, M. (2016). *Unwritten, the Story of a Living System: A Pathway to Enlivening and Transforming Education.* Wyatt-MacKenzie Publishing.

'Distracted puppy party', www.youtube.com/watch?v=sZd0isWgsJw (accessed 10 September 2019).

Domoney, C. (2018). *The Magic Is Inside You,* 2nd edition. CreateSpace Independent Publishing Platform.

Draper, S. M. (2016). *Out of My Mind.* Atheneum Books for Young Readers.

Ecker, B., Ticic, R., & Hulley, L. (2012). *Unlocking the Emotional Brain: Eliminating Symptoms at Their Roots Using Memory Reconsolidation.* Routledge.

Ering, T. B. (2008). *Necks Out for Adventure.* Candlewick.

Falkoff, M. (2015). *Playlist for the Dead.* HarperCollins.

'Flea in a glass jar experiment', www.youtube.com/watch?v=TK2Hd9a05HM (accessed 10 September 2019).

Forney, E. (2013). *Marbles: Mania, Depression, Michelangelo, and Me: A Graphic Memoir.* Robinson.

Fussell, S. (2015). *Sad, the Dog.* Candlewick Press.

Greder, A. (2008). *The Island.* Allen & Unwin Children's Books.

Green, D. (2017). *The Adventures of Your Brain.* Red Shed.

'Guess the sound game', www.youtube.com/watch?v=IZsssS_I_2Y (accessed 10 September 2019).

Hallowell, E. (2004). *A Walk in the Rain with a Brain.* HarperCollins.

Hammill, K. (2018). *We Are What We Think.* Kristy Hammill.

Hammond, T. (2017). *I Have Bees in My Brain.* Friesen Press.

Harrison, J. (1996) *When Mum Turned into a Monster.* Picture Lions.

Harvey, N. (2018). *Silly Limbic.* Naomi Harvey.

Hawkins, K. (2017). *Mindful Teacher, Mindful School: Improving Wellbeing in Teaching and Learning.* Sage.

Hebb, D. O. (1949/2002). *The Organization of Behavior: A Neuropsychological Theory,* re-edition. Psychology Press.

Hoestlandt, J. (1996). *Star of Fear, Star of Hope.* Bloomsbury U.S.A. Children's Books.

Howarth, H., & Howarth, D. (2019). *What Makes Me Sad?* Sky Pony.

'How to learn major parts of the brain quickly', www.youtube.com/watch?v=FczvTGIuHKM (accessed 10 September 2019).

'How to memorize fast and easily', www.youtube.com/watch?v=OnFkQ4cQhME (accessed 10 September 2019).

'How you treat people is who you are! (kindness motivational video)', www.youtube.com/watch?v=mTsvSAltPqA (accessed 10 September 2019).

'I had a black dog, his name was depression', www.youtube.com/watch?v=XiCrniLQGYc (accessed 10 September 2019).

'Imaging reveals patterns in neuron firing', www.youtube.com/watch?v=t3TaMU_qXMc (accessed 10 September 2019).

'Individual social responsibility', www.youtube.com/watch?v=gWff2Ne4v78 (accessed 10 September 2019).

Isadora, R. (1991). *Ben's Trumpet.* HarperTrophy.

Jeffers, O. (2010). *The Heart and the Bottle.* HarperCollins Children's Books.

Joëls, M., Pu, Z., Wiegert, O., Oitzl, M. S., & Krugers, H. J. (2006). 'Learning under stress: how does it work?' *Trends in Cognitive Sciences,* 10(4), 152–158.

Johnston, T. (2008). *The Harmonica.* Charlesbridge Publishing.

Johnstone, M. (2007). *I Had a Black Dog.* Robinson.

Jordan, D. (2008) *Salt in His Shoes: Michael Jordan.* Simon & Schuster Books for Young Readers.

Kamkwamba, W., & Mealer, B. (2012). *The Boy Who Harnessed the Wind.* Dial Books.

Kelly, M. (2009). *Why Am I Here?* Blue Sparrow.

Krosoczka, J. (2018). *Hey, Kiddo.* Scholastic.

'Learned Optimism by Martin Seligman – animated book review', www.youtube.com/watch?v=2hHNq45rEnU (accessed 10 September 2019).

Letran, J. (2016). *I Would, but my DAMN MIND Won't Let Me!: A Teen's Guide to Controlling Their Thoughts and Feelings*, 2nd edition. A Healed Mind.

'Life vest inside – kindness boomerang – "One Day"', www.youtube.com/watch?v=nwAYpLVyeFU (accessed 10 September 2019).

Litwin, E. (2014). *Pete the Cat and his Four Groovy Buttons.* HarperCollins Children's Books.

Llenas, A. (2015). *The Color Monster: A Story about Emotions.* Templar Publishing.

Lloyd-Jones, M. (2015). *The Princess and the Fog: A Story for Children with Depression.* Jessica Kingsley Publishers.

'Look after your brain – Brainsmart – BBC', www.youtube.com/watch?v=12pbrkcfRDI (accessed 10 September 2019).

McAllister, A. (2016). *A Mouse So Small.* Little Tiger Press.

McCloud, C. (2015). *Have You Filled a Bucket Today?*, 10th anniversary edition. Bucket Fillers.

McDonnell, P. (2014). *A Perfectly Messed-Up Story.* Little, Brown Young Readers.

McEwan, I. (2004). *Rose Blanche.* Red Fox.

Malcolm, D. (2015). *Meh: A Story About Depression.* ThunderStone Books.

Mantchev, L. (2016). *Strictly no Elephants.* Simon & Schuster/Paula Wiseman Books.

Moses, B. (2017). *Poems About Emotions.* Wayland.

'Mr Motivator Beautiful Morning No 1', www.youtube.com/watch?v=1M5-HzxswPw (accessed 10 September 2019).

Neimark, J. (2015). *The Hugging Tree.* Magination Press.

'Neuron time lapse video', www.youtube.com/watch?v=A9zLKmt2nHo&pbjreload=10 (accessed 10 September 2019).

'Neurotransmitters - What are neurotransmitters and what do they do in the body?, www.youtube.com/watch?v=Mz3Plvyu3ew (accessed 10 September 2019).

Niven, J. (2015). *All the Bright Places.* Penguin.

Olson, K. (2014). *The Invisible Classroom: Relationships, Neuroscience and Mindfulness in School.* W.W. Norton.

Oram, H. (1999). *Badger's Bad Mood.* Picture Lions.

Pascual-Leone, A., Amedi, A., Fregni, F., & Merabet, L. B. (2005). The plastic human brain cortex. *Annu. Rev. Neurosci.*, 28, 377–401.

Paulsen, G., *Hatchet.* Macmillan Children's Books.

Peters, A. Fusek (2015). *The Colour Thief: A Family's Story of Depression.* Wayland.

'Positive self-talk – Ginther Elementary School', www.youtube.com/watch?v=8AQQqJEwkjw (accessed 10 September 2019).

Quick, M. (2014). *Forgive Me.* Leonard Peacock Headline.

Rakic, P. (2002). 'Progress: Neurogenesis in adult primate neocortex: an evaluation of the evidence', *Nature Reviews Neuroscience,* 3(1), 65.

Reynolds, P., & Reynolds, P. (2014). *Going Places.* Atheneum Books for Young Readers.

Rosen, M., & Blake, Q. (2011). *Michael Rosen's Sad Book.* London: Walker Books.

Ryden, L. (2016). *Rosie's Brain.* Peace of Mind Press.

Santat, D. (2016). *The Adventures of Beekle: The Unimaginary Friend.* Andersen Press.

Siegel, D. J. (2015a). *The Developing Mind: How Relationships and the Brain Interact to Shape Who We Are,* 2nd edition. Guilford Publications.

Siegel, D. J. (2015b). *Brainstorm: The Power and Purpose of the Teenage Brain.* Penguin.

Smith, C. (2018). *The Wonky Donkey.* Scholastic.

Spires, A. (2017). *The Thing Lou Couldn't Do.* Kids Can Press.

Stevens, L. (2016). *Not Today, Celeste!: A Dog's Tale about Her Human's Depression.* Jessica Kingsley Publishers.

'The bystander effect', www.youtube.com/watch?v=OSsPfbup0ac (accessed 10 September 2019).

'The bystander effect – the science of empathy', www.youtube.com/watch?v=Wy6eUTLzcU4 (accessed 10 September 2019).

'The chemical mind – Crash Course Psychology #3', www.youtube.com/watch?v=W4N-7AlzK7s (accessed 10 September 2019).

'The marshmallow test', www.youtube.com/watch?v=QX_oy9614HQ (accessed 10 September 2019).

'The negativity bias and how to beat it', www.youtube.com/watch?v=0LfteZ9k8YU&t=51s (accessed 10 September 2019).

'The science of kindness', www.youtube.com/watch?v=O9UByLyOjBM (accessed 10 September 2019).

Thompson, L. (2015). *Emmanuel's Dream: The True Story of Emmanuel Ofosu Yeboah.* Schwartz & Wade.

Ttofa, J. (2017). *The Tale of Two Fishes.* Routledge.

'Unit 1, clip 1 of Helpful Thinking and Self Talk (SenseAbility)', www.youtube.com/watch?v=YQz11MmUoY0 (accessed 10 September 2019).

'Unit 2, clip 2 of Helpful Thinking and Self Talk (SenseAbility)', www.youtube.com/watch?v=AS7tUD97k7g (accessed 10 September 2019).

Vander Zee, R. (2013). *Erika's Story,* reprint edition. Creative Paperbacks.

Verde, S. (2018). *I Am Human.* Abrams Books.

Walden, L. (2018). *Feelings: Inside My Heart and In My Head.* Caterpillar Books.

Watt Smith, T. (2016). *The Book of Human Emotions.* Wellcome Collection.

The Wellcome Trust: Simmonds, A. (2014). 'How neuroscience is affecting education: Report of teacher and parent surveys', Wellcome Trust.

'What is the limbic system in the brain? Definition, functions & parts', https://tinyurl.com/y3mklph9 (accessed 10 September 2019).

'Where are memories stored?', www.youtube.com/watch?v=R0wbTR95VEs (accessed 10 September 2019).

Whitehead, C. (2017). 'Neuroscience in the classroom', *SEEN,* Southeast Education Network Magazine, 19(1), Summer 2017, 16–19, www.seenmagazine.us/Articles/Article-Detail/ArticleId/6486/NEUROSCIENCE-IN-THE-CLASSROOM (accessed 17 September 2019).

Willis, J. (2009). 'How to teach students about the brain', *Educational Leadership*, 67(4), 40–44.

Winn, D. (2010). *The Higgledy-Piggledy Pigeon*. Cardboard Box Adventures.

Witek, J. (2014). *In My Heart: A Book of Feelings (Growing Hearts)*. Abrams Appleseed.

Yabuki, A. (2016). *Ishi*. Powerhouse Books.